D1317961

DONALD
TRUMP

IS NOT MY SAVIOR

———

DONALD TRUMP

IS NOT MY SAVIOR

AN EVANGELICAL LEADER
SPEAKS HIS MIND ABOUT THE
MAN HE SUPPORTS AS PRESIDENT

MICHAEL L. BROWN, PH.D.

DESTINY IMAGE® PUBLISHERS, INC.
P.O. Box 310, Shippensburg, PA 17257-0310
"Promoting Inspired Lives."

This book and all other Destiny Image and Destiny Image Fiction books are available at Christian bookstores and distributors worldwide.

For more information on foreign distributors, call 717-532-3040.

Reach us on the Internet: www.destinyimage.com.

ISBN 13 TP: 978-0-7684-4993-8

ISBN 13 eBook: 978-0-7684-4994-5

ISBN 13 HC: 978-0-7684-4996-9

ISBN 13 LP: 978-0-7684-4995-2

For Worldwide Distribution, Printed in the U.S.A.

1 2 3 4 5 6 7 8 / 22 21 20 19 18

Contents

PREFACE

F OR those of you who are not familiar with my work, you might be wondering, "Is this guy for Trump or against Trump? The title sounds negative, but the subtitle more positive." I understand your confusion!

During the primaries, I staunchly opposed Donald Trump, feeling there were quite a few Republican candidates who could do a better job than him. But as Trump continued to win, I began to recognize that something else was going on and that God might have some surprises for us. Once it was a matter of Trump vs. Hillary, I voted for him, but with a little trepidation. Would he keep his promises? Was he truly conservative? And what of his volatile character? Now that he is our president, I am thrilled with so many good things he has done but grieved by other aspects of his presidency that do more harm than good. What are we to make of Donald Trump?

It is the purpose of this book to take you on a journey with me over the last three years, helping all of us better evaluate perhaps the most polarizing man on the planet today. In particular, we'll look at the unique (and unexpectedly close) relationship between Trump and evangelical Christians, asking if this relationship has helped us (and our nation) or hurt us. I'm sure you have your strong opinions too! But first, a quick note about the unique history of this book.

Quite out of the blue, in the middle of August, I felt an urging to write a book on the relationship between President Trump and evangelical Christians and to get it out before the midterm elections—quite ridiculous for an author and virtually impossible for a publisher. Yet I felt it could (and should) be done. At the same time, I wondered, "But I haven't I already addressed all this in writing?" After all, since my first open letter to candidate Trump in August, 2015, I had penned scores of Trump-related articles, never from a purely political perspective but always from a biblical, or moral, or spiritual perspective. Perhaps I could draw on that material?

The morning of August 16, I was gripped in prayer, and suddenly, everything was clear: I saw the rough title and subtitle of the book; I had a plan of action (writing fresh new essays for the beginning and end of the book and compiling all relevant Trump articles from August 2015 until August 2018); and I knew the editor and publisher to contact: Larry Sparks and Destiny Image.

Larry and his team, from the senior leadership down, immediately felt this was the right thing to do, and by Tuesday, August 21, I had written all the new material and compiled all the relevant articles in chronological order, the last article being, "Some Candid Questions for Evangelical Supporters of President Trump," dated August 11, 2018. By Thursday, August 23, the amazing cover design was completed, and the editing and final layout processes well on their way. Only a few weeks later, and, incredibly enough, this book is in your hands. My deep appreciation to Don Nori, Jr., Larry, and the entire Destiny Image team (including Tina and Eileen and John and Meelika and Brad and Tammy and others). May God bless the labor of your hands!

My great hope in writing this book is that it will help those of us who claim to be people of faith and character, who claim to honor the Scriptures and are jealous for the reputation of Jesus, to be able to take a more nuanced position when it comes to our president—a man raised up by God for such a time as this but a deeply flawed man at that. I also hope it will encourage us to get and out vote for the right issues, not paralyzed by the media frenzy on the left and on the right. Each new election cycle feels more critical than the last.

Last (but not least), for each of you reading this book from a different perspective (perhaps non-faith or, at the least, non-evangelical), I do hope that you'll gain insight into how evangelicals think and why we do what we do. Perhaps all of us can actually sit down across the table (or, in my case, across phone lines on my daily talk radio show) and have civil interaction in the midst of our differences? Perhaps we can even work together for the common good?

Once you've read the book, I'd love to hear from you. Through our website and social media and radio show, I'm quite accessible. A good place to start is right here: AskDrBrown.org, with links to all our social media accounts as well. Let's connect! And may God bless you as you read the pages that follow.

Evangelicals and Donald Trump: A Match Made in Heaven or a Marriage with Hell?

MANY of us are now used to the words "President Trump." But if you predicted four years ago, "Donald Trump will be the next President of the United States," you would have been laughed to scorn. "President Donald Trump? Are you kidding me?"

This, in fact, happened to conservative pundit Ann Coulter when she appeared on the liberal Bill Maher show on June 19, 2015. When asked who the best candidate would be to win the general election, she said without hesitation, "Donald Trump." The audience roared with laughter.[1] Donald Trump?

But what if your prediction went further? What if you said, "Actually, Trump will crush a host of Republican candidates, including senators, governors, and former governors—candidates like Jeb Bush, Ted Cruz, Marco Rubio, John Kasich, Mike Huckabee, Chris Christie, Rick Perry, Scott Walker, Rand Paul, Carly Fiorina, Ben Carson, and others. Then, he will beat Hillary Clinton."

People would have been absolutely incredulous. "That could never happen," they would say with conviction. "Trump could never beat a pack of candidates like that."

But people would have been sure you had lost your mind if you said, "Actually, Donald Trump will be elected with the help of evangelical Christians who will support him in large numbers because of his strong pro-life, pro-Christian stance."

"Are you crazy?" you would be asked. "Hell will freeze over before evangelical Christians will rally around an ungodly, immoral narcissist like Trump. For that matter, hell will freeze over before Trump becomes a pro-life champion and a staunch defender of Christian liberties."

Yet that is exactly what happened. Eighty percent of white evangelical voters reportedly voted for Donald Trump.[2] And they are among his staunchest supporters today. How did this happen?

How is it that the same evangelicals who rejected Bill Clinton in the strongest possible terms—in particular because of his sexual immorality—became some of the greatest supporters of Donald Trump, a thrice-married, self-confessed adulterer? How is it that the same people who once shouted "Character matters" now proclaimed, "We're voting for a president, not a pastor"?

Did these evangelicals (especially the leaders) sell their souls for Donald Trump? Did they compromise their convictions to gain a seat at the table? Did they prove themselves to be shameless hypocrites? Or did these Bible-quoting, church-attending Christians sense that God had a purpose in raising up Trump?

It is one thing to vote *for* Trump in order to vote *against* Hillary Clinton. It's another thing to venerate him as a man chosen by God for such a time as this to the point that he can virtually do no wrong. How did so many evangelical Christians, among whom are many fine men and women, end up anywhere near the Trump camp?

Richard Land is the president of Southern Evangelical Seminary and a highly respected Southern Baptist leader with a Ph.D. from Oxford University. On my radio show, he stated that of the seventeen Republican candidates, Trump was his seventeenth choice. Today, Dr. Land serves on the president's Faith Advisory Council.[3] What changed his mind?

James Robison is a world-renowned evangelist and Christian TV host, the founder of LIFE Outreach International. He has been a friend of past presidents and will tell you with a smile that he gave Mike Huckabee his first job. Although he does not endorse candidates for office, he urged Dr. Ben Carson *not* to endorse candidate Trump.[4] Today, Rev. Robison also serves on the president's Faith Advisory Council.[5] How can this be?

As you will see in the pages that follow, I spoke out publicly against Donald Trump during the primaries, warning evangelicals not to vote for him. I said he could not be trusted. I questioned whether he would keep his promises. I told fellow evangelicals that we could not look to a man like this to protect our rights.

At the same time, I had read prophetic words from respected colleagues like Jeremiah Johnson and Lance Wallnau, both of whom likened Donald Trump to a Cyrus figure. (Cyrus was a pagan king who was raised up by God to help the Jewish people; see Isaiah 44:24-45:6.) They said that Trump would be like a bull in a china closet, like a divine wrecking ball, and they pointed to him as our next president.[6]

I remember getting on my knees in prayer and saying, "Lord, I just don't see it. I don't see what these men are seeing. Am I missing something?" And so, I continued to oppose candidate Trump, even as he shocked many of us by staying at the top of the pack.

But as he continued to win decisively, I began to wonder, "Is there something about Trump that I'm missing? Are millions of Americans that stupid? Are the Christian leaders who support him that blind?"

I felt like a person sitting in the audience as a comedian performed, but I was not laughing at any of his jokes. "This guy is not funny at all." Yet the rest of the audience was howling with laughter. Perhaps I simply wasn't getting the jokes?

I had to ask myself, "What is his great appeal?" And, more importantly, "Is it possible God is raising him up for a purpose?"

It was during that time that James Robison also called me, saying, "Michael, I think God is up to something with Trump. Let's keep praying."

Subsequently, James spent more than one hour alone with Trump, preaching the gospel to him in the strongest of terms and assuring me that Trump listened attentively. Other friends of mine met with him in small group settings—these were also respected evangelical leaders—and they too told me, "Something is going on. He really likes evangelicals and he believes in our cause. And in a strange sort of way, he even seems to fear God." Could it be true?

Once Trump became the Republican candidate, I began to lean toward supporting him. And ultimately, when the choice was between Trump and Hillary, I felt I had to oppose her presidency, convinced that she would be a champion of abortion and an obstacle to our religious freedoms. As for the Supreme Court, her appointees would certainly be to the radical left, and that would be disastrous.

So, on November 8, 2016, with some trepidation, I voted for Donald Trump, hoping that he would keep his promises. My wife, Nancy, also voted for him, but with great trepidation, fearing that he would be a deeply divisive figure, that he would degrade the presidency, indeed, that he would degrade our national character. *In my opinion, in the first two years of his presidency, he has lived up to my highest expectations and confirmed Nancy's greatest fears.* Donald Trump has, indeed, been a divine wrecking ball. The man once dubbed "God's chaos candidate" has become the chaos president.[7]

On the one hand, President Trump has been incredibly effective. His first Supreme Court appointee, Neil Gorsuch, has been stellar, and many of his federal court appointees appear to be outstanding as well. And as I write these words, confirmation hearings for Brett Kavanaugh are about to begin. Could he, too, become a tremendous asset to the Court?

When it comes to Israel, President Trump not only promised to move our embassy to Jerusalem. He actually did it. Yes! What Presidents Bill Clinton and George W. Bush and Barack Obama failed to do, he did. Not only so, but he has already proven to be a true friend to Israel.

He has also proven to be a true friend to evangelical Christians, speaking out on behalf of our liberties and pushing back against radical LGBT activism. And he is quite fearless in doing so.

He also met with North Korean leader Kim Jong-un, and, if the reports are true, that despotic country is in the process of destroying its nuclear facilities. Who predicted this?

The economy is humming. The military is getting more support. Other nations are being challenged to do their part and not depend so much on American aid. All this is positive.

At the same time, President Trump has deepened the national divide, often unnecessarily so. His derogatory and inflammatory tweets have gone far beyond fighting back and taking a stand. They are not just "unpresidential." They are nasty. They are ugly. And they are immature. He also hurts his cause by often playing fast and loose with the truth.

Of course, I understand that many Americans are so fed up with politics that they are glad to see Trump being "unpresidential." They're glad he fights back. They're glad he speaks his mind. They're glad he is not tepid or timid. But does the President of the United States need to call a former employee a "dog"? Does he need to label a TV commentator "psycho"? Does this advance his cause or unite Americans around his agenda?

Political commentator Ben Shapiro claimed that,

> Trump won the Republican primaries because he was—by far— the most aggressive, no-holds-barred candidate. Republican primary voters wanted to see Hillary Clinton pummeled on stage, and Trump offered the best promise of that. After brutalizing Jeb Bush and reducing Senators Marco Rubio and Ted Cruz to frustrated stammering, Trump proceeded to pile drive Hillary Clinton at every opportunity. Republican primary voters got precisely what they bargained for.

He continued,

> What's more, backing Trump lent Republican voters a sense that they were *in the fight*. After Mitt Romney's destruction at the hands of Barack Obama in 2012—after the Democrats turned the cleanest politician of the modern era into a gay-bashing, dog-hating sexist who wanted to put black people "back in chains"—Republicans were fully on board with the Sean Connery line from *The Untouchables*: "They pull a knife, you pull a gun. He sends one of yours to the hospital, you send one of his to the morgue. *That's* the *Chicago* way." Trump was the knife, and the morgue, and all the consequences wrapped up into one giant bag of *id*, topped with a puzzling hairdo.[8]

What was odd, then, was not that so many Americans could support this pugnacious leader, but that *so many evangelicals* could support him without flinching and without apology or caveat. "Trump is God's man! If you oppose him, you're opposing God."

Why have so few evangelical leaders been willing to say, "We support our president, but we sometimes grieve over his behavior"? Why are such statements considered treasonous or disloyal by other evangelical believers? Worse still, why do many evangelicals now sound just like President Trump when they comment or tweet or post? It's as if his fleshly behavior legitimized theirs.

And how is it that we can just look the other way when charges of sexual sin and marital infidelity are raised against him? Some of us who railed against President Clinton because of pre-presidential adulteries now say, "Who cares what Donald Trump did in the past? He's a good president, and that's all that matters."

Can we see why we are constantly ridiculed by the leftwing media? Do we understand why we are frequently called hypocrites? Can we recognize why some people are genuinely perplexed by our unswerving allegiance to a man who at times can be quite carnal?

I absolutely believe President Trump has been a divine wrecking ball. He is wreaking havoc on the political status quo. He is breaking the traditional rules. He is exposing the extraordinary bias of the liberal media and the radical core of the Democratic Party. Some would even say that he is the "worst nightmare" of the New World Order (whatever that is).[9]

Yet a wrecking ball swings back and forth, and I believe President Trump has also exposed some weaknesses (and more) in our evangelical circles. Have we refrained from any criticism so we can keep our seat at the table? Have we ignored major character issues to preserve our political power? Have we become more identified publicly with our President than with our Savior? Have we confused patriotism with the kingdom of God?

To be perfectly clear, if the elections were held today and it was Trump vs. Hillary for president, I would vote for him in a heartbeat, without hesitation. In fact, I would have far less concern than when I voted for him on November 8, 2016. He *is* keeping many of his promises, and it was with that hope that he got my vote. And it appears that evangelical leaders have made a lasting impact on the president.

Not only so, but I will not let the secular media dictate my behavior. As I wrote on July 3, 2018, I will not play the game of denouncing Donald Trump to prove my loyalty to Jesus.[10] And I don't for a moment believe that, if I speak against Trump, the leftwing media will suddenly say to me, "By all means, tell us why you're pro-life. We'd love to hear more about your position. And please, do tell us why you do not recognize homosexual marriage. Perhaps we're missing something here."

Not a chance. The same people telling us that, say, Rev. Franklin Graham has lost his credibility by supporting President Trump are the very ones who rejected his moral and spiritual views in the past. To repeat: I'm not playing the secular media's game.

Yet I do recognize that our failure to criticize the president, our failure to distance ourselves from his worst words and actions, our failure to be nuanced in our support of him has damaged our witness in the eyes of many. And when we become like him in our fleshly behavior and are almost idolatrous in our pro-Americanism, something is profoundly wrong. We have definitely gotten off track.

In many ways, we are just as politicized as those on the left. We slavishly follow the conservative media as much as others blindly follow the liberal media. We hardly stand out from the world. Is this how we function as salt and light?

For me, the matter is simple (and yet complex). Here are three essential points.

First, Donald Trump did not die for our sins. Consequently, the allegiance we have to Jesus must be infinitely greater than the allegiance we have to the president. We cannot allow our loyalty to President Trump to compromise our loyalty to Jesus. Our greatest priority is to maintain our witness before a watching world.

Second, tens of millions of babies have been slaughtered since 1973 and Donald Trump will do far more to stop that slaughter than Hillary Clinton (not to mention quite a few Republican candidates). It's the same with a number of other, very important moral and cultural issues, including the brutal persecution of Christians worldwide. Trump will do a better job. That's why he continues to have our support.

Third, the media and public opinion cannot dictate our responses. When the president deserves praise, he should get it; when he deserves appreciation, he should get it; when he deserves respectful criticism, he should get it. This is the ultimate expression of righteous loyalty. This is Christian consistency. We will not dance to the media's tune.

What, then, does this mean for the future? Where do we go from here? I am personally thrilled that President Trump has a Faith Advisory Council. I am thrilled that he has a largely evangelical cabinet (some say the most evangelical ever, plus there is Vice President Mike Pence). I am thrilled that he seems steadfast in his pro-life, pro-liberty, pro-family, pro-Israel convictions. All this is wonderful, representing a push-back against a dangerous swing to the far left in recent years.

Yet, when it comes to national transformation (in the best and highest sense of the word), we must not put our hope in President Trump. (Even less can we put our trust in the Republican Party as a whole, let alone in the political system.) We must remain more committed to the advancement of the gospel in America than to "making America great again." Put another way, we must be more concerned with the spiritual and moral transformation of our nation than with our world prominence and dominance.

As I wrote in *Saving a Sick America* in 2016, "America can only be great to the extent that America is good, and for America to be good, it must recapture its biblical heritage."[11] Does President Trump have this in mind when he promises to "make America great again"? For the most part no, which reminds us: He has his job to do and we have ours. Let's not blur those lines.

What, then, should our attitude be when it comes to the 2018 and 2020 elections? And to what extent should we be defenders or critics of our president? I'll return to these questions in the last chapter of the book. Right now, we'll take a journey together, beginning with my first article about Donald Trump, dated August 27, 2015, and in the form of an open letter to him. And as we make our way through the short chapters that follow, each of which was published as an article online, we'll be better equipped to answer the question of whether evangelicals and Trump represent a match made in heaven or a marriage with hell.

So, turn the page, and let's go back to August, 2015. What follows has not been edited or revised. Where my views have changed, they have changed. Perhaps yours have changed (or will change) too?

Part One

OPPOSING TRUMP
DURING THE PRIMARIES
★ ★ ★ ★ ★

August 27, 2015–May 3, 2016

August 27, 2015

AN OPEN LETTER
TO DONALD TRUMP
★ ★ ★ ★ ★

Dear Mr. Trump,

LIKE millions of Americans, I am intrigued with your meteoric rise to the top of the polls. You have truly captured the imagination of this nation.

Because I would love to see you succeed, I've got some unsolicited advice for you. And you're going to love this. It's free!

If you'll allow me to introduce myself, I'm a Jewish follower of Jesus (just like Peter and Paul and John and the rest of the apostles), an author, professor, minister, and national talk radio host. My wife, Nancy, and I have been married for almost 40 years, and we have two wonderful daughters (and sons-in-law) and four amazing grandkids. And for the record, I'm not registered Republican or Democrat, but I'm a strong conservative.

Now, as to your campaign, it's very obvious that you have a tremendous amount going for you.

For one, you speak your mind and let the chips fall where they may. Americans like a straight shooter.

And you can't be bought with money because of your massive wealth. That means that no special interest group can own you. Wonderful!

You've also taken on the political establishment without fear. We've been waiting for someone to do that.

We also believe you're a man of action, and if you say you're going to build a wall, you're going to build it.

A lot of people also think that a businessman like you could help turn our economy around, and since you don't seem to be afraid of people, you'd be a great one to stare down the likes of Russia's Putin or Iran's Khamenei. I bet you'd get our hostages back too.

But there are some big problems, and most of them are self-inflicted. Why do you keep shooting yourself in the foot?

Although I'm not a political candidate, I've spoken before some large crowds (as many as 300,000) as well as been in the hot seat with the media and engaged in public debates at universities, and so I was really surprised to see you act so defensively during the first presidential debate, almost right out of the gate.

There you were, the frontrunner in the polls, standing in the central, number-one position on the stage, and you acted like the victim. Could it be that underneath the bravado there's some insecurity? Could it be that a real, living, vibrant relationship with God would give you that deeper sense of security?

When you were asked recently about your Christian faith, you referenced the sermons of Norman Vincent Peale, whose church you used to attend. But Rev. Peale died in 1993, and he was more of an upbeat, motivational speaker than an expositor of the Scriptures. Perhaps hearing some fresh, new sermons from some fine contemporary pastors would do your soul good?

I would hate to have to point back to food more than two decades old when asked about the last healthy meal I ate.

That being said, I was glad to hear that your favorite book is not one that you wrote (*The Art of the Deal*) but the Bible. Good choice!

But here's what concerns me. You don't seem to know what the Bible says, let alone live by it.

For example, in the same interview where you referenced Peale, you said you had never really asked God for forgiveness, apparently not wanting to be a burden to Him but rather wanting to take responsibility for your actions.

With all respect, sir, while it's important to take responsibility for your actions, you're a rotten sinner like the rest of us, and the central message of the Scriptures is that Jesus died for our sins because all of us need forgiveness. How could you miss that?

Of course, you're an incredible businessman and a major presidential candidate rather than a theologian, but certainly, you must know that the Bible teaches ethics and not just theology, and this is a big area where, sad to say, you're turning lots of people off.

I ask again, Why shoot yourself in the foot when you have a legitimate chance of becoming the president of the United States?

Proverbs 15:1 says, "A soft answer turns away wrath, but grievous words stir up anger" (MEV).

I'm not a defender of Fox News or Megyn Kelly (or some others whom you have attacked), but if you spoke the truth with civility, stating your viewpoint plainly and without equivocation but without the gutter-level attacks, you'd make fewer enemies.

Really now, do you think that the Bible, your favorite book by far (you said it!), really supports your unkind assaults against others? Do you really think you become bigger when you belittle others? And shouldn't a presidential candidate be more of a statesman than a mudslinger?

Again, I'm thrilled to see someone throw caution to the wind and speak his mind. I simply wish you would do it with civility and respect.

And here's one more verse from the Bible (this is another biggie): "Pride goes before destruction, and a haughty spirit before a fall" (Prov. 16:18 MEV).

There's often a fine line between confidence and arrogance, between self-assurance and pride (often, the line is anything but fine), and, to many of us following you with interest, you seem to have crossed that line. Pride really does kill!

So, my heartfelt suggestion to you, sir, is that you humble yourself before your Creator, that you recognize your sins and shortcomings, asking Him for forgiveness through the cross, and that you ask Him to help you to be the kind of man that America (and the nations) need at this critical time in world history.

It's a painful process, but it's a glorious process, and if you take my friendly advice, you'll never look back with regret.

So, what will it be? Donald Trump, the self-made billionaire who fell short of his goal, or the new Donald Trump, ready to change the nation?

September 25, 2015

DONALD TRUMP AND THE DIFFERENCE BETWEEN CHUTZPAH AND RUDENESS

★ ★ ★ ★ ★

ALONG with many other Americans, I like someone who shoots straight and doesn't pull punches, someone who will tell it like it is without fear of being politically incorrect.

For many Americans, that "someone" is Donald Trump, a man who has said more politically incorrect things in a few months of presidential campaigning than many politicians say in a lifetime.

For some, this is very refreshing.

For others, it's deeply disturbing, not because of his boldness but because of his rudeness.

Now, to be clear, as a New York Jew (currently living in North Carolina but with that aggressive New York spirit alive and well within me), I understand the "art" of sarcasm, and I don't believe in candy coating our differences with some kind of Southern, genteel charm.

In fact, when my wife, Nancy, and I lived near Pensacola, Florida from 1996–2003, we experienced almost daily culture shock (I'm sure the people around us experienced some culture shock too; Nancy is also a New York Jew).

It was not just that everything seemed to move so slowly.

It was also that our direct manner of speech was perceived as being impolite (or worse), while on our part, while we loved the sweetness of the people and found much of the culture to be far more Christian than our previous milieu, we often wondered what was behind the lovely smiles.

New Yorkers might be brusque, but at least you knew what they were thinking.

All that to say that I have no problem with Trump's forthrightness and I would much rather have a bold lion running for a president than someone who tip-toed around the issues for fear of sounding offensive.

Tell me the truth, the whole truth, the hard truth, and tell me straight and plain.

That's what I want to hear and that's what so many Americans want to hear.

But there is a difference between gutsy truth-telling and abrasiveness, and unfortunately, Donald Trump is consistently guilty of the latter, which might well be the undoing of his campaign.

Really now, can you picture the president of the United States attacking world leaders the way Trump has attacked political rivals, newscasters, and others?

To repeat: I'm not looking for a sissified candidate, and I would reject a spineless candidate in a split second, no matter what other appeal he or she had.

But America needs someone with chutzpah, not rudeness, and there is a world of difference between the two.

Chutzpah is a Jewish (Yiddish) word that comes from a Hebrew/Aramaic root and speaks of a particular nerve or courage that would cause people to say, "I can't believe he had the gall to say that. What chutzpah!"

As classically explained by the Yiddish scholar Leo Rosten, chutzpah is "that quality enshrined in a man who, having killed his mother and father, throws himself on the mercy of the court because he is an orphan."

Chutzpah is an impudence that borders on shamelessness, but when it is in the cause of right, it is courageous and commendable.

It took real chutzpah for Ronald Reagan to stand at the Brandenburg Gate near the Berlin Wall on June 12, 1987 and say, "Mr. Gorbachev, tear down this wall!"

Is that what you say to the leader of the Soviet Union while standing next to the wall that his country helped build?

Absolutely, if you're committed to doing what is right rather than bowing down to fear of conflict or selling out to toothless diplomacy.

It also took real chutzpah for Elie Wiesel to confront[1] President Reagan two years earlier when Wiesel was at the White House to receive the Congressional Gold Medal of Achievement, the highest honor that the government gives to civilians.

President Reagan was scheduled to go to Germany and visit the Bergen-Belsen concentration camp, where Anne Frank died, and then, the same day, to attend ceremonies at the Bitburg military cemetery, where, it was learned, 47 SS soldiers, members of the Nazi elite guard, were buried.

As he stood to receive his prestigious gold medal, Wiesel said to the president (while declaring his respect and admiration for him), "The issue here is not politics, but good and evil. And we must never confuse them. For I have seen the SS at work. And I have seen their victims. They were my friends. They were my parents. Mr. President, there was a degree of suffering in the concentration camps that defies imagination."

He continued with this appeal: "May I, Mr. President, if it's possible at all, implore you to do something else, to find a way, to find another way, another site? That place, Mr. President, is not your place. Your place is with the victims of the SS."

What chutzpah to say this to the leader of the free world when he is personally honoring you with a congressional award in the White House.

Now, contrast the chutzpah of Reagan and Wiesel with Donald Trump's attacks on Megyn Kelly (she "had blood coming out of her whatever"), Carly Fiorina ("Look at that face!"), and Marco Rubio ("He sweats more than any young person I've ever seen in my life"), just to name a few, and you see the difference between chutzpah and rudeness.

Just imagine how much more effective Donald Trump could be if he learned the difference between the two.

November 30, 2015

WHY EVANGELICAL CHRISTIANS SHOULD NOT SUPPORT DONALD TRUMP

★ ★ ★ ★ ★

I understand the tremendous popularity of Donald Trump in America in 2015.

He is a larger-than-life reality TV star; he is incredibly rich and not beholden to anyone; he is fearless and speaks his mind; he articulates the frustrations and anger of millions of his countrymen; he gives the impression that he can fix our economy and will put an end to illegal immigration; he is not a Washington insider; he could be a strong leader who could face down our global enemies; he can even be winsome and self-effacing at times.

Yes, I do understand all this to the point that, for some weeks, I wondered to myself if I could get behind Trump as a candidate. And the question still remains, if the presidential race was between Hillary Clinton and Donald Trump, could I cast a vote for Trump? (I could not possibly vote for Hillary Clinton.)

But let's not deal in hypotheticals now. The immediate question is: Should evangelical Christians support Donald Trump as the Republican candidate? I do not see how we can if the Word of God is to be our guide and if it's important to us that a candidate have a solid moral compass and a biblically based worldview—and I mean to be our president, not our spiritual leader, since we are electing a president, not a pastor or priest.

The Scriptures teach that out of the abundance of the heart the mouth speaks (Luke 6:45), and so Trump's consistent pattern of reckless speech points to deeper issues which could make him unfit for the office of the presidency.

I'm not just talking about his silly attacks on Megyn Kelly (blood), Carly Fiorina (face), and Marco Rubio (sweat) or his more serious attacks on Mexican immigrants (accusing the many of what the few do) and others. I'm talking about his character assault on Ben Carson, comparing him to a child molester who has pathological problems and, most recently, his apparent mocking of the disability of *New York Times* reporter Serge Kovaleski.[1]

Worse still, rather than apologizing for his most recent remarks, he claims he is being unfairly attacked for his comments and alleges that he doesn't even know what Kovaleski looks like. Is he lying?

Notice that he referred to Kovaleski, who suffers from arthrogryposis, which visibly limits flexibility in his arms, as a "nice reporter," before saying, "Now the poor guy, you've got to see this guy," flailing his arms as he pretended to be Kovaleski.

Is this the man you want to be our president? The warnings in Proverbs are strong: "Do you see a man who is hasty in his words? There is more hope for a fool than for him" (Prov. 29:20). And, "A fool gives full vent to his spirit, but a wise man quietly holds it back" (Prov. 29:11).

We need a statesman, not an irresponsible flame thrower, and one can be a strong political leader who is cutting and fearless with words—think of Winston Churchill—without making a fool of oneself.

What of Trump's claim[2] that, "I have no idea who this reporter, Serge Kovalski is, what he looks like or his level of intelligence," and, "Despite having one of the all-time great memories, I certainly do not remember him"?

If this is true, why did he refer to him as a "nice reporter" and what did he mean when he said, "Now the poor guy, you've got to see this guy"? And did he merely flail his arms mocking someone who, he claimed, couldn't quite remember things correctly—this was Trump's defense—or was he making fun of Kovaleski's arms? (Watch for yourself and you be the judge as to whether he is telling the truth.)

Kovaleski, for his part, states that, "Donald and I were on a first-name basis for years. I've interviewed him in his office. I've talked to him at press conferences. All in all, I would say around a dozen times, I've interacted with him as a reporter while I was at the *Daily News*."

How could Trump have forgotten someone with Kovaleski's condition?

Trump pointed to the large sums he has given to help people with disabilities, and I don't doubt that he has, nor do I doubt that he cares about the disabled and handicapped.

But what is undeniable is that he is often irresponsible and reckless in his speech, something that could be utterly disastrous for the president of the United States of America. As noted by Jay Ruderman, an advocate for the disabled, "It is unacceptable for a child to mock another child's disability on the playground, never mind a presidential candidate mocking someone's disability as part of a national political discourse."[3]

Yet there's something that concerns me even more when it comes to evangelicals supporting Donald Trump and that is the issue of pride, the sin that is often at the root of a host of other sins (Isa. 14:11-15), the sin which God resists (James 4:6), the sin which leads to destruction (Prov. 16:18).

Trump seems to have little understanding[4] of what it means to ask God for forgiveness, while his very open, unashamed boastfulness is part and parcel of his persona. Trump and pride seem to walk hand in hand, quite comfortably at that.

So, while I do understand why many Americans are behind Donald Trump and while I do believe he could do some things well as president, I cannot understand how evangelicals can back him, especially when we have a number of solid, God-fearing, capable alternatives.

(See my video commentary on this, with the relevant clips from Trump.[5] The ugly comments from Trump supporters are quite telling.)

December 2, 2015

THE FOLLOWERS OF DONALD TRUMP DECLARE WAR

★ ★ ★ ★ ★

I knew that there would be a strong backlash when I raised concerns about evangelical Christians supporting Donald Trump as the Republican presidential candidate. (I did this by video and article.) But it is the nature of the attacks that concerns me, since it appears that for some staunch Trump supporters, you cannot be a strong leader unless you are nasty, overbearing, and rude. To fail to be so is to display your weakness.

Here's just a tiny sampling of some of the comments that came my way after the video and article were released:

- You are obviously on Medicare and you will lose it if our economy is not improved. Unbelievable!!!!

- This quack is an arm of the establishment trying to keep Trump out.

- Dr brown you wimp. Goooooo Trump.

- OMG you Evangelical "Christians" are such blasphemers. You don't even really believe in God. You live in your little Whiteopia away from the rest of the country, you have no idea what the real problems with this country.

- You're a heretic "Dr." Brown. You're preaching another Gospel, which is not another. First get saved and then perhaps we'll listen to you.

- Spoken like a liberal...how blind are these people. Christians like Mike are the very reason why we have lost our Christian youth. Mike allows the world to steal and brain wash our Christian children right out of their Christian faith and world view. Guys like Mike give the go ahead for the world to trample and put out the Christian voice. Obviously Mike. lacks foresight and godly wisdom into the future. MIKE IS A SECRET DEMOCRAT LIBERAL WORKING TOWARDS THE NEW WORLD ORDER. MIKE YOU HAVE BEEN EXPOSED, EXPOSED, EXPOSED, EXPOSED, EXPOSED, EXPOSED.

- Screw you, Michael Clown. Trump is GOD!

- You freaking idiot…You fool…Are you masochist? Is this some kind of Jewish disease within certain sects of Judaism, that they have the tendency to grapple up to [expletive]s. You did last time in Nazi Germany.

- Dr. Brown types are the reason the Democrat party surrogate (a.k.a. Republican party establishment) loses elections…

- You are part of the fringe liberal left of evangelicals.

- Another beta male necon chickenhawk fraud trashing the man from NY.

- Mr. you have lied to the people…and you Mr. making this video are very evil and you are the devil.

And on and on it goes, with one common theme: We need a real man to turn our country around, even if that man may not be a paragon of moral virtue, and anyone who opposes him is a wimp, a shill, a tool of the Republican establishment (or Democratic party), a supporter of Obama, and an enabler of Hillary.

The fact is you can be bold without being rude.

You can be a strong leader without being egotistical.

You can be fearless without being vulgar.

You can take controversial positions without demeaning your opponents in kindergarten terms.

Unfortunately, for some Trump supporters, strength and rudeness go hand in hand.

Worse still, some evangelicals have no problem overlooking Trump's obvious moral weaknesses, saying, "We're not electing a pope or pastor or priest. We're electing a president."

But don't they understand the importance of our president having a strong moral compass? Don't they recognize that when it comes to dealing with international leaders, we need a statesman—not a wimp, not a compromiser, not a man-pleaser but a statesman—and that a president given to shooting recklessly from the hip could do real harm?

I did a poll on Twitter, asking for a response to this statement: "We're not electing a pastor, but I believe the president should be a person of real integrity. Do you agree?"

98 percent of those responding said Yes.

Before that, I conducted a poll asking, "Do you believe the president of the United States should be a God-fearing individual?"

92 percent responded with Yes to that poll.

Why then is it so hard to understand that I have grave concerns about putting Donald Trump forward as the Republican candidate, especially when I believe we have strong alternatives, some of whom are proven political leaders and some of whom are either anti-establishment or outside the establishment?

It's one thing for Trump to appeal to the fears and frustrations and anger and crudeness of many Americans, but it's another thing to be able to make that appeal to biblically based followers of Jesus. Are we so easily influenced?

And is Trump the only politician who can't be bought with money? Can only an independently wealthy candidate run for office?

As I've said repeatedly, there's much to like about Donald Trump and it appears that there are certain things he could do well as a president. And under no circumstances could I vote for any of the current Democratic candidates.

But when I see the irrational response of so many of his supporters, coupled with their demonizing of those who oppose him (along with, often, the demonizing of the other candidates), this only heightens my concerns.

I will certainly pray for Donald Trump and for God's best for America. At the same time, I will raise concerns as I see them, since my goal is to see our nation blessed.

January 18, 2016

IS DONALD TRUMP
A DOUBLE-MINDED MAN?

★ ★ ★ ★ ★

W E all understand that politicians will be political, emphasizing one point to one audience and another point to another audience. We also understand that people's views can genuinely change, including the views of politicians.

But when a political leader completely flip-flops on issues and then flip-flops again, the trustworthiness of that leader must be questioned.

Does Donald Trump fit the description of a double-minded, untrustworthy leader?

Judge for yourself.

Trump claims that his views on abortion changed based on personal experience.[1]

Let's give him the benefit of the doubt, although at best, he is still not a strong, consistent pro-life candidate.

He has also taken a more negative stance on gay issues than he did in the past (although at no time did he fully support same-sex "marriage").[2] Is this simply a calculated political shift in order to win the Republican nomination?

Perhaps, but once again, let's give him the benefit of the doubt, although here too, he is hardly an articulate champion of conservative moral values.

Other shifts in his views cannot be so easily explained.

Let's consider Trump's views on Hillary Clinton.

As *Time Magazine* reported July 17, 2015, last year Donald Trump called Hillary Clinton the "worst Secretary of State in the history of the United States," and a "desperate" and "sad" candidate.[3]

Trump's insults this year have gotten even worse, to the point of him calling Hillary's bathroom break during a presidential debate "disgusting." And that is only the tip of the iceberg.[4]

Trump is also renting out a theater in Iowa so voters can see the new movie *13 Hours: The Secret Soldiers of Benghazi* for free. According to a Trump spokesperson, "Mr. Trump would like all Americans to know the truth about what happened at Benghazi."[5]

Contrast this with Trump's comments in 2007 when Hillary was running for president on the Democrat side while Rudy Guiliani was running on the Republican side.

Trump said he was torn between them, stating, "They're both terrific people, and I hope they both get the nomination."[6]

Yes, these were the words of Donald Trump.

Then, in 2012, he told Greta van Susteren on Fox News, "Hillary Clinton I think is a terrific woman," he told Greta Van Susteren. "I am biased because I have known her for years. I live in New York. She lives in New York. I really like her and her husband both a lot. I think she really works hard. And I think, again, she's given an agenda, it is not all of her, but I think she really works hard and I think she does a good job. I like her."[7]

As to Hillary's record as Secretary of State, Trump opined on Live Leak that she probably did "above and beyond everybody else and everything else."[8]

He also dismissed the importance of Benghazi and said that, if Hillary ran again for office, he was "sure" she would do a "good job" of defending her record as Secretary of State.

Is this not a glaring example of being double-minded?

How do you trust the words of someone who one day says that Hillary did her job as Secretary of State "above and beyond everybody else and everything else" and another day brands her the "worst Secretary of State in the history of the United States"?

Which is his real opinion, the old one (from just a few years back) or the current one? And if his current opinion is his real opinion, why did he speak of Hillary with such praise before?

For another glaring example, consider how Trump has flipped, then flopped, then flipped again in terms of his evaluation of Ted Cruz.

On December 13, 2015, Trump stated that Cruz has acted like "a little bit of a maniac" in the Senate and doesn't have "the right temperament" or "the right judgment" to be president.[9]

Two days later, when CNN's Dana Bash asked Trump about those comments during that night's presidential debate, he replied, "Let me tell you, as I have gotten to know him over the last three or four days, he has a wonderful temperament, he's just fine, don't worry about it."

Perhaps Trump was sincere during the debate.

Perhaps the first comments were just political rhetoric and perhaps he really did get to know Cruz better and genuinely believes that "he has a wonderful temperament" and "he's just fine."

Then how do we explain Trump's comments just one month later—and a month in which Trump made significant gains in the race—blasting Cruz in even more extreme terms?

Speaking to George Stephanopoulos on ABC News on January 17th, Trump said of Cruz, "Look, the truth is, he's a nasty guy.... Nobody likes him. Nobody in Congress likes him. Nobody likes him anywhere once they get to know him. He's a very—he's got an edge that's not good. You can't make deals with people like that and it's not a good thing. It's not a good thing for the country. Very nasty guy."[10]

Trump also called him "a total hypocrite."

So, what does Trump really believe?

Is Cruz "a little bit of a maniac" and "a nasty guy," a "very nasty guy" whom "nobody in Congress likes"? Or is Cruz "just fine" with "a wonderful temperament"?

Either Donald Trump is double-minded and therefore untrustworthy, or his words cannot be taken seriously, since there's no way of knowing what he really believes.

If you are one of his loyal supporters, I urge you to give this some calm, rational thought.

Can you really trust him with your vote?

January 27, 2016

AN OPEN LETTER TO JERRY FALWELL JR.

★ ★ ★ ★ ★

Dear Mr. Falwell,

IN light of your not-unexpected endorsement[1] of Donald Trump for president, I have some candid questions for you.

But I write with the utmost respect for Liberty University and with real appreciation for your own labors, not to mention those of your esteemed father.

I raise these questions for you as well as for other evangelicals who also support Mr. Trump for president, but in doing so, I recognize that there is far more that unites us than divides us, and I do not intend to lose sight of that.

That being said, my concerns are very deep, addressing the fundamental questions of: 1) What are America's most pressing needs right now? And: 2) What qualities should we look for when voting for the President of the United States?

You had previously pointed to your father's support of Ronald Reagan, noting that, "When he walked into the voting booth, he wasn't electing a Sunday school teacher or a pastor or even a president who shared his theological beliefs; he was electing the president of the United States with the talents, abilities and experience required to lead a nation. After all, Jimmy Carter was a great Sunday school teacher, but look at what happened to our nation with him in the presidency. Sorry."

So on the one hand, you have stressed that as evangelical Christians we can back someone who does not share our theological beliefs as long as that person has "the talents, abilities and experience required to lead a nation."

At the same time, you stated in your endorsement that Mr. Trump is "a successful executive and entrepreneur, a wonderful father and a man who I believe can lead our country to greatness again," adding, "In my opinion, Donald Trump lives a life of loving and helping others as Jesus taught in the great commandment."

Are you, then, seriously endorsing Mr. Trump as a man following the example of Jesus?

One colleague wrote to me after learning of your endorsement, saying, "I just don't understand how a true Christian can so easily dismiss all this.... Wife posed nude, married three times, nasty, crude, cruel, proud, dishonest, manipulative, casino owner and promoter, bankrupted several companies, 'hates' abortion but agrees to make it legal, gutter mouth...and on and on and on. It's not necessary for the president to be a Christian, but doesn't integrity and a moral compass count for the highest office in the land? How about someone who can reign in their tongue?"

Conservative Christian leader John Stemberger has raised similar concerns in detail, and I have asked whether Mr. Trump's words can be trusted based on his consistent flip-flopping, right until now. (It appears that he has changed political parties at least five times. Are you sure you can trust where he stands today?)

Mr. Falwell, in light of Mr. Trump's attacks on those he happens to dislike at the moment—be it Megyn Kelly, Ted Cruz, Jeb Bush, or Rosie O'Donnell—attacks in which he behaves more like a spoiled, petulant child than a presidential candidate, how can you point to his Christlike character?

I cite this as one small example out of many, but isn't it true that out of the abundance of the heart the mouth speaks? And does it not concern you that it seems that no matter what he says or does, his followers still back him?

I'm sure Mr. Trump can be a very kind man, and I've been told that, in private, he is very genuine and caring. And I don't doubt that he helps lots of people with his wealth, and it's great to hear that his kids love and respect him. But to extol his allegedly Christlike ways is, in my view, quite absurd.

You might say, "But this is where you're missing the point. He is the man for the job, the man who can get things done and restore our nation to greatness."

Yet this is where I have my greatest issue with evangelicals backing Donald Trump.

Simply stated, I firmly believe that our greatest problems are moral and spiritual, not economic or otherwise, and to think that we can make America great again by securing our borders, defeating ISIS, and rebuilding our economy without first addressing the moral rot in our society is to deceive ourselves gravely.

Donald Trump is hardly the man to address America's moral demise!

Proverbs 14:34 states, "Righteousness exalts a nation, but sin is a reproach to any people." This is true for all peoples and all nations, and without addressing our deepest issues first, we will be guilty of repeating the error of Israel's false prophets who superficially treated the fracture of their people (see Jer. 6:14; 8:11).

Looking at some of our most pressing moral issues, when it comes to same-sex "marriage," Mr. Trump has stated that it's the law of the land whether he likes it or not. In contrast, a number of the other Republican candidates have made clear that they will work against this unjust Supreme Court ruling.

Similarly, while we have a number of true, proven pro-life Republican candidates, Mr. Trump can hardly be viewed as a pro-life champion, despite his recent editorial touting his pro-life sympathies.

Our next president could appoint as many as four new Supreme Court justices, and those justices could potentially shape the nation for decades to come.

Will Mr. Trump cut a deal with his opponents when it comes to appointing justices, or will he appoint righteous justices who will help restore our country's moral sanity? Can you really say you're confident you know what he will do?

You stated that, "He cannot be bought, he's not a puppet on a string like many other candidates...who have wealthy donors as their puppet masters."

But here too you appear to have missed something of great importance.

Perhaps Mr. Trump is not beholden to his donors—at least, not at this early stage of the campaign—but he does seem beholden to the gods of money and fame, and he is as driven by material wealth and popularity as any candidate in memory (perhaps even more than any candidate in memory).

Do not these gods blind one's eyes even more than gifts from wealthy donors? And do you have concrete proof that all the other candidates have strayed from their convictions in order to gain financial support? It would seem clear that some of them have done quite the opposite.

It is absolutely true that we are not electing a pastor or priest or pope. But it is of the utmost importance that our president be a man of integrity, a man of strong moral character, a man who can address the most fundamental needs of our nation.

Nothing I have seen or heard in recent months has given me any indication that this describes Donald Trump.

Rush Limbaugh has pointed to the new divide between nationalism and conservatism, with Donald Trump being viewed as the nationalist/populist leader and Ted Cruz being viewed as the conservative leader.

For me, as an evangelical follower of Jesus, the contrast is between putting nationalism first or the kingdom of God first. From my vantage point, you and other evangelicals seem to have put nationalism first, and that is what deeply concerns me.

Accordingly, if we put the kingdom of God first (by which, of course, I do not mean trying to impose a theocracy but rather putting biblical values first), we can also rebuild the economy, address the immigration issue, and strengthen our national defense.

But if we put nationalism first, the most pressing issues will be relegated to second place, and it will be a distant second place at that. And like Israel of old, we will look for a king to make us great rather than looking to the Lord.

I welcome your response to these questions and concerns however you choose to respond—in writing, on my radio show or in private—and I pray that regardless of our differences, God will use you to draw Mr. Trump to Jesus as his Savior and Lord.

February 3, 2016

MR. TRUMP,
WHAT IS "NOT WORTH IT"?

★ ★ ★ ★ ★

I N the aftermath of Donald Trump's second-place finish to Ted Cruz in Iowa, his Twitter feed was surprisingly silent for 15 hours, a near eternity for the very vocal, Twitter-friend billionaire.

When he did resume tweeting, he did it with typical aplomb, first with positive words about Iowa, and then with one tweet that generated a lot of attention and criticism. But what exactly did he mean?

At 11:39 A.M., Feb. 2, he tweeted: "I don't believe I have been given any credit by the voters for self-funding my campaign, the only one. I will keep doing, but not worth it!"

A headline on the *Daily Caller* exclaimed, "Donald Trump Is Disappointed In You, Iowa: 'Not Worth It!'"

A headline on the *Washington Examiner* stated, "Donald Trump, angry at voters, media, growls, 'It's not worth it.'"

But what, exactly, did he mean? What is "not worth it"?

Only Donald Trump can answer that question, so, with the hope that we can get an answer, I'll ask him for clarification, with the hope that even putting the questions on the table will be enlightening.

Mr. Trump, by "not worth it" do you mean that it's not worth your money to run for president and lose? In that case, one might think this was more about you than about the people of America.

Do you mean that if people are not going to recognize your sacrificial efforts on their behalf, then they don't deserve it, that you're only willing to use some of your massive wealth to fund your campaign if people will give you credit for it?

To put it more bluntly, sir, is this campaign about the people or about you? Are you running for president in order to serve our country and save us from disaster or are you doing it because you want to be president?

I would think that if your heart is to serve your country, a country that I'm sure you love deeply, then no sacrifice would be too great, and if you had to spend every dime you had to be elected and to prove that you could not be bought, it would be worth it.

I would also think that it would be worth it regardless of whether you got credit or not. Isn't real virtue found in the doing of a good thing rather than in being acknowledged for it?

Someone very close to me—actually, my bride of almost 40 years, an incredibly perceptive and clear-headed woman—posted this on Facebook, and I believe her comments were right on.

She wrote, "What's shocking is that one would expect that his claims for loving this country and wanting to 'Make America great again' would overshadow any other feeling he might have. My expectation for a presidential candidate would be one who thinks that it certainly *is* worth it, no matter how under-appreciated they might feel…it's all worth it, whatever the sacrifice may be, it's worth it. So many other candidates have been ridiculed, trashed, and humiliated, yet they keep on going without complaining about the American people. Trump's statement shows *tremendous* weakness. Any individual, working hard toward a goal, who states, 'it's not worth it'…I mean, really, why would I want to support any candidate with that attitude even if they keep on going? Running for the highest office in the land is not for the faint of heart."

She then added, "The thing that struck me about this particular comment of his was that it's the antithesis of strength (which is what he is touted for). It's the antithesis of a heart that is truly fighting for the cause. His dedication seems hollow, even if he is willing to fund his own campaign. A true leader and dedicated fighter for the cause is not looking for the accolades of men."

And that brings us back to you, Mr. Trump.

What exactly did you mean when you said, "It's not worth it"?

We can't seem to find a good construction to put on it, especially one worthy of the potential President of the United States.

February 15, 2016

COGNITIVE DISSONANCE AND THE
FOLLOWERS OF DONALD TRUMP

★ ★ ★ ★ ★

WHEN the legendary boxing promoter Bob Arum was challenged about the veracity of one of his past statements, he famously replied, "Yesterday I was lying, today I am telling the truth."

This leads to the obvious question, "But Mr. Arum, what will you tell us tomorrow?"

There is something about Arum's line that reminds me of Donald Trump, except that: 1) Arum was not running for the office of the President of the United States; and 2) Trump could say the same thing that Arum did but it appears that many of his followers would say, "You see! He's not a politician. He tells the truth."

Have you ever seen the like with a political candidate? And who but Trump could boast that he could shoot someone in broad daylight in New York City and his followers would still follow him? Who but Trump would want to boast of such a thing?

By all fair accounts, Trump did not perform well in the South Carolina debate on Saturday night, but this didn't matter much to his followers, as evidenced by the Drudge Report poll which, as always, declared him the overwhelming winner.

So when the crowd boos him for his vile behavior, that's just proof that the crowd has been stacked against him.

When competing candidates rightly confront his vacillating positions, they're branded liars, corrupt politicians, and, worse, all to the delight of his followers.

"We need an alpha male," they exclaim. "Trump will get things done."

As to how, exactly, he will do it, no one seems to know.

But be assured that, despite four Trump bankruptcies (which surely affected many people, even if Trump was not personally affected) and the failures of Trump Airlines, Trump Vodka, Trump Mortgage, Trump: The Game, The China Connection, Trump Casinos, Trump Steaks, Trump Magazine, and GoTrump. com, Donald Trump will get the job done.

He always does.

He only wins—as in wins, wins, wins.

And when he doesn't win (as in Iowa)? Actually, second was really first, since, we're told, the winner cheated. And his followers cheer him on.

But this is nothing to laugh about. The future of our country is at stake, especially with the sudden death of Antonin Scalia, which makes the question of the appointing of new Supreme Court justices all the more urgent.

Last August 26—so, barely six months ago—Trump stated that his sister would make a "phenomenal" Supreme Court justice, despite her strong support for partial-birth abortion.

Now, after being challenged about what kind of justices he would appoint if president, Trump says that he was only joking about his past comments about his sister: "Just so you understand, I said it jokingly. My sister's a brilliant person, known as a brilliant person, but it's obviously a conflict."

Shades of Bob Arum.

"I was joking yesterday, but today I'm being serious."

Dear followers of Donald Trump, are you sure this is your man?

But it gets worse.

During the Saturday night debate in patriotic, pro-George W. Bush South Carolina, Trump said that Bush lied about Iraq and claimed that he, Trump, was the only one to oppose the war in Iraq. In fact, at a debate last September he said, "You can check it out, check out—I'll give you 25 different stories."

When asked for proof of this on Sunday, he responded, "I wasn't a politician so people didn't write everything I said."

Really? No proof of 25 different stories you told us to check out? No documentation of your very outspoken opposition to the war? You spoke loudly and clearly back then but no one noticed it because you weren't a politician?

Unfortunately for Trump loyalists, Andrew Kaczynski has documented that "in his 2000 book *The America We Deserve*, Trump noted Iraq was developing weapons of mass destruction and targeted Iraq strikes had little impact on their overall capabilities. The Donald [*sic*] said the best course might be against Iraq to 'carry the mission to its conclusion.'" (Kaczynski provides the exact quote.)

It wasn't until August of 2004 that Trump expressed clear opposition to the war, long after it had started and long after the problems with our engagement there had emerged.

This revelation led to the clever tweet from *New York Post* columnist Robert A. George, "Trump knew Iraq had WMDs before Bush lied abt [*sic*] Iraq having WMDs and followed Trump's advice to finish job in Iraq!"

In response to all this, I posted on Facebook and Twitter, "Trump could say tomorrow 'I've been lying about everything!' And his followers would say 'That's our man! He tells it like it is.'"

And how did some of his followers respond to my comment?

"So explain to me who is better than Trump."

And, "No he wouldn't. Nobody is ideal, but you have it in for Trump. He is better than all of the socialists and other deceptive liars running."

And, "[People would] much rather give Trump the benefit of the doubt because he does not answer to any special interest groups and because he proves that you can fight the leftwing media and their strongest weapon 'political correctness.'"

What makes this all the more disturbing, not to mention downright scary, is that a substantial percentage of his supporters profess to be evangelical Christians, and it still appears that there is almost nothing he could say or do that would dampen their support for him.

"After all," they lamely repeat, "we're not electing a pastor; we're electing a president."

And if I might borrow a quote, "Yesterday he was lying; today he's telling the truth."

Let the voter beware.

February 19, 2016

Can We Judge the Christianity of Donald Trump?

★ ★ ★ ★ ★

DONALD Trump has challenged the Christianity of Ted Cruz while also raising questions about the nature of Ben Carson's faith. In the past, he also suggested that President Obama might be a Muslim rather than a Christian. Now, the pope has questioned the Christianity of Trump.

It appears that what goes around, comes around.

Trump's immediate response was to call Pope Francis's comments "disgraceful" and to state that, "No leader, especially a religious leader, should have the right to question another man's religion or faith."

So, Trump can question the faith of others but the pope cannot question his?

In defense of Trump, Jerry Falwell Jr. has stated that, "I have no doubts that he is a man of faith, that he's a Christian."

Welcome to the 2016 version of the presidential race, representing reality TV at its most unscripted and bizarre.

Two serious questions, though, are begging to be asked.

First, according to the Bible, do we have the right to judge someone's profession of faith, let alone the mandate to?

Second, if we are called to judge, what are the criteria?

On the one hand, the Bible tells us repeatedly that only God knows the heart and, in that sense, only He knows who belongs to Him and who doesn't. At the same time, the Bible repeatedly calls us to examine what a professing Christian believes and to evaluate how that person lives, to judge the tree by its fruit, as Jesus put it.

Using that criteria, we know, for example, that Richard Dawkins is not a Christian, since he denies the existence of God, the authority of Scripture, and the atoning death and bodily resurrection of Jesus. We also know that Osama bin Laden was not a Christian, since he was a radical Muslim and an unrepentant mass murderer.

In the same way, albeit in a much less extreme fashion, we know that our friendly next-door neighbors are not Christians when they demonstrate no understanding of their own sin, no recognition of their need for forgiveness, and no knowledge of who Jesus really is or why He died on the cross. And we can say this with certainty even if they attend church services every year at Easter and Christmas.

A Christian believes core Christian doctrines and lives a basic Christian lifestyle.

The Christian faith begins with an acknowledgment of our sin and a profession of faith in our Savior and is then evidenced by a godly life—not a perfect life, but a godly life. As Jesus said, "Not everyone who says to me, 'Lord, Lord,' will enter the kingdom of heaven, but the one who does the will of my Father who is in heaven" (Matt. 7:21).

James (Jacob) echoed this saying, "Show me your faith apart from your works, and I will show you my faith by my works" (James 2:18b).

In other words, talk is cheap. Let's see how you live.

That's why Paul could contrast the works of the flesh with the fruit of the Spirit (Gal. 5:17-23), adding, "And those who belong to Christ Jesus have crucified the flesh with its passions and desires" (Gal. 5:24).

That's why Paul could also state plainly that no adulterer or drunkard or practicing homosexual would enter God's kingdom (among other lifestyles; see 1 Cor. 6:9-10; Eph. 5:5-7; Gal. 5:17-21), also noting, "And such were some of you. But you were washed, you were sanctified, you were justified in the name of the Lord Jesus Christ and by the Spirit of our God" (1 Cor. 6:11).

How does Donald Trump line up?

We know that in the past he boasted about his numerous adulterous affairs and that he built the first casino in America with its own strip club, actually featuring 36,000 square feet of adult entertainment. Yet he sees no need to ask for forgiveness for these past acts (which are just a small sampling of ungodly behavior) because he is "a very good person."

This is the opposite of Christianity, which begins with a recognition of guilt and an open confession of our need for forgiveness. As for Donald Trump, at no point in any interview that has ever been conducted with him has he offered the slightest understanding of the heart of the gospel.

That alone would indicate that Trump is a not a real Christian.

As for his conduct, while we have no idea how he lives in private, and while he presumably has many good qualities that are commendable, we do know that his public conduct is often deplorable, with his tweets and comments violating almost every standard of Christian decorum.

This is the standard Paul laid out for followers of Jesus: "Do not let any unwholesome talk come out of your mouths, but only what is helpful for building others up according to their needs, that it may benefit those who listen" (Eph. 4:29 NIV).

Trump's vitriolic, nasty, often vulgar, sometimes patently false attacks on others violate this verse from beginning to end, both in spirit and in letter. And remember that it was Jesus who told us that it was out of the abundance of the heart that the mouth speaks.

Jesus also "told this parable to some who trusted in themselves that they were righteous, and treated others with contempt [does this sound familiar to you at all?]:"

> *Two men went up into the temple to pray, one a Pharisee and the other a tax collector* [remember that in New Testament times, tax collectors were notoriously corrupt].
>
> *The Pharisee, standing by himself, prayed thus: "God, I thank you that I am not like other men, extortioners, unjust, adulterers, or even like this tax collector. I fast twice a week; I give tithes of all that I get."*

But the tax collector, standing far off, would not even lift up his eyes to heaven, but beat his breast, saying, "God, be merciful to me, a sinner!"

I tell you, this man went down to his house justified, rather than the other. For everyone who exalts himself will be humbled, but the one who humbles himself will be exalted (Luke 18:9-14).

Which one sounds like Donald Trump, the Pharisee or the tax collector? And which is more characteristic of Mr. Trump, the person who exalts himself or the person who humbles himself?

Again, God is the ultimate judge, but He does tell us to judge the tree by its fruit, and that means that Donald Trump could really use our prayers.

You may still plan to vote for him to be president, even though he shows no true signs of being a genuine Christian (although it's clear he believes he is one). That's obviously your call entirely.

But let's not foolishly proclaim him to be a Christian when, until recently, many of his ardent supporters acknowledged that he was not.

And just consider what a world changer Donald Trump could be if he really knew the Lord. Through prayer and God's mercy, it could happen.

February 26, 2016

DONALD TRUMP:
THE VACILLATOR-IN-CHIEF

★ ★ ★ ★ ★

I F Donald Trump ends up being our next president, I will pray that he will be the greatest president we have ever had and I will fervently hope that I'm absolutely wrong about all of my concerns. Until then (or at least until we decide on the Republican nominee), I will sound the alarm and raise my voice as loudly and clearly as I can.

Do not be duped by Donald Trump!

The issue is not whether he's a true Christian.

The issue is whether he can be trusted and whether we even know what his real positions are.

So I ask you, if you are a Trump supporter, with all respect for your zeal and with affirmation of your frustration with status-quo politics, how can you know what Trump really believes or what he will actually do if elected?

He changes his views from one day to the next—sometimes diametrically—and flatly contradicts his previous positions, then insults and mocks those who challenge him, often in the most puerile ways. No other candidate in memory—perhaps in our nation's history—has vacillated so wildly and dramatically in such a short period of time.

Trump truly is the vacillator-in-chief.

Let's remember that we're talking about who will be the next President of the United States, arguably the most powerful person in the world, so this is not the time for blind loyalty. The stakes are very high.

Please look at the facts honestly, and if you have the courage, look at them through the eyes of a critic or skeptic.

Last week on MSNBC, when pressed by Joe Scarborough, he pledged to stay neutral on the Israeli-Palestinian conflict until elected president, not only an ambiguous answer but a weak answer. Less than seven days later, speaking at Regent University, he pledged "100 percent support" for Israel.

Which position, if either, is true? What will Trump do if elected? Who knows?

And is it at all curious that on the infamously liberal MSNBC, hardly a pro-Israel bastion, Trump would not openly stand with Israel, while at the famously pro-Israel Regent University, he promised to stand with Israel?

Trump is either lying or vacillating or both, but either way, he's untrustworthy.

Earlier this month, when asked by Chris Wallace on Fox News if he would nominate Supreme Court justices who supported overturning the Obergefell decision that redefined marriage, Trump said he would "strongly consider" it. Less than one week later, he assured a lesbian reporter that under his administration, there would be great progress for LGBT Americans.

When pressed by ABC's George Stephanopoulos as to how both of these positions could be true at the same time, he answered (to paraphrase), "Well, it's a long way off, George, but trust me. We're going to have great judges and everybody will love them."

This prompted the gay website PinkNews to opine, "It's all very clear: if you're a lesbian voter he will support your marriage, but if you're an evangelical voter he'll oppose lesbian marriage. If you ask on Fox News then he will absolutely consider it, but if you ask on NBC then he hasn't decided whether he will decide to decide yet."

Trump also vacillated wildly when asked whether his sister (of pro-partial birth abortion fame) should be nominated as a Supreme Court justice including: yes, no, I was joking, I wasn't joking, I have no idea what she believes. (This is a partial, very rough summary.) Then add to the mix that in 2000 he said there should be no abortion litmus test for federal judges.

And the list goes on and on, almost endlessly.

During Thursday night's debate, Leon Wolf tweeted this quote from Trump: "I have great respect for Justice Scalia," followed by, "Trump Less than 5 months ago...slammed Scalia for not supporting affirmative action."

Others called him out during the debating for reversing his position on Libya's Qaddafi, contrasting his remarks in the debate ("[Cruz is] saying I was in favor of Libya? I never discussed that subject. I was in favor of Libya? We would be so much better off if Gadhafi were in charge right now.") with his 2011 comments that, "Now we should go in, we should stop this guy which would be very easy and very quick. We could do it surgically, stop him from doing it, and save these lives."

So, not only did he deny ever discussing the subject—either an outright lie or an example of a terrible memory—but he also reversed his earlier position.

Then there are his contradictory statements on government funded healthcare, Planned Parenthood, and a host of other important subjects.

As Dr. Bunsen Honeydew (@DunsScottus) tweeted during the debate, "Trump is actually just Sanders in a toupee. 'I'm gonna give you coverage for pre-existing conditions but no individual mandate.' Magic!"

Not surprisingly, immediately after the debate the Cruz campaign released a video from the debate where, in answer to Cruz's "true or false" question, Trump said it was "false" that he ever said that the government should pay for everyone's healthcare. This was followed by a clip from Trump's Sept. 27, 2015 *60 Minutes* interview in which he stated emphatically that, "The government's gonna pay for it."

Speaking of Cruz, let's not forget Trump's vacillating comments on him, ranging from: He's "a little bit of a maniac" to "he has a wonderful temperament, he's just fine, don't worry about it," back to he's a "Very nasty guy," a "total hypocrite," a "liar," and "a very unstable guy" (all in the course of a month).

And we can't leave out his statements on Hillary Clinton as Secretary of State, going from "I think she really works hard and I think she does a good job. I like her" (2012) to "worst Secretary of State in the history of the United States" (2016).

Shall we also mention Trump's completely absurd statements, such as his suggestion after the debate that "maybe" he's being audited because he's "a strong Christian"?

Or what of Trump's righteous indignation over former Mexican President Vicente Fox's statement that Mexico is "not going to pay" for that "[expletive] wall"? Trump said to Wolf Blitzer during the debate, "This guy used a filthy, disgusting word on television, and he should be ashamed of himself, and he should apologize, OK?" And he said this with a straight face.

And in a post-debate interview with Chris Cuomo he actually said, "And I could tell you I would not use that word, but if I did use that word, uh, I probably wouldn't have even been allowed on the stage tonight."

This prompted Cuomo to laughingly respond, "You do understand there's a touch of irony in that...." To say the least!

What's really sad, though, is the response from his supporters, even when he's exposed.

I posted this on my Facebook page after the debate: "Come on Trump supporters! Wake up and face reality. You cannot believe what this man says—unless you really believe he's being audited because he's a strong Christian. Stop drinking the Kool-Aid!"

Trump supporters responded with gems like these:

- 🐦 "Ur a moron and as evil as Obama is" [*sic*].
- 🐦 "U DONT HAVE A CLUE...TRUMP 100 %...we need a strong man and he is all we have...Christian or not...that is not your call...lol...and who are U...or who do U think U R...an old joke..." [*sic*].
- 🐦 "Gooo TRUMP!!! Please stop the bashing thank u" [*sic*].
- 🐦 "And ur a Christian. U prove my point because ur not just a money hog or prob will burn in hell Ur a Christian. Hahaha. Maybe so is Obama Yep same cockroaches" [*sic*].
- 🐦 "You are a Christian leader on here attacking us on you're site??? Way uncool?? What other Christian leaders would do this??? Report this site and delete!! U don't need to be rude!! Not a Christian at all" [*sic*].

And there was this truly insightful comment: "I spoke to a Trump supporter today and he told me, 'it's part of life to flip flop on issues because your learning new things every day'" [*sic*]. Unreal.

One day earlier, I had conducted a poll on Twitter in which the vast majority of those who responded said that, of Trump, Cruz, Rubio, or Carson, it was Trump who was the least honest. In response to this, the "Trump Revolution" tweeted back, "Bad poll. Trump is the most honest!"

As I said two weeks ago, Trump could say he's been lying all along and his supporters would commend him for his honesty.

And so, Trump can decisively lose a debate to Marco Rubio and Ted Cruz with headlines proclaiming, "Donald Trump Was Badly Exposed," yet his followers, who apparently dominate Drudge Report, can crown him the overwhelming victor. (When checked at 3:00 A.M., EST, the Drudge voters gave Trump 60 percent of the vote with a combined 34 percent going to Cruz and Rubio.)

May I make one more appeal for sober reflection and sanity?

March 7, 2016

AN OPEN LETTER TO PASTOR ROBERT JEFFRESS

★ ★ ★ ★ ★

Dear Pastor Jeffress,

I have the utmost respect for your many years of faithful ministry, for your gracious and unflinching witness for the Lord, and for your devotion to His people over decades of service.

It is in that spirit of respect as brothers that I appeal to you to reconsider your position that "any Christian who would sit at home and not vote for the Republican nominee [if it were Trump]...that person is being motivated by pride rather than principle."

Pastor Jeffress, is this really your carefully considered, prayerful position?

I fully understand your argument that, while many of us are not convinced that Donald Trump is a true pro-life conservative, we know that Hillary Clinton certainly is not, and so we have a chance of going in the right direction with Trump but the certainty of going in the wrong direction with Hillary.

That is why influential thinkers like Dennis Prager have stated that, as distasteful as the prospect is, he would vote for Trump rather than Hillary with the hope that Trump might appoint one or more good Supreme Court justices while Hillary would do her best to appoint as many radical liberals as possible.

I certainly understand these arguments, and they do carry weight.

But, my dear brother, do you honestly believe that those who could not in good conscience vote for Trump, should he be the Republican nominee, must be acting on pride rather than principle?

To the contrary, it is principle that drives many of those in the #NeverTrump camp.

Consider, for example, the words of Christian attorney (and Iraq Bronze Star veteran) David French.

He wrote, "I have spent my entire adult life advocating against abortion and working to protect the unborn. I didn't endure the taunts and jeers of my law-school classmates, work countless days and nights away from home to protect the free-speech rights of pro-life protestors, and defend the freedoms of the unsung heroes in crisis-pregnancy centers only to vote for a man who's a walking Planned Parenthood commercial."

That, sir, is the voice of principle, not pride.

He adds, "There are those who say that the #NeverTrump crew should 'get a life,' but we are opposed to Trump because of our lives: our life's work, to be precise. No, not our careers—they will go on—but rather the long and vital work of building a conservative movement that represents our nation's best hope for the greatness Trump claims to crave."

There are many other Christians who feel just as French does, who cannot imagine pushing the button or pulling the lever in support of Trump, a man who has managed to bring the Republican Party to all-time lows and who has made a mockery of the campaign process.

Many of us have had it with politics as usual and have tremendous distrust for the political establishment, yet we would feel like we were selling our souls to help a man like Trump become the representative of our nation. And we feel this way not so much because of who Trump was in the past but because of who he is today.

Pastor Jeffress, do you have any regret for telling the *Christian Post* that, when it comes to Christians who will not vote for Trump, "I think the Bible has a word for people like that—it's fools"?

You have frequently pointed to the 1980 presidential race between Ronald Reagan and Jimmy Carter, the former being a twice-married former Hollywood actor, the latter being a born-again Sunday school teacher.

But Donald Trump is not Ronald Reagan and Ted Cruz (Trump's leading competitor) is not Jimmy Carter, so the comparison is not only inapt, it is irrelevant.

You have also stated in speeches and TV commentaries that evangelical Christians have lost faith in Washington, so they are ready to elect a businessman to get the government in order while the church focuses on moral and spiritual issues.

But is there no vital intersection between the government and society? And isn't the very reason so many of us opposed Barack Obama and now oppose Hillary Clinton because of the national damage that bad government can bring about?

You stated that "if Donald Trump is elected president of the United States, we who are evangelical Christians are going to have a true friend in the White House. God bless Donald Trump!"

But how do you know this for sure? In the recent past, he has completely reversed major positions in the course of a week, while in the course of the last debate, he reversed a previous position on immigration, only to issue a different statement after the debate.

The same happened with his position on torture and killing the families of terrorists, which over a matter of days changed from "I will order the military to break all international laws, and you better believe they will obey me" to "Of course I understand the rule of law and would not ask the military to break the law" to "If elected, I will expand the law."

How can you be so sure of what he will do if elected when he has vacillated so wildly already? This is the man who thundered at one debate, "Bush lied!" (about WMDs in Iraq)—an ugly, unfounded accusation—only to mollify his statement within hours.

This is the man you want us to trust?

And what potential damage could Trump cause as President? Could he lead us into a needless war? Could he alienate our allies? Could he provoke racial or ethnic strife (and even violence) in our nation by making inflammatory remarks?

Perhaps rather than saying, "God bless Donald Trump!" you should have said, "May God bring Donald Trump to repentance and salvation!"

When it comes to the issue of pragmatism, both Cruz and Rubio have consistently polled better against Hillary than Trump (Trump's unlikability numbers are off the charts), so it could be argued that a vote for Trump today is a vote for Hillary tomorrow.

Even if Trump did secure the Republican nomination, some would still argue against voting for him based on both principle and pragmatism.

Principle, because they cannot do so in good conscience.

Pragmatism, because Christians would be forced into an all-out (nonviolent) moral and cultural battle if Hillary were elected, because the church would be forced to go after God with a greater desperation for our nation, and because the Republican leadership would be forced to take a stand.

In contrast, it could be that a President Trump (which is still hard for me to wrap my mind around) would be the ultimate compromiser and dealmaker, just adding to the current morass.

In other words, a Hillary victory, as much as I deplore the thought and could not under any circumstance vote for her, could be the final straw that breaks the back of American Christian complacency, leading to an awakening.

That being said, I have not yet made a final decision of what I would do if it came down to Hillary vs. Trump. I simply ask you to recognize that the issue for me and many others is one of principle, and we are wrestling with it in the fear of Almighty God.

You said in your interview with the *Christian Post*, "Every Christian has the right to choose a candidate he thinks is best. But no Christian has the right to make his preference a litmus test for somebody else's Christianity or spirituality."

I certainly concur with you on this and, despite my profound reservations concerning Donald Trump, I cannot judge your reasons for supporting him now.

In that same spirit, I encourage you to retract your comments that Christians who would not support Trump in the general election are fools who are acting on pride rather than principle.

March 10, 2016

IS DONALD TRUMP A MODERN-DAY CYRUS?

★ ★ ★ ★ ★

EVER since Donald Trump began to surge as a candidate last year, Christians have been pointing to the book of Isaiah and comparing Trump with the ancient Persian King Cyrus. Some have even claimed that God has revealed to them that He will use Trump for the good of America just as He used Cyrus for the good of the Jewish people, even though Cyrus was a "pagan" king.

Could this be true?

Let's first look at the biblical and ancient Near Eastern evidence.

Cyrus (whose name was pronounced "ko-resh" in Hebrew) became king of Persia in 559 B.C. and conquered Babylon in 539 B.C. He is mentioned in a majestic passage in Isaiah where the Lord says of Cyrus, "'He is My shepherd, and shall perform all My desire'; and he declares to Jerusalem, 'You shall be built,' and to the temple, 'Your foundation shall be laid'" (Isa. 44:28 MEV).

In other words, Cyrus would be the one who would cause Jerusalem to be rebuilt after it had been destroyed decades earlier by the Babylonians.

But there's more that Isaiah says about Cyrus as the prophecy continues into chapter 45:

> *Thus says the Lord to Cyrus, His anointed, whose right hand I have held—to subdue nations before him and to loosen the loins of kings, to open doors before him so that the gates will not be shut: I will go before you and make the crooked places straight; I will break in pieces the gates of bronze and shatter the bars of iron. And I will*

*give you the treasures of darkness and hidden riches of secret places
so that you may know that I, the Lord, who calls you by your name,
am the God of Israel. For Jacob My servant's sake and Israel My
chosen one, I have even called you by your name; I have named
you, though you have not known Me* (Isaiah 45:1-4 MEV).

Notice the beginning and the end of this passage. First, Cyrus, a non-Israelite king, is called God's anointed, a term elsewhere only used for Israelite leaders. Second, Cyrus, although called by the God of Israel, doesn't actually know the God of Israel. Instead, like the vast majority of people in the ancient world, he worshiped different deities in the form of idols.

In fulfillment of this prophecy, the Scriptures record how Cyrus made this decree to the Jewish people living in Babylon, where they had been taken in exile: "The Lord [meaning Yahweh] God of heaven has given me all the kingdoms of the earth, and He has commanded me to build for Him a house at Jerusalem, which is in Judah. Whoever is among you of all His people, may the Lord [Yahweh] his God be with him. Let him go up" (2 Chron. 36:23 MEV).

So a pagan king encouraged the Jewish people to return to their homeland and rebuild their temple, also helping to finance the endeavor.

But Cyrus did not only do this for the people of Israel.

This became a standard Persian policy, allowing exiles to return to their homelands and rebuild their temples as subjects of the Persian Empire.

We know this from the famous Cyrus Cylinder that was discovered in 1879. There, we read that Marduk, the chief god of the Babylonian pantheon and called "the king of the gods" in the text, "took the hand of Cyrus...and called him by his name, proclaiming him aloud for the kingship over all of everything."

We also read in the text that Cyrus restored the various idol temples in his empire, which gives further confirmation to the biblical account.

So here, it is Marduk who is given credit for the reign of Cyrus. In the Bible, it is Yahweh, the God of Israel and the only true God, who takes the credit. Obviously, Cyrus did not know Him, just as Isaiah said.

Could Donald Trump, then, be a modern-day Cyrus? Could it be that Trump, like Cyrus, clearly does not know the Lord in a real and personal way but could still be used by God to accomplish His purposes?

As the saying goes, let God be God, meaning, it's up to Him to do what He wants to do. Only He can answer this question for sure.

Or, from a more secular perspective, only time will tell.

What's clear, though, is that God did not raise up an idol-worshiping king to rule the nation of Israel. That would have been a curse rather than a blessing.

In contrast, Christians are talking about God raising up Trump to lead America, which would be very different than Cyrus being used to help the exiles return to Jerusalem and rebuild it.

That doesn't mean, of course, that Trump could not be a Cyrus-type of figure. It simply means that the parallel breaks down when applied.

But there's another possibility to consider.

There was another ancient king named Nebuchadnezzar, the Babylonian leader who, decades before Cyrus became king, led his armies to destroy Jerusalem, burn down the temple, and send the Jewish people into exile in 586 B.C.

He too was an idol worshiper, yet shockingly, Yahweh called him "My servant," stating plainly, "I will send and take all the families of the north, says the Lord, and Nebuchadnezzar the king of Babylon, My servant, and will bring them against this land [meaning Judah] and its inhabitants, and against all these surrounding nations; I will utterly destroy them, and make them an astonishment, a hissing, and perpetual desolations" (Jer. 25:9 MEV; see also 27:6; 43:10).

So Cyrus was anointed by God to restore the Jewish people from captivity and to rebuild Jerusalem after Nebuchadnezzar, as a vessel of divine judgment, was called by God to send the Jewish people into exile and to destroy Jerusalem.

Two pagan kings, one raised up to bring judgment and the other raised up to bring restoration.

Is Donald Trump a Cyrus or a Nebuchadnezzar, if either?

Let God be God, and only time will tell.

But while we wait and watch and vote and act, let's not forget to pray: God, have mercy on America!

The one thing of which we are sure is that this is a very critical season in the history of our nation.

March 13, 2016

DONALD TRUMP, ANGER, AND VIOLENCE

★ ★ ★ ★ ★

L ET me make three unequivocal statements about the wave of protests and violence at recent Donald Trump events.

First, anyone attempting to attack Trump supporters, let alone trying to attack Trump directly, is completely wrong and without any justification.

Second, the protesters that shut down the Friday night Trump rally in Chicago were not just anti-Trump. It appears that many of them were ultra-liberal and would be no friends of the conservative movement as a whole.

Third, Trump bears some responsibility for these outbreaks because of his inflammatory and irresponsible rhetoric.

As Senator Marco Rubio stated, words have consequences, and you cannot run for the highest office in the land and be so irresponsible with your speech without expecting unfortunate results.

Again, this does not justify the spirit of the protesters, but it does illustrate that, for the most part, Trump is bringing out the worst in Americans, not the best, and this is hardly the way to make America great again.

Last August, in an Open Letter to Donald Trump meant to be constructive rather than destructive, I wrote, "Why shoot yourself in the foot when you have a legitimate chance of becoming the President of the United States?

Proverbs 15:1 says, "A gentle answer deflects anger, but harsh words make tempers flare" (NLT).

I continued, "I'm not a defender of Fox News or Megyn Kelly (or some others whom you have attacked), but if you spoke the truth with civility, stating your viewpoint plainly and without equivocation but without the gutter-level attacks, you'd make fewer enemies."

Can anyone argue with this now?

Last December I wrote, "The Scriptures teach that out of the abundance of the heart the mouth speaks (Luke 6:45), and so Trump's consistent pattern of reckless speech points to deeper issues which could make him unfit for the office of the presidency."

I added: "The warnings in Proverbs are strong: 'Do you see a man who is hasty in his words? There is more hope for a fool than for him' (Prov. 29:20). And, 'A fool gives full vent to his spirit, but a wise man quietly holds it back' (Prov. 29:11)."

Today, we are seeing some of the negative fruit of Mr. Trump's irresponsible and incendiary rhetoric, and things could get much worse in a hurry, especially when he continues to make provocative comments.

And can you imagine what could happen with our relationship to other nations if Donald Trump became President? Could you imagine what unnecessary, violent hostility could be needlessly provoked against Americans around the world, not to mention what larger, anti-American actions could be provoked?

Earlier in the day last Friday, just hours before the Chicago protest and while waiting for protesters to be removed from his rally, Trump remarked unhappily that "...part of the problem and part of the reason it takes so long is no one wants to hurt each other anymore and they're being politically correct the way they take them out so it takes a little longer."

So, it would have been better for police to smash non-violent protesters over the head with a night stick or something like that? Perhaps to rough them up a little and teach them a lesson? And the only reason the police don't do that is because they're being "politically correct"?

It should be obvious to see how this kind of speech is so dangerous, especially when many Americans are already concerned about their own safety and are fearful about Islamic terrorism and angry with a weak government.

Couple this with Trump's oft-quoted comments about wanting to punch protesters in the face or wishing that the crowd would rough them up, assuring his people that he'd foot the legal bill, and you have a potent recipe for disaster.

Last week, one of his supporters sucker-punched a protester in the face as he was being escorted out of the building, but in light of Trump's previous statements, is it any surprise?

Trump had said: "So if you see somebody getting ready to throw a tomato, knock the crap out of 'em, would you? Seriously. Okay? Just knock the hell—I promise you, I will pay for the legal fees. I promise. I promise."

Yes, do this if you see someone about to throw a tomato—hardly a deadly or dangerous weapon—and yet Trump won't back down from his words or take any responsibility for them.

At another rally, as a protester was being led out, "Trump lamented that he wasn't closer. 'I'd like to punch him in the face, I tell ya,' he said."

This is reckless, and if Donald Trump wants to be our next President and Commander in Chief, he needs to apologize for these statements, renounce them, and step higher.

Unfortunately, even in his stated policies, his words are often incendiary, not just by broad-brushing his statements, only to nuance them slightly later (for example, regarding Mexican illegal immigrants or Muslims), but by saying that the best way to fight terrorism is to be similar to the terrorists (like ISIS).

In his own words, "We have to play the game the way they're playing the game. You're not going to win if we're soft and they're, they have no rules."

The truth be told, if we become like ISIS we are no better than ISIS, and if we intentionally target and kill the families of terrorists—including small children—we are terrorists ourselves.

We can be strong and powerful and strike deadly fear into the hearts of our enemies without becoming like them.

We can also look evil in the face, as Ronald Reagan did, and say, "Mr. Gorbachev, tear down this wall!" without engaging in personal insults.

Reagan did not make fun of Gorbachev's famous birthmark, nor did he ridicule him as Lyin' Mikhael or Little Gorbie, nor did he call out the "Filthy Commies" or the like.

Instead, he spoke truth to power, with precision and without fear, and the Iron Curtain, along with the Berlin Wall, came tumbling down.

That's the kind of strong leadership we need today, and I actually believe that, if Donald Trump could have a fundamental heart change, he could be a leader like that.

Right now, though, his angry, irresponsible rhetoric is doing much more harm than good. The sooner he and his supporters realize that, the better.

April 21, 2016

DONALD TRUMP IS NOT YOUR PROTECTOR: A WARNING TO EVANGELICAL CHRISTIANS

★ ★ ★ ★ ★

D ONALD Trump has presented himself as a protector of conservative Christians and as the best friend Christians will ever have.

He has held up his mother's Bible and pledged to bring Christ back into Christmas.

But when the rubber meets the road, he is anything but the defender of conservative Christians and their values.

This became crystal clear yesterday morning (April 21), when Trump, appearing on the *Today* show, answered questions on abortion, North Carolina's Bathroom Privacy Act, and transgender rights.

When he was asked if he would like to change the Republican Party platform on abortion, which allows no exceptions for rape, incest, or the life of the mother, Trump replied without hesitation, "Yes, I would, absolutely, for the three exceptions. I would."[1]

In response, conservative leader Richard Viguerie told LifeSiteNews, "... he has zero chance of accomplishing that. The Republican Party is not going to change. We are a pro-life party, and the Republican Party is not going to change that."[2]

Certainly, the questions of rape, incest, or the life of the mother are terribly painful questions that deserve thoughtful and compassionate answers, especially from other women.

But if you're pro-life, you're pro-life. As Kristan Hawkins of Students for Life for America asked, "Does he want to put an exception into the platform saying it's OK to murder a two-year-old child whose father is a rapist, too? Or is he only OK with it as long as the child hasn't been born yet?"

In the words of Rebecca Kiessling, herself conceived by a rape, "Donald Trump has the audacity to suggest that the Republican grassroots has been wrong to believe in protecting innocent children like me who were conceived in rape. My message to Donald Trump, and others like him is this: Punish rapists, *not* babies!"

So much for Donald Trump being a pro-life champion and defender of conservative Christian values.

But it gets worse.

He actually criticized North Carolina's HB2, designed to protect the safety of women and children, stating, "North Carolina did something that was very strong, and they're paying a big price. There's a lot of problems."[3]

He indicated it was best to let people use the bathroom they felt comfortable with, showing no concern for all the people affected by that decision.

Yet across America, it is conservative Christians who have raised their voices the loudest in support of bills like HB2, standing up for the safety and privacy of women and children and not wanting heterosexual predators to use the loophole of "transgender rights" to prey on our wives, children, or grandchildren.

Senator Cruz had no trouble voicing his support for HB2, stating last week that these laws made perfect sense because "men should not be going to the bathroom with little girls."[4]

He said, "That is a perfectly reasonable determination for the people to make."

But of course.

In stark contrast, Trump said that Bruce (Caitlyn) Jenner would be welcome to use the ladies' room in one of his buildings.

I wonder how his wife and daughters would feel if they were in a bathroom and a burly transgender "woman" came walking in?

Or what if they were coming out of the shower stalls at a gym, with their towels wrapped around them, only to find a biological male sitting there in his underwear?

Would he have no problem with this?

Perhaps Donald Trump is not only failing to protect the rights and liberties of babies in the womb and conservative Christians but also of women in general?

In response to Trump's remarks, Ted Cruz issued this statement:

Donald Trump is no different from politically correct leftist elites. Today, he joined them in calling for grown men to be allowed to use little girls' public restrooms. As the dad of young daughters, I dread what this will mean for our daughters—and for our sisters and our wives. It is a reckless policy that will endanger our loved ones.

Yet Donald stands up for this irresponsible policy while at the same time caving in on defending individual freedoms and religious liberty. He has succumbed to the Left's agenda, which is to force Americans to leave God out of public life while paying lip service to false tolerance.

Whether you like Cruz or not (I have endorsed him, but we each have to make our own choices), if you're a conservative Christian, you have to be more comfortable with his position on these issues than with the positions of Donald Trump.

And in light of the growing tide of an increasingly irrational transactivism,[5] Cruz was right to ask, "Have we gone stark raving nuts?"[6]

If you're a Trump supporter, you might say, "I know he's not a Christian and I don't even think he's a real conservative, but I'm voting for him because I believe he's the best man to fix our economy and protect our borders."

I beg to differ, but I can respect that position.

But please don't look to him to be a defender of conservative Christian values or a protector of religious freedoms.

Barring dramatic divine intervention in his life, you will be sadly disappointed.

Be forewarned.

April 28, 2016

WHEN BIBLE-QUOTING TRUMP SUPPORTERS DROP THE F-BOMB

★ ★ ★ ★ ★

I T'S one thing when non-religious supporters of Donald Trump attack their candidate's detractors in the most profane and vile way. It's another thing when Bible-quoting, professing Christians do the same. Yet this is a phenomenon I see with increasing frequency. What can we learn from it?

On a daily basis, I receive lovely responses to my articles and videos, with comments like: "YOU'RE A F—ING IDIOT. duuuuumb" (This was in response to my video as to why we should boycott Target.[1] As with all the quotes that follow, the profanity was spelled out in full.)

And, "I've never heard such s—. This jerk is a f—ing stupid morn. F— Israel." (This was in response to my video, "Is Israel an Evil Occupier?"[2])

And, "Damn Brown is ugly" (This was in response to my video "A Warning to Conservative Christians Supporting Donald Trump."[3])

An atheist named Adam took real exception to this same Trump video, with comments including: "AskDrBrown you have been f—ing warned. You subhuman scum, TRUMP 2016. By speaking against Trump you are committing treason against us."

In fact, it seemed the F-bomb was Adam's lexeme of choice, as he used it in post after post, even in the most ungrammatical ways. (I doubt he's losing sleep over his poor grammar.)

And since, in the video, I brought up the issue of Trump's most recently stated position on abortion, Adam wanted me to know that, "IT'S NOT A F—ING

BABY if it's a tiny clump of cells you moron. It becomes a baby during the 3rd trimester. Period. So f—ing shut up."

But ugly rhetoric like this is not surprising from someone who also wrote, "There is no god. The sky daddy is a f—ing myth. The person who comes closest to a god would be Trump. TRUMP 2016-2028 AND BEYOND."

What is surprising, though, is when someone starts their comment to this same video with the words, "You are a f—ing idiot!!!!!" and then proceeds to preach to me from the perspective of a Bible-believing Christian. Talk about hypocrisy.

Here's what Kim M. wrote in full on the AskDrBrown YouTube channel:

> You are a f—ing idiot!!!!! Trump will win POTUS and when he DOES and he makes this country great again by getting back ALL THAT WAS STOLEN FROM HER, I am going to laugh in your face, and say, "YOU WERE WRONG AND NEED TO SHUT YOUR PIE HOLE MOUTH!" You are a deceiver and you are leading Christians down a road of utter SUFFERING for speaking against God's ANNOINTED ONE WHOM HE HAS CHOSEN AND THAT IS TRUMP! You should be ASHAMED OF YOURSELF. Funny how you could not back one thing that came out of your lying mouth with scripture! READ YOUR BIBLE YOU WICKED PLOTTING POS! And I don't care that I cuss at you because I was made this way, and I KNOW who I AM in The Lord Jesus Christ!!!! You will be held accountable on the day of the great white throne judgement and you will have God asking you, 'Why have you led my sheep astray!?' Good luck on THAT DAY, because YOU are going to NEED IT, May God have mercy on you!! Bring on the backlash for my comment. Anyone that gives me crap for this comment, your part of this world's PROBLEM and know NOTHING! I am confident in what I say here and I will risk it for the sake of the Saints who are true Saints and are WAKING UP!! Like I said before, may the Lord have mercy on you. You deserve what's coming to you for spreading lies about God's ANNOINTED one Donald J. Trump!

Yes, this poor soul is rebuking me in righteous indignation for my warning that Donald Trump cannot be trusted to protect the interests of conservative Christians, his critical comments on North Carolina's HB2 being a case in point. And she is warning me that on the Day of Judgment, God Himself will rebuke me for leading His sheep astray—because I have been critical of Trump.

And she does all this while violating virtually every biblical standard of speech and decorum, all while shouting that she knows who she is in the Lord Jesus.

Extraordinary.

Yet in this, she is typical of many "Christian" supporters of Trump: they are often more vile than godly, more unruly than reasonable, more worldly than spiritual, and more American than Christian. Kim M. speaks for so many of them.

Somehow, I couldn't see Bible-quoting supporters of Mike Huckabee or Ben Carson or Ted Cruz defending their candidates with filthy rhetoric like this, yet for Bible-quoting Trump supporters it is hardly uncommon. (I hear from them on a regular basis.)

This is not to deny that there are plenty of gracious, godly, fair-minded Christians who support Trump, believing that he's the best man for the job. As much as I differ with them, I don't judge the quality or depth of their faith.

But when we hear how many "evangelicals" are zealously backing Trump, we can be fairly sure that many of them are as spiritually deficient as Kim M., sounding more like the Donald than the Savior.

In this, they provide a sad commentary on much of the nation's "evangelical" church.

It is as revealing as it is disturbing.

May 3, 2016

DONALD TRUMP:
THE *NATIONAL ENQUIRER*
CANDIDATE
★ ★ ★ ★ ★

IT is altogether fitting that Donald Trump became the all-but-certain presidential nominee of the Republican Party on the same day that he cited the ridiculous allegations of the *National Enquirer* that Ted Cruz's father, Raphael, had involvement in the assassination of JFK.

This is not so much an indictment on Trump as it is an indictment on the American people. God could well be giving us exactly what we deserve.

After all, we are the generation raised on a steady diet of amoral and immoral reality TV, also feasting on shows like Jerry Springer and Howard Stern and regurgitating meaningless sound bites as though they were pearls of wisdom.

No wonder, then, that Donald J. Trump appeals to so many Americans. He is a *National Enquirer* candidate for a Jerry Springer generation. What a match!

Of course, there are fine people who also believe in Trump's candidacy, people of conscience, spiritual people, patriotic people.

I certainly do not condemn all of their judgments, nor is it my place to do so.

I have also listened carefully to the prognosticators who have predicted for months that Trump would be our next President—some even claimed prophetic inspiration for these predictions—and that he would be a tool in God's hand to destroy the corrupt political establishment and do good to our nation.

I fervently hope that these prophecies will prove true and that I will have to eat every word I have written—and I am writing.

I have no desire to be right; I do have an intense desire to America blessed; and I would far rather say, "I was so wrong about Donald Trump," than say, "I told you so!"

That being said, it appears today in America that God has given us over to delusion, a phenomenon mentioned several times in the Bible when God takes away a people's moral and spiritual sensibilities as a judgment on their sin.

In other words, because people reject Him and His standards, He says, "Go ahead then. Have at it," further pushing us into our folly.

That seems to be the only way to explain how we are suddenly at the point in America where people are saying there's nothing wrong with grown men using women's locker rooms and bathrooms and where states like California have ruled that boys who identify as girls can play on the girls' sports teams and share their shower stalls and changing areas.

This is cultural insanity, yet many are too blind to see.

How else do we explain college students telling[1] a young Caucasian man that if he identifies as a woman, he is; if he identifies as Chinese, he is; if he identifies as a 7-year-old, he is—but if he identifies as 6 feet 5 inches, he is not—how else do we explain this unless we have been given over to a spirit of delusion?

I see the Trump candidacy in the same way.

Tens of millions of Americans are not put off by his blatant, well-documented lying.

Tens of millions of Americans are not put off by his consistent practice of vile character assassination for the purpose of political gain.

Tens of millions of Americans are not put off by his vulgarity and profanity.

Tens of millions of Americans are not put off by his ignorance of critical issues and his complete flip-flopping of major positions.

And among these tens of millions of Americans is a significant percentage of professing evangelical Christians, despite Trump saying he has never asked God for forgiveness, despite his failure to renounce his previous adulteries or to acknowledge the wrongness of making money off casinos and strip clubs, despite his taking offense at the distribution of the near-nude photo of his wife Melania— not because he thought it was a bad picture but because it was made out to be bad.

And evangelicals continue to flock to him.

How do we explain this phenomenon?

Trump is obviously a brilliant salesman and promoter, a master of the media.

And he has masterfully appealed to American fears and anger—fears of terrorism, fears of economic collapse, anger with the political system, anger with American weakness—to the point that his supporters are looking to him as a quasi-savior figure. Only he can get the job done!

But in almost any other time in American history, Trump's negatives would have so outweighed his positives that he would have quickly disqualified himself as a candidate.

Not today.

Instead, we find ourselves with the increasingly likely possibility that either Donald Trump or Hillary Clinton will be our next president, and to me, there is only one satisfactory explanation for this: God is giving us what we deserve and handing us over to judgment.

All the more, then, should we be on our faces, repenting of our own sins.

All the more, then, should we be asking ourselves, "How much is Donald Trump a reflection of each one of us?"

All the more, then, should we who profess to know the Lord be asking Him, "How have we failed as Your people? How have we failed in our calling to be salt and light? How did things sink so low on our watch?"

All the more, then, should we be praying for Donald Trump and Hillary Clinton.

Barring merciful divine intervention in their lives, America is on the verge of a great and fearful shaking.

Part Two

GETTING BEHIND
REPUBLICAN CANDIDATE TRUMP

May 24, 2016–November 7, 2016

May 24, 2016

"I WAS WRONG": THREE WORDS THAT COULD CHANGE DONALD TRUMP'S LIFE

★ ★ ★ ★ ★

SINCE my open letter to Donald Trump on August 27th, 2015, I've raised many concerns about his candidacy, feeling strongly that there were other Republican candidates who were far more qualified for the job.

And I urged voters to consider these other candidates, warning that Donald Trump could turn out to be a *National Enquirer* candidate for a Jerry Springer generation, a vulgar and mean-spirited reality TV star who would stop at nothing to be elected.

But now that he's the presumptive Republican nominee and his only real competition looks to be Hillary Clinton or Bernie Sanders, candidates I couldn't possibly vote for because of their staunchly pro-abortion, pro-LGBT activist positions (among other things), I want to offer Mr. Trump some words of wisdom—words that could radically change his life if he would only take heed.

Last August, in my open letter, I wrote:

My heartfelt suggestion to you, sir, is that you humble yourself before your Creator, that you recognize your sins and shortcomings, asking Him for forgiveness through the cross, and that you ask Him to help you to be the kind of man that America (and the nations) need at this critical time in world history.

It's a painful process, but it's a glorious process, and if you take my friendly advice, you'll never look back with regret.

So, what will it be? Donald Trump, the self-made billionaire who fell short of his goal, or the new Donald Trump, ready to change the nation?

Since that time, a number of Christian leaders have met with Trump, sharing the gospel plainly with him and encouraging him to moderate his tone and watch his words, but to date, without much outward success.

Yet that doesn't mean that we don't keep trying (and praying), so, with that in mind, I want to suggest that Donald Trump learn to say (and mean!) these three simple words: *I was wrong*.

It takes a strong, confident man to admit to his failures.

It takes a secure, mature man to acknowledge that he messed up.

The weak, the insecure, the immature, those lacking confidence—they are the ones who point the finger at others, who make excuses, who play the blame game, who deny personal guilt.

Those who are honest have no problem saying, "I was wrong. I blew it. Please forgive me."

Those are liberating words!

As the Bible says, "God opposes the proud but gives grace to the humble" (James 4:6).

And other people give grace to the humble as well—to those willing to shoulder the blame for what they did; to those who show true contrition; to those who make a change.

Americans in particular are forgiving people, and many of us would think a lot more highly of candidate Trump if he plainly said, "Look, I've been foolish and full of myself, and I now regret my words and actions."

Many Americans who have been turned off by his rude and crude ways would reconsider his candidacy if he said, "*I was wrong* when I insulted Megyn Kelly and Heidi Cruz and other women. *I was wrong* when I built that strip-club casino. *I was wrong* when I destroyed my first marriage with adultery. With God's help, I intend to put the past behind me, learn from my mistakes, and lead America into a much brighter future."

That's the kind of leader America needs, one who finds strength in humility and power in honesty.

If Mr. Trump would learn the secret of getting low, he could still be a decisive, fearless, even visionary leader, but he'd do it with the wind at his back.

Otherwise, if he hardens his heart in pride, he could find God Himself resisting him.

Worse still, he could even be headed for a fall.

So, let's pray that Donald Trump will discover the life-changing power of saying *I was wrong*. And if you're close to him and you read this article, please pass it on to him.

May 30, 2016

IF OBAMA WAS NOT THE POLITICAL SAVIOR, NEITHER IS TRUMP

★ ★ ★ ★ ★

EIGHT years ago, massive crowds gathered to hear Barack Obama's stirring message of hope and change.

This young senator was not just a rising star, he was a superstar, and even overseas, crowds thronged to hear him.

Eight years later, rather than hope and change there is widespread pessimism and disgust, and the dramatic changes that have occurred under the Obama administration are, for the most part, negative and even destructive.

Now, a new star has risen, a quite unlikely one at that.

The crowds are also thronging to hear him, and his followers are convinced that this man, their man, Donald Trump, will singlehandedly make America great again.

The political system is corrupt, say his loyal supporters, and America has become a shell of what she used to be, both nationally and internationally.

Donald Trump will save the day.

Donald Trump knows how to get it done.

Donald Trump will not back down.

Donald Trump is the alpha male we need.

Some even claim that God Himself has raised up Donald Trump for such a time as this.

Others firmly believe that Bernie Sanders is the man. We need nothing less than a revolution, they say, and he is the man to lead it!

Bernie Sanders is also drawing crowds, and his supporters are equally passionate and devoted.

From a personal perspective, whoever our next president is, I will pray that he (or she) will be the greatest president we have ever had, just as I have prayed for Barack Obama (with evident disappointment).

And although I could not vote for Bernie or Hillary because of their militantly pro-abortion and pro-LGBT activist views, and although I have grave concerns about a Trump presidency, assuming that one of them will be our next president, that person will be my president. I will honor their authority, do my best to be of help in realizing our national goals, and speak out when I feel they are seriously wrong.

All that being said, my great concern is that we make the mistake of putting our trust in a political leader.

As one who endorsed Senator Cruz and felt that he could have helped lead America in a righteous revolution, I constantly reminded myself, "Ted Cruz is not the answer. Only Jesus is the answer."

All the more do I say that when it comes to Trump or Bernie or Hillary.

Five years ago, in 2011, I wrote an article entitled "Don't Put Your Trust in a Political Savior," warning Americans of the danger of looking to a political leader to save the day.

One year later, as we approached the 2012 elections, I wrote these words: "If the elections were held today, I would vote for Mitt Romney rather than sit out the elections or cast a protest vote for a third party candidate. But I would do so with extremely limited hopes, and my very act of voting in November would be a reminder to me that I cannot expect the radical changes America needs to come from the White House."

Today, when the crises surrounding us seem all the more intensified and when the world around us seems all the more unstable, it is all the more imperative that we do not put our trust in a man (or woman), exalting that person into quasi-divine status, looking to him or her as some kind of heroic deliverer.

Without a doubt, a good president can do much good and a bad president can do much harm, but there is only so much one individual can do—even the President of the United States—and we set ourselves up for failure and disappointment when we look to a human being as if he or she were some kind of super-being.

But that is what some people are doing.

In his victory speech in Bismark, North Dakota, Trump said to his jubilant supporters, "Politicians have used you and stolen your votes. They have given you nothing. I will give you everything. I will give you what you've been looking for for 50 years. I'm the only one."[1]

Unfortunately, many of his supporters believe this, leading Brandon Morse to say on Redstate.com, "This Feels Less Like An Election and More Like the Establishment Of Religion."[2]

Let the voter beware.

Writing for *The Federalist* on May 28th, M.G. Oprea penned an insightful article entitled, "What The Arab Spring Can Teach Us About America's Populist Revolution."

The subtitle read, "'A Rage For Order' chronicles the dangers of political strongmen and popular revolts. Should Americans nervously eyeing Donald Trump and Bernie Sanders be asking if it can happen here?"

After summarizing what happened in the Arab world, where, in several countries, the Arab Spring became the Sharia Fall, she gave this word of warning: "It's easy to look down on the people in these countries for their naïveté in believing that a single man could provide all the answers and being so easily carried from one extreme to the other. But, it would be unwise to throw the first stone at a time when this is truer in America than many of us are comfortable admitting."

And, she added, "Whenever a party, or a people, put their hopes in one man, the promises of democracy begin to fade into the background."

We have lived through eight years of political demagoguery and executive orders, and we surely do not need four (or, worse still, eight) more years of the same. And while we do our best to advocate for the candidate whom we feel is best suited to lead our nation, and while we may have very strong feelings about who that candidate is, the warning remains the same: By all means, work for and with the best candidate, but do not put your trust in a political savior.

Only Jesus is the Savior. Everyone else serves, for better or for worse.

June 30, 2016

WHY I'M ACTUALLY ROOTING FOR DONALD TRUMP

★ ★ ★ ★ ★

BEFORE you overreact to the title of this article, let me make clear that I still have grave concerns about a potential Trump presidency, that I have not personally endorsed him, that if the elections were held today I do not know that I could vote for him, and that if there were other qualified Republican candidates still in the race, Trump would not be my first choice.

Nonetheless, when I say that I'm actually rooting for him, what I mean is that I could not possibly vote for Hillary Clinton, and with Trump surrounding himself with so many godly Christian leaders, I'm hopeful that something will sink in and that God will deal with him in a radical way. Perhaps he is listening to some of the solid evangelical leaders who have become close to him?

That failing, I'm hoping that even in his Christian ignorance, even with his glaring character faults, even with his waffling on major positions, he still desires to be a champion of Christianity and genuinely desires to see America turned around and will therefore make the right decisions if elected.

Now, to be perfectly candid, I have no place whatsoever for some of the evangelical fawning over Trump, including a recent article that ended with a quotation from Isaiah 40:30-31, shockingly applied to Trump in quasi-divine terms: "Trump is our energy.... Trump renews our strength.... With Trump we mount up with wings like eagles.... With Trump, we run, we are not weary."[1]

Readers familiar with this scriptural passage will recoil with this interpretation which replaces the God of Israel with Donald Trump!

This is fawning to the point of near blasphemy.

I also believe that critics[2] of last week's choreographed New York meeting where Trump spoke before 1,000 evangelical leaders have raised valid concerns: first, regarding our gullibility (did we actually expect anything other than a humble Trump who would answer softball questions in an evangelical-friendly way?); and second, regarding our failure to probe more deeply (as Tom Delay asked,[3] why not ask him where he gets his values from or if he's read the Constitution and, if so, what he thinks of it?).

Not only so, but we must be cautious in believing reports that Trump has recently become born-again, especially when one of the reports[4] claimed that a well-known televangelist had led him to Christ years ago. (If true, this would speak eloquently to the bankruptcy[5] of some of our contemporary "gospel" preaching.) The old adage remains true, namely, that the only proof of the new birth is the new life (James Edwin Orr).

And still, I am hoping and praying that Donald Trump will indeed have a change of heart and that, by surrounding himself with so many godly leaders— some of whom are known for their no-compromise stands—something will rub off and he will provide a genuine alternative to Hillary Clinton.

Earlier this week, attorney and columnist (and almost presidential candidate) David French expressed eloquently to my radio listeners why he remains Never Trump,[6] and his arguments sound as strong as ever. And it was I who asked him to share his thoughts with my audience.

French echoed concerns I and others have had about Trump for months, to the point that I warned in May that he could be a *National Enquirer* candidate for a Jerry Springer generation, bringing divine judgment rather than divine blessing to our nation.

Nonetheless, even as one who endorsed Senator Ted Cruz fairly early in the race, I have consistently asked myself if the prophetic word[7] about Donald Trump could be true, specifically, that he would be our 45th president and, like King Cyrus, a foreign king who did not know the Lord and who was spoken of in Isaiah 45, he would do good for the people of God. (Naturally, such "prophecies" have been roundly mocked[8] by others, and with every presidential election, there are all kinds of alleged prophecies, most of which do not pan out.)

Now that he continues to defy the odds, with the latest poll[9] showing him ahead of Hillary, I continue to wonder if there is a divine inevitability to his presidency.

Again, it could be part of God's plan to judge and abase our nation, and a Trump presidency could be an unmitigated disaster, even if he appointed a good Supreme Court justice or two. (Wasn't it Reagan who appointed Justice Kennedy, the infamous swing vote in last year's redefinition of marriage?) And it remains very possible that Trump will not make it to the White House after all.

But as the one real alternative we have to Hillary, I'm hoping for the impossible and praying for God to do something radical in the life of Donald Trump for the good of the nation and of the Church.

Stranger things than this have happened in history, and given the bizarre nature of the current presidential elections—more importantly, given the nature of God—all things are possible.

As I've said several times before, I truly hope that I have been wrong about Trump. Having to eat my words would be a joy.

July 9, 2016

THE IRONY OF DEMOCRATS CALLING DONALD TRUMP ANTI-SEMITIC

★ ★ ★ ★ ★

ANYONE who has followed me over the last 12 months knows that I am not a Donald Trump surrogate. I was an early endorser of Ted Cruz and have often been critical of the presumptive Republican nominee. But at no point did I feel he was an anti-Semite.

If you're an anti-Semite, you don't embrace a Jewish son-in-law, much less embrace your own daughter converting to Judaism (which means your grandchildren will be considered Jewish), much less take public pride in this. In this regard, it's important to hear what Jared Kushner, the Jewish son-in-law of whom I speak, says about his father-in-law, Donald Trump.[1]

It's also doubtful that you could have the New York business connections Trump has while being an anti-Semite, and if you're really anti-Semitic, you don't give strong, pro-Israel assurances to evangelical leaders, even if you're pandering for their votes.

While only God knows what Trump would do if elected, I do believe that he wants to be a friend of Israel—notwithstanding previous comments he made regarding wanting to maintain a neutral posture between Israel and the Palestinians until elected—and I'm not one who's easily duped when it comes to Israel and anti-Semitism.

I've written about anti-Semitism in Church history and have delivered lectures on worldwide anti-Semitism, and I can certainly spot an anti-Semite, many of whom are proud of their antagonism toward the Jewish people and their hostility to Israel.

The fact that many white supremacists are anti-Semites and that some white supremacists support Trump does not by extension make him an anti-Semite (unless you truly believe that he has not denounced these followers quickly enough because he agrees with them), and in my opinion, the near-hysterical attacks on Trump for retweeting an anti-Hillary meme with an apparent Jewish star are absolutely baseless.

You could easily argue that he should have spotted the Star of David image immediately (he and his team have claimed it was a sheriff's star and argued that the six-pointed star is featured in other, non-Jewish settings), and you could condemn him for not recognizing the original source of the meme (a white supremacist), but again, in my view, it is misguided to accuse him of anti-Semitism because of this meme.

That's why my good friend and frequent debating opponent Rabbi Shmuley Boteach could be critical of Trump's lack of Jewish values while also decrying the idea that he was anti-Semite. He wrote, "But Trump a Jew-hater? Let's not be ridiculous."[2]

What makes these attacks on Trump so ironic, though, is the fact that the ones most aggressively attacking Trump are Democrats, yet solidarity with Israel has not been one of the strengths of the Obama administration.

It is widely known that the relationship between Obama and Netanyahu has been quite strained, and four years ago there was overt hostility expressed toward Israel at the Democratic National Convention, with many delegates publicly voicing their opposition to recognizing Jerusalem as Israel's capital.[3]

This year, "The Democratic Party platform drafting committee is top heavy with veterans of political battles over Israel—some friendly, some critical, and including at least one major backer of the Boycott, Divestment and Sanctions [BDS] movement."[4]

Significantly, three of the committee members selected by Bernie Sanders are "Cornel West, a philosopher and social activist; James Zogby, the president of the Arab American Institute, and Rep. Keith Ellison, D-Minn., the first Muslim elected to Congress" and they "are known in part for their criticisms of Israel."

Indeed, "West is a prominent BDS backer and Zogby has spoken forcefully against attempts to marginalize the movement...."

Clearly, though, "The standout appointment is West, a fiery speaker who has called the Gaza Strip 'the "hood" on steroids' and, in 2014, wrote that the crimes of Hamas 'pale in the face of the U.S. supported Israeli slaughters of innocent civilians.'"

In an open letter to Professor West in 2015, Judea Pearl, who is Chancellor's Professor of Computer Science and Statistics at UCLA and president of the Daniel Pearl Foundation, urged West to excuse himself from delivering a commemorative lecture at UCLA on a noted Jewish intellectual, Rabbi Abraham Joshua Heschel.[5]

She pointed to West's support of the BDS movement, a movement rightly condemned for its militant anti-Israel bias. She also pointed to an August 12, 2014 interview with Sean Hannity in which West "could not find even one historical link between the Jewish people and the land of Israel. None! *Nada!* Blank! Not one word of empathy for a multiethnic society of immigrants who've fought 67 years of besiegement and hostility. None! *Nada!* Blank!"

As for Bernie Sanders, although nominally Jewish, he has hardly been a friend of Israel,[6] and he remained committed to making an impact on his party's platform this year.

Yet it is not Sanders or West who find themselves in the crosshairs of accusations of anti-Semitism, but it is Donald Trump, primarily over a retweeted meme.

This is not just ironic; it is downright hypocritical.

By all means, if you're a Democrat, call out Trump on that meme if you question his judgment. But do it while requiring your own party to live up to the same standard, and point the finger where it belongs, placing the positions of Cornel West and others side by side with those of Trump.

Then we'll see whose positions smack more of anti-Semitism.

August 4, 2016

HILLARY CLINTON, DONALD TRUMP, THE PRESIDENTIAL ELECTIONS, AND THE SOVEREIGNTY OF GOD

★ ★ ★ ★ ★

MORE than 2,500 years ago, the prophet Daniel declared that God "removes kings and sets up kings" (Dan. 2:21), and throughout the Old Testament, we see the Lord orchestrating history according to His plans, either to bless His obedient people or to judge His disobedient people. So, there is human responsibility and there is divine activity, but it is clear that God has the ultimate word.

What does that imply for the 2016 presidential elections in America? What is God saying to our nation today?

I understand that America, which is a Democratic Republic, is not ancient Israel, which was first a theocracy and then a theocratic monarchy. God made a covenant with Israel at Mount Sinai, and the whole nation swore allegiance to Him. That cannot be compared with the founding of our nation. And the children of Israel did not get to vote for their king whereas we get to vote for our president.

Still, since God remains sovereign, doing what He sees fit on the earth, and since America was founded largely on biblical, Christian principles (and still remains majority Christian by profession), it is only fair to ask: What is God doing in these elections? Put another way, if an Old Testament prophet were writing the history of our nation, what insights would he give us in terms of a Hillary or Trump presidency?

On the one hand, we ourselves will choose our next president, going to the ballot box and voting and making up our own minds, for better or for worse. From that perspective, we chose Barack Obama and George W. Bush and Bill Clinton and George H.W. Bush and Ronald Reagan.

On the other hand, the Lord is not a passive spectator in world events, especially when His people pray for His will to be done "on earth as it is in heaven," in which case we might conclude that we elected the presidents God chose for us to elect. If so, why did He choose Obama or Bush or Clinton or Reagan or Nixon or Kennedy? To what purpose? With what message? Or does He simply give us what we deserve (or choose), for better or worse?

Many Americans are upset that we are left with Hillary Clinton and Donald Trump as candidates, pointing to their extraordinarily high unfavorability ratings. Yet on the Democratic side, Hillary has been the expected candidate for some years now, so that is hardly a surprise.

But how do we explain the Trump candidacy? He defeated 16 other Republican candidates, including respected governors and senators, some of whom had massive funding behind their campaign. And his campaign was hardly flawless, leaving him open to all kinds of attack that should have brought him down, yet he still defeated a strong, tenacious field.

Is any of this God's doing?

As much as there are natural explanations for the ascendancy of Trump—his nationalistic appeal, his outsider appeal, his reality TV star appeal, his appeal to our fear and anger—there could well be supernatural explanations as well. Has God raised up Donald Trump for a specific purpose in history?

Others have speculated on what a Trump presidency could mean, pointing either to the Persian king Cyrus, who was used to bless Israel, or the Babylonian king Nebuchadnezzar, who was used to curse Israel. Although I have written about this in the past, I believe the jury is still out on what the implications of a Trump presidency would be, although I would fervently pray for blessing rather than cursing should we elect President Trump.

But there's another angle to consider, and that's what concerns me most.

What if Donald Trump was raised up by God to defeat 16 Republican candidates, some (if not most) of whom could have readily defeated Hillary Clinton? What if he was raised up, not to become president, but to pave the way for a Hillary presidency? And what would it mean if, after eight years of President Obama, we would then have President H.R. Clinton?

To me the message would be clear: Despite President Obama's radical policies, policies which have directly (and, for the most part, quite negatively) affected our families and our freedoms, the Church in America is still largely asleep, still largely oblivious to our nation's steep moral and spiritual decline, still largely unaware of the perilous situation in which we find ourselves in the world today.

The bad news is that a Hillary presidency would mean divine judgment on a sleeping Church and a sinning nation.

The good news is that, with true repentance, that judgment could become a mercy, provided that we wake up.

The best news is that the elections are still three months off and we can wake up today, asking God to have mercy on our land, getting out of our self-satisfied complacency, and praying for the Lord to turn us in the right direction without the help of His smiting rod.

Obviously, I can only offer these thoughts as spiritual surmisings, also recognizing that the Lord has no political affiliation[1] and that there is good and bad in each party. And whoever our next president is, that person will be my president and I will pray for him or her.

My hope, though, is that the thought of Trump being raised up to pave the way for Hillary, all for the purpose of divine judgment, would provoke us to a greater sense of prayerful urgency. It is certainly called for today.

August 17, 2016

THE BOOK OF PROVERBS AND A WINNING STRATEGY FOR CANDIDATE TRUMP

★ ★ ★ ★ ★

Dear Mr. Trump,

I'D like to offer you some free advice that will almost certainly guarantee your victory in the November elections. In fact, if you put into practice what I'm about to share with you, you could become a fine president as well. It will only take you about 15 minutes a day.

Do I have your ear?

We both know that, for the most part, a political campaign is a battle of words. Words spoken on the campaign trail. Words exchanged in a debate. Words sent out via social media. Words that run in a TV ad. Words that are printed in newspapers and online.

Wise words will win a campaign and foolish words will destroy a campaign—I'm not telling you anything you don't know—and so it makes sense to see what God has to say about the words we speak. And since you've openly stated that the Bible is your favorite book, I want to point you to the book in the Bible that has the most to say about the power of words.

I'm talking about the Book of Proverbs, which actually states that, "Death and life are in the power of the tongue, and those who love it will eat its fruits" (Prov. 18:21).

So, here's my counsel: Start every day by reading one chapter from Proverbs out loud, together with your closet staff or family or advisers, if possible. Then note what Proverbs says about wise people and fools, examine your conduct and your words in light of what you read, and then ask God for wisdom.

There are 31 chapters in Proverbs, which means you'll be reading it about once a month, and every day, as you read, ask yourself this question: "Am I acting like a wise man or a fool?"

Let me give you some examples of how beneficial it is to listen to the wisdom of Proverbs.

Proverbs 12:16 says, "Fools show their annoyance at once, but the prudent overlook an insult" (NIV).

What if you had read this verse right after you were attacked on national TV by Khizr Khan at the DNC? Obviously what he said upset you, and you felt personally insulted.

What does a foolish person do? That person shows his annoyance at once.

What does a wise person do? That person overlooks an insult.

And what would have been a good way to respond to Mr. and Mrs. Khan? Proverbs 15:1 says, "A soft answer turns away wrath, but a harsh word stirs up anger."

You could have tweeted out, "As a fellow-American, I mourn the loss of Mr. and Mrs. Khan, I celebrate their son's sacrifice, and I call on them to stand with me in fighting radical Islam."

And if you wanted to add (with a smile), "And thanks for the offer of a copy of the Constitution, but I have a few copies myself, and we agree it's a great document."

Had you done that, you would have saved yourself days of negative media frenzy, you would not have taken such a hit in the polls, and you would have stayed on message.

These proverbs are pretty wise after all!

Here's some more free counsel from this important book.

Proverbs 17:27 says, "Whoever restrains his words has knowledge, and he who has a cool spirit is a man of understanding."

There are times when silence is better than speech (the very next verse actually says, "Even a fool who keeps silent is considered wise; when he closes his lips, he is deemed intelligent"), and at all times, a cool head must prevail.

That's why Proverbs repeatedly warns against being short-tempered, stating, "Whoever is slow to anger has great understanding, but he who has a hasty temper exalts folly" (Prov. 14:29).

Put another way, someone with a hasty temper is holding up a sign for the whole world to see, stating in big bold letters, "I AM A FOOL."

You might think that your sharp responses show your toughness or display your alpha male traits, and many in your audience might love your retorts too. But for the general public, they degrade you more than they degrade your opponents.

You can be strong, decisive, forceful, and persuasive without making a fool out of yourself in the process. Why give your opponents free ammunition?

Here's some more wisdom from Proverbs: "Do not reprove a scoffer, or he will hate you; reprove a wise man, and he will love you. Give instruction to a wise man, and he will be still wiser; teach a righteous man, and he will increase in learning" (Prov. 9:8-9).

Often, when people come to us with constructive criticism, we reject it because of our pride. "How dare you tell me I'm wrong!" That's what fools do.

But a truly wise man welcomes constructive correction and input. It only makes him wiser. And since you have surrounded yourself with many fine, godly, Christian counselors, you do well listen to their words. As Proverbs also states, "for with guidance you wage your war, and with numerous advisers there is victory" (Prov. 24:6 NET).

So, here's your winning strategy in a nutshell. Learn to live by the wisdom of Proverbs, and you'll make a great president. Scorn it, and you'll only have regret.

August 19, 2016

Has Donald Trump Turned a New Leaf?

★ ★ ★ ★ ★

IT was just one speech—really, it was just one very small part of one speech—but it drew immediate and massive media attention: Donald Trump expressed regret for things he had previously said.

How big a deal was this?

The coverage on CNN.com was typical, calling this "an astonishing act of contrition."[1]

The CNN article, written by Jeremy Diamond and David Mark, began with, "Donald Trump on Thursday shelved his guiding mantra—never back down, never apologize—and did what he has refused to do in public in more than a year of campaigning."

What exactly did he do? "He expressed regret."

According to spokesperson Kellyanne Conway,[2] the words were Trump's own and not those of a scriptwriter, and while we have no way of verifying this beyond a doubt, when you listen to the audio of his remarks in Charlotte, North Carolina, it seems to confirm that this is something he wanted to say.

After stating that he was not going to be politically correct, he explained, "Sometimes, in the heat of debate and speaking on a multitude of issues, you don't choose the right words or you say the wrong thing. I have done that."

Yet the crowd did not see an apology coming, cheering him on for his incorrectness, in other words, for *not* choosing the right words.

He then said, "And believe it or not, I regret it," to which the crowd started chanting, "Trump! Trump! Trump!" It's as if they were saying, "Keep saying the wrong things! Keep speaking your mind, whatever happens! Be Donald Trump!"

It also seems that some (or many) in his audience were genuinely confused. What? Our man regrets some of the things he has said? Seriously?

Now, had he been insincere in these remarks, just following the latest script given to him to read, this would have been the perfect time to say, "Yes, I regret not being even stronger! I regret not going after my opponents more aggressively!"

The crowd would have loved it, much as they loved his "apology" for calling Elizabeth Warren "Pocahontas." He apologized to Pocahontas!

But not this time. Instead, he continued, "And I do regret it"—as far as I can tell, these words were not on the teleprompter but rather reflected his desire to prove his sincerity. He then returned to the teleprompter to say, "particularly where it may have caused personal pain. Too much is at stake for us to be consumed with these issues."

Of course, if he was sincere, this raises other questions, which is why the CNN headline read, "Campaign reboot: Trump expresses regret for saying 'the wrong thing,' doesn't specify."

Conservative pundit John Hawkins also tweeted, "Not sure it was a good idea for Trump to say he regrets some of the things he said. Sounds good, but he will be asked about specifics a lot."

Will he apologize privately or publicly to Ted Cruz and his family or to others he attacked personally? This remains to be seen.

But there's only one thing that matters to me right now. Did Donald Trump really mean what he said? Does he truly regret some of the words he has spoken, especially those that caused personal pain?

A reader on my Facebook page named Christopher wrote, "Hahahaha y'all foolin yourselves if you believe Trump is going to humble out and change. He is a rude, egotistic, bigoted individual and that's how he is going to be. Nothing about that man is presidential and he will do nothing to help the American people."

As one who has raised warnings about Trump for the last year, beginning last August and frequently thereafter, urging him in May to learn to say "I was wrong" and offering him wisdom from Proverbs as recently as Thursday, just hours before he made his "I regret" comments, I do understand Christopher's concerns and I don't fault him for being cynical.

But when you're praying for a man to humble himself and apologize for past errors and he takes a major step in that direction, shouldn't you say, "Perhaps God is answering our prayers?" And shouldn't you encourage him to keep moving in that direction rather than mocking his first big step?

When Donald Trump does something he's never done before, namely, expresses regret openly and publicly for words he has spoken, calling them "wrong" and acknowledging they brought "personal pain," isn't this itself an act of humility?

Now, some will argue that this has nothing to do with humility and is simply a political ploy, which could well be true. Politicians have been known to say and do just about anything to get elected.

On the other hand, everyone I know personally who has had a private (or small) audience with Trump has talked about how gracious and humble he was in that setting, contrasting that with his public persona. Perhaps the "humble Trump" does exist after all?

The Bible speaks of "the fruits of repentance," which means we must prove our repentance by our deeds. So if Trump is being sincere, we'll see a change in the weeks ahead, with no more crude, childish, personal attacks even as he launches an all-out assault on the record of Hillary Clinton.

I for one am hoping he was sincere, choosing to be neither gullible nor skeptical. Only time will tell. For now, we can say that this was a big step in the right direction.

September 5, 2016

DO CONSERVATIVE CHRISTIANS HAVE THE LOVE OF CHRIST FOR OBAMA AND HILLARY?

★ ★ ★ ★ ★

ALONG with many other conservatives, I believe Barack Obama has been one of our worst presidents and I dread the thought of a Hillary Clinton presidency. I believe both of them have damaged our country in significant ways, and I steadfastly oppose some of their most cherished policies.

But that does not give me permission to despise them as human beings or to have a visceral hatred for them. God forbid.

Yet attitudes like this are all too common in our conservative Christian circles, circles which could better be described as "CONSERVATIVE christian," circles in which those whom we oppose can be vilified in the name of righteousness.

We feel justified in mocking their appearance or denigrating their families or criticizing them for the most minor infraction, and we do it because we have moved from opposing their destructive policies to despising them as people, as if they deserve our self-righteous scorn.

We're even happy to see Hillary have another coughing fit on the latest YouTube video. Maybe we'll retweet it and add a snappy comment too. After all, she's wicked! And just look at that pathetic pants suit!

I wonder how the Lord feels about all this? I wonder if we have forgotten Paul's directive which stated, "Do not be overcome by evil, but overcome evil with good" (Rom. 12:21)?

Do you remember what Christopher Hitchens wrote when Rev. Jerry Falwell died? Hitchens referenced Falwell's "carcass" and proclaimed, "Like many fanatical preachers, Falwell was especially disgusting in exuding an almost sexless personality while railing from dawn to dusk about the sex lives of others." Hitchens opined that, "The evil that he did will live after him," then ended his article by stating, "It's a shame that there is no hell for Falwell to go to."[1]

Yet Hitchens felt perfectly justified in expressing these ill-timed sentiments because he judged Falwell to be evil.

Are we no better than this deceased atheist?

More recently, with the passing of conservative icon Phyllis Schlafly, hostile voices began to pile on, with tweets[2] like these: "On the one hand it's a shame Phyllis Schlafly died, but on the other it's always heartwarming when Satan calls one of his own home" (Jeb Lund, now with *RollingStone*); and, "God never takes a Gene Wilder without relieving us of a Phyllis Schlafly" (Julie Klausner, with over 100,000 Twitter followers); and, "We absolutely get to celebrate the passing of someone who worked for 70 years to reinforce oppressive, violent systems in this country" (Katie Klabusich, host of the *Katie Speak Show*).

How do you feel when you read these words, words which display such a deep disdain for Schlafly that they were posted the same day she died?

It's one thing for her ideological opponents to oppose her while she's alive and to hold to those differences after her death, but to mock her on the day of her death is to cross an ugly line.

Yet the truth be told, some "conservative Christians" would have a hard time restraining their glee if something tragic happened to President Obama or candidate Clinton. After all, we think to ourselves, they are terrible people who are hurting our great nation. And so, we justify our sinful attitudes in the name of righteous indignation.

A black pastor told one of my white colleagues that when he and his friends hear someone criticizing Obama, it's as if that person was criticizing their own son.

I have found that comment to be useful, and so, while I speak forcefully and freely about my staunch disagreements with our president, I always do so with several things in mind: 1) he is the first African-American president, bringing a real sense of pride to many African Americans, therefore I will speak carefully; 2) he is my president, like it or not, therefore I will speak with respect; and 3) I also want to say something redemptive, such as, "I'm praying that he will be our greatest president, but so far, he has been a terrible disappointment."

When Bill Clinton was president, I agreed with many of Rush Limbaugh's salvos against him, but I would never call him "Slick Willy" as Rush famously did (and does). Yet other conservative Christians had no problem echoing these words, believing that Clinton's failings deserved such scorn, even saying things like, "Jesus called Herod a fox (Luke 13:32), so I can call Clinton Slick Willy."

They conveniently forgot that they were far closer to the character of Clinton than to the character of Jesus.

I'm all for denouncing what I believe to be the sinful policies of Obama and Hillary, as well as exposing and rebuking corruption wherever it is found (including Hillary's email server). If someone's actions are wicked, we can brand them as such.

But let us do so with a heart that longs to see these leaders transformed by God's love, that prays for them as we would pray for a family member, that is determined to walk in undefiled light, and that recognizes that we too have failings that call for repentance and contrition.

We can do that if we put *Christian* first and conservative second; we will fail miserably if we reverse the two.

October 9, 2016

WHAT KING DAVID COULD TEACH DONALD TRUMP

★ ★ ★ ★ ★

FOR many months now, critics of Donald Trump have asked his Christian supporters, "So, you heard about the latest scandal with your candidate? He's a vulgar, immoral man. How can you possibly vote for him?"

His supporters have responded: "Well, look at King David in the Bible. He committed adultery and murder, and God still used him. He was even called a man after God's own heart! So, if God could use a man like David, he can certainly use Donald Trump."

To be candid, comparing Trump to David is like comparing apples to Learjets—in other words, the two are so different that they're not even in the same category—but that doesn't mean that Trump could not learn a lot from David, especially at a time like this, when the Trump campaign is still reeling from the latest scandal, the video tape of Trump with Billy Bush.

But before I explain what David could teach Trump, let me emphasize how inapt the comparison is between them.

First, David was a man after God's own heart, meaning, a man who loved the character of God and the ways of God and the Word of God, a man who sought to please God, a man who longed deeply for God. None of this, even faintly, can be said of Donald Trump—at least, to this point in his life.

Just consider these words of David written in the Psalms and see if you can imagine Donald Trump speaking them sincerely, let alone writing them:

The law of the Lord is perfect, reviving the soul; the testimony of the Lord is sure, making wise the simple; the precepts of the Lord are right, rejoicing the heart; the commandment of the Lord is pure, enlightening the eyes; the fear of the Lord is clean, enduring forever; the rules of the Lord are true, and righteous altogether. More to be desired are they than gold, even much fine gold; sweeter also than honey and drippings of the honeycomb. Moreover, by them is your servant warned; in keeping them there is great reward (Psalms 19:7-11).

Or how about these words?

Vindicate me, O Lord, for I have walked in my integrity, and I have trusted in the Lord without wavering. Prove me, O Lord, and try me; test my heart and my mind. For your steadfast love is before my eyes, and I walk in your faithfulness. I do not sit with men of falsehood, nor do I consort with hypocrites. I hate the assembly of evildoers, and I will not sit with the wicked. I wash my hands in innocence and go around your altar, O Lord, proclaiming thanksgiving aloud, and telling all your wondrous deeds" (Psalms 26:1-7).

Shall I quote hundreds of other verses like this, verses which Trump has likely not even read his entire life?

I join many others in praying that Donald Trump would become a man after God's own heart, but to compare him to David is to miss the point badly.

Second, David's sin with Bathsheba, committing adultery with this married woman and then having her husband, Uriah, killed, was an absolutely horrific act, one for which he paid dearly. In fact, you could argue that his life was never the same after his sin. But it was the exception to the rule of his life, which is why Scripture said that "David did what was right in the eyes of the Lord and did not turn aside from anything that he commanded him all the days of his life, except in the matter of Uriah the Hittite" (1 Kings 15:5).

In the case of Trump, ungodly behavior has been the pattern of his life, the rule rather than the exception, something for which he was known and of which he was proud.

Again, the comparison breaks down dramatically.

Third, when David was confronted with his sin, he pointed no fingers, offered no justification, and did not seek to minimize his guilt. Instead, he confessed his sin in the most humble, broken, and contrite terms, pleading for undeserved mercy.

And this is where King David could teach Donald Trump a valuable lesson.

When the video comments were released over the weekend, Trump immediately tweeted out an extremely tepid "apology," minimizing his guilt, attacking Bill Clinton, and apologizing "if anyone was offended."

This was extremely disappointing, since what matters now is not what he said and did more than a decade ago—is anyone really surprised by that?—but rather how he responds today. That is ultimately how he be will judged and how his supporters will evaluate his character.

A few hours after his tweeted "apology," he issued a more substantial apology on video, repudiating his 11-year-old comments but still pointing a finger at former president Bill Clinton.

I would encourage Mr. Trump to get on his knees, all alone, to take out his favorite Bible, and to read Psalm 51 out loud. (Remember: This is the man who said publicly that he didn't feel the need to ask forgiveness.) Let him read these words of repentance written by David after he was confronted by the prophet Nathan about his adultery and murder.

David pointed the finger at himself alone, stating, "Against you, you only, have I sinned and done what is evil in your sight" (Ps. 51:4), and he didn't minimize his sin: "For I know my transgressions, and my sin is ever before me" (Ps. 51:3).

He also recognized how utterly polluting his sin was, pleading with God to cleanse him: "Wash me thoroughly from my iniquity, and cleanse me from my sin! ...Hide your face from my sins, and blot out all my iniquities. Create in me a clean heart, O God, and renew a right spirit within me" (Ps. 51:2, 9-10).

Americans are a forgiving people, also tending to side with the victim, and given the media's frenzied attacks on Trump now, he could easily be perceived as the victim rather than as the womanizing victimizer of the past—but only if he humbles himself deeply.

So here's what he must do (maybe even in the debate tonight?). With heartfelt contrition, he must restate how utterly ashamed he is of his past transgressions, which he does not minimize or deny; he must say that he has asked God to forgive him, asked his family to forgive him, and asked his supporters to forgive him.

Then he must reaffirm that although that is the man he once was—and he is ashamed of it—that is not the man he now is, as his family and friends can attest. And because he has done wrong in the past, he is the ideal person to do what is right in the future, having learned from his errors. He can be the poster boy of reformed behavior!

And he must do this without comparing his sins to the even worse sins of Bill Clinton and without, for the moment, talking about the campaign.

There will still be several weeks to promote his campaign agenda and, when he is criticized, to expose the media's hypocrisy, covering for Bill Clinton (and Hillary Clinton) while crucifying him.

But now, let him act in the spirit of Psalm 51. Whether he wins the election or not, he will be a better man for it, and the nation will be the better for it as well.

And David would surely tell him, "Whatever you do, don't let pride dictate your actions. In this case, it could be the difference between the White House and a failed campaign, if not between life and death."

October 10, 2016

WHY ALL THE FUSS OVER THE TRUMP SEX-COMMENTS TAPE?

★ ★ ★ ★ ★

I'M not writing this to defend Donald Trump or to minimize the despicable nature of his comments captured on video in 2005. Not a chance.

Nor am I writing this to convince NeverTrumpers to vote for him.

My own wife, Nancy, has told me repeatedly that she could not vote for him, despite the possibility of Hillary getting elected. (Of course, she will not vote for Hillary either.)

Instead, I'm writing this to ask those who once supported Trump, like my highly esteemed Christian brother Wayne Grudem, a fellow-professor and theologian, why the video tape changed things.

Professor Grudem wrote, "There is no morally good presidential candidate in this election. I previously called Donald Trump a 'good candidate with flaws' and a 'flawed candidate' but I now regret that I did not more strongly condemn his moral character. I cannot commend Trump's moral character, and I strongly urge him to withdraw from the election."[1]

Certainly, I commend Professor Grudem for his integrity and for acknowledging what he now feels was an erroneous endorsement of Trump. In fact, just a few days ago, I wrote a piece questioning whether I will endorse another candidate in the future, having previously endorsed Senator Cruz.[2]

But my issue is simply this: Why the surprise now? Did any of us really think that the Donald Trump revealed on that tape was not related to the Donald Trump of 2005 (and, in all likelihood, after that as well)? Did any of us think that he didn't sexualize women, that he didn't lean into his star power, that he didn't boast about his many (alleged) sexual trysts? Why the outrage and shock now?

Even if Trump changed in certain ways since 2005—perhaps he has been more faithful to Melania and more involved with their kids—the character he displayed throughout the election process indicated some very deep moral flaws, making him the least likely poster boy for the evangelical right.

During the primaries, I issued numerous words of warning and concern about Donald Trump, in writing, on radio, and on video, also making clear that these warnings were in the context of the primaries, when we had other, more viable candidates for president. (Obviously, this was simply my opinion.)

Once it came to Trump vs. Hillary, my posture has been that I cannot vote for Hillary but that Trump could earn my vote, and that remains my position until today.

I would like to be able to vote for him, and I do hope that he will heed the godly advice that is being given to him and learn to humble himself before God and people. But his failings and flaws are such that I still have concerns about helping to elect him as president, despite the dire possibility of a Hillary presidency.

But these are just my personal opinions, and I do not write this to persuade or to influence. My purpose in writing is to ask those who once backed Trump but do so no longer: Why the surprise at his past conduct? Weren't his weaknesses and flaws shouting aloud to the nation over the last year via tweet and spoken word?

I never for a moment bought into the "Saint Donald," rhetoric, questioning other Christian leaders who embraced him as such. (I don't mean to deny that he has helped people privately and has a compassionate, caring side. I simply mean that to present him as a wonderfully Christian man is to be self-deceived.)

And I understand the convictions of the NeverTrumpers, although I have never identified with this group. (I once used the hashtag in a tweet but decided not to do so again.)

My issue is with the political leaders and Christian leaders who endorsed Donald Trump and who worked to help elect him but are now distancing themselves from him in shock and dismay. Who did you think you were dealing with?

I know he can be gracious and humble in person, and there are surely many positive qualities about him.

But if you're going to endorse him, do so with your eyes wide open, or don't endorse him at all.

The man who once boasted about his adulterous encounters with famous women and who opened a casino with a massive strip club inside but felt he didn't need to ask God for forgiveness is the man you endorsed for President.

Had he renounced with shame his past life, that would be one thing.

Had he not insulted and degraded his political opponents (and other perceived opponents) in the most vile and cruel ways, crushing them at any cost so that he could advance politically, that would be one thing as well.

But he did not renounce his past or change his public ways, because of which, the only issue with the 2005 tape should not have been the tape itself but rather how he responded to it today.

I have colleagues who believe that God is raising up Trump the way He raised up Cyrus, pointing out that Cyrus was used by the Lord although he was a pagan king who did not know the God of Israel (see Isa. 45:1-6, and note carefully the phrase "although you do not know Me" in verses 5-6).

I have no problem with this concept at all. As the old saying goes, let God be God (in other words, let Him do what He chooses to do in His way and for His purposes). So be it. As I've written before, I personally hope it's true.

But for those who are having cold feet about Trump now, I ask again: Wasn't it clear from day one that this was the man you were endorsing?

For all of us, then, from here on in, the lesson is simple and clear: Whatever we do, let's do it with our eyes wide open and with our trust in God alone.

October 13, 2016

Is Donald Trump "God's Chaos Candidate"?

★ ★ ★ ★ ★

I T was former governor Jeb Bush who first referred to Donald Trump as the "chaos candidate." Now, Lance Wallnau, an out-of-the-box Christian thinker and businessman, has dubbed Trump "God's chaos candidate," writing a book by this title (with the subtitle, "Donald J. Trump and the American Unraveling").

Wallnau believes that God is using Trump as a "wrecking ball to the spirit of political correctness," claiming that, "His emergence is such a destabilizing threat to the vast deal making machinery embedded in both parties that he has the unique distinction of being rejected by both liberal Democrats and establishment Republicans at the same time."

Whether Wallnau is right in all of his beliefs remains to be seen (I'm scheduled to interview him next Wednesday, October 19, live, from 2-3 P.M., EST, and I'll be sure to ask him lots of probing questions, since he strongly supports Trump for president), but what is clear to me is that God is using Trump as a wrecking ball of sorts, and the results are not pretty.

What has this human wrecking ball helped bring to the surface?

1. Trump has helped to expose the carnality of the culture.

It was Donald Trump who initially delighted his crowds by dropping F-bombs, and it is Donald Trump whose borderline profane tweets ignite his followers today. The crasser, the better!

But Trump is not alone in his carnality. His words and actions have encouraged his supporters to engage in the most profane rhetoric as they not only defend him but also feel empowered by his example.

2. Trump has helped to expose the superficiality of the culture.

Candidate Trump remains a reality TV star, and much of his political appeal is tied to his rock star status.

To be sure, candidate Obama took on rock star status during his first presidential campaign, but as undeserved as Obama's stardom was, it had a very different feel than the stardom of Trump. That's why I wrote back in May that he was "a *National Enquirer* candidate for a Jerry Springer generation."

Now, in saying this, I do not mean that Trump has not struck a chord with many Americans, for whom he has provided a voice, and I don't mean that people are not voting for him because of his policies. I simply mean that his candidacy has helped bring our superficiality to the surface.

3. Trump has helped to expose the vulgarity of our culture.

Forget about the release of the 2005 videotape with Trump's horrific comments about women. That's news from 11 years ago.

We're talking about the candidate who boasted about the size of his manhood during a debate in the primaries.

And now, with his running mate's husband being an even easier target, the most recent presidential debate (I use the term "presidential" with hesitation) degenerated into rhetoric like, "Yeah, what I said was bad, but what he did was even worse."

The other day, I spent a few seconds browsing the Drudge Report and then the Huffington Post, in both cases just looking at the most prominent headlines, after which I felt like I needed to take a shower to get the dirt and grime off of me. These websites were absolutely in the gutter.

Does anyone think that if the battle for the White House was between, say, Jeb Bush and Bernie Sanders, the headlines would be as vulgar and debased? (And yes, on Drudge, there are now accusations of impropriety directed against President Obama as well.)

4. Trump has helped to expose an unhealthy nationalism.

I certainly recognize that many Americans are deeply upset with the direction of our nation (for good reason), and Trump has appealed to their frustration and anger, promising to turn the ship around.

But Trump has also helped stir up an almost rabid, America-first nationalism (whether intentionally or not), one that can easily lead to xenophobia, racism, and more, one that feeds on these very attitudes and mindsets. In keeping with this, a white supremacist website claimed that it was "the Jews" who were behind the release of the damning 2005 video tape.[1]

I am *not* connecting Trump with this website (obviously) and I am not stating that he himself is a racist or a xenophobe. I'm simply saying that his campaign has caused these sentiments to surface with a vengeance.

5. Trump has helped to expose the corruption of the political system.

There are many Christians who feel that the Hillary vs. Trump presidential race is a sure sign of divine judgment on America, as if God is giving us over to our foolishness.

At the same time, Trump's refusal to play the standard political game has helped reveal the power of the political establishment, both Republican and Democrat, and with that, the corruption of the political establishment. Will we ever look at these parties in the same way again?

6. Trump has helped to expose the massive divisions in the evangelical church.

This is not just a matter of a difference of opinion. It is a matter of one evangelical leader claiming that any Christian who votes for Trump is guilty of idolatry and another evangelical leader claiming that any Christian who does not vote for

Trump will be held accountable by God and will have the blood of the unborn on his or her hands.

One group asks, "As a Christian, how can you possibly vote for such a narcissistic, proud, vulgar, potty-mouthed, short-tempered, inexperienced man who is absolutely unfit for the presidency?"

The other group responds, "As a Christian, how can you not vote against Hillary Clinton and how can you not recognize that we're not electing a pastor in chief but a Commander in Chief? God is raising up Trump!"

Again, I'm not blaming Donald Trump for these divisions (and I've barely scratched the surface in detailing them). To the contrary, these divisions were already there (even down to the meaning of "evangelical"); Trump's presidential run has just helped to reveal them.

7. Trump has helped to expose the collusion of the liberal media with the Democratic Party.

I don't doubt for a moment that if Ted Cruz was the Republican candidate, the liberal media would be doing everything in its power to bring him down, and this would have been true 10 years ago (and longer) as well as today.

But it appears that the media that gave Trump endless free time on its networks during the primaries is the same media now seeking to bring him down, lending credence to the allegation that the liberal networks (at least some of them) helped prop Trump up during the primaries because he would be the easiest target to bring down in the general election.

Whether or not this is true, the media's radical liberal bias and pro-Hillary sentiments cannot be denied, to the point of almost being shouted out by the moderators during the presidential debates. Or should we think nothing of a moderator arguing a policy position with Trump, as if he was debating her (Martha Raddatz) rather than Hillary?[2]

The bottom line for me is simple, regardless of who you plan to vote for (and I don't write this to discourage a vote for Trump): God has used Trump to expose a lot of what is wrong with America, and it is not a pretty sight.

October 23, 2016

WHY I WILL VOTE FOR DONALD TRUMP

★ ★ ★ ★ ★

BEFORE you applaud me for my integrity or condemn me for selling out, allow me to explain my decision to vote for Donald Trump on November 8.

First, I'm writing this because I have been asked incessantly for months how I would be voting, not because I think I'm someone special or that what I do should influence you.

Second, I'm not endorsing Donald Trump. In my mind, there's a world of difference between endorsing a candidate and voting for a candidate.

Third, I respect those in the #NeverTrump camp and I share many of their concerns, including the possibility of his further vulgarizing and degrading the nation, the possibility of him deepening our ethnic and racial divides, and the possibility of him alienating our allies and unnecessarily provoking our enemies, just to name a few. Among the #NeverTrump voices I respect are columnists like David French and Ben Shapiro, bloggers like Matt Walsh, and evangelical leaders like Russell Moore and Beth Moore.

Fourth, I take strong exception to evangelicals who have fawned over Trump as if he were some kind of savior figure, supporting him as if he was Saint Donald. I also take issue with evangelical leaders who want us to minimize some of Trump's failings, constantly saying, "Let him who is without sin cast the first stone" (see John 8:7). This is not a question of condemning the man but rather a question of making a moral assessment as to his readiness to serve our nation.

Fifth, my decision to vote for Trump, barring something earth-shattering between now and November 8, is consistent with my position, which has been: 1)

During the primaries, I issued strong warnings against voting for Trump while we had other excellent choices. I did this in writing, on video, and on the radio, but always stating that, if Trump won the nomination, I would reevaluate my position. 2) Once Trump became the Republican candidate, I wrote that I was rooting for him to take steps in the right direction and thereby win my vote. 3) I have stated repeatedly that under no circumstances would I vote for Hillary. (Here are two strong warnings[1,2] about Hillary.)

So, what has convinced me that I should now vote for Donald Trump?

First, I believe that he actually is serious about appointing pro-life, pro-Constitution Supreme Court justices. When he said during the last debate that, if you're pro-life, you want to see Roe v. Wade overturned, and when he reiterated at his Gettysburg speech that he will be drawing from his list of 20 potential appointees, he helped me feel more confident that he would not suddenly flip-flop if elected.

Second, one reason I endorsed Senator Cruz was because he took on the political establishment, both Democrat and Republican, to the point of calling it the Washington cartel. Trump is an absolute wrecking ball to the negative parts of the political system (although, unfortunately, he's been a wrecking ball to some of the good parts of the system), so my vote for him is also a protest vote.

Third, I am voting for the Republican platform, not the Republican Party, which means I'm in agreement with the platform while at the same time having very little confidence in the party as a whole.

Fourth, while I have always felt that the line, "We're electing a president, not a pastor," was overstated and superficial, if we rephrased it to say, "We're electing a general to train hand-to-hand combat warriors, not a pastor," it might have more relevance. In other words, we are not looking for Trump to be a moral reformer (even if he does appoint righteous judges), and, at this point, he certainly is anything but a moral example (although we pray he will be truly converted and become one). Rather, out of our choices for president, which are stark, we are voting for the one most likely to defeat Hillary and make some good decisions for the nation, not be the savior. And with things so messed up in America, the hand-to-hand combat analogy is closer to home.

Fifth, within the first few minutes of the last debate, the massive differences between Hillary and Trump were there for the world to see, she a pro-abortion radical and an extreme supporter of the LGBT agenda, and he unashamedly speaking out against late-term abortions and wanting to appoint justices who would defend our essential liberties. Since I have the opportunity to vote, I feel that I should vote for Trump.

Sixth, Trump continues to be drawn to conservative Christians, and not just ones who tickle his ears. One of my dear friends has spent hours with Trump and members of his family, and he has told me that in 55 years of ministry, no one has received him as openly and graciously as has Trump. Yet my friend continues to speak the truth to him in the clearest possible terms. While I am not one of those claiming that Trump is a born-again Christian (I see absolutely no evidence of this), the fact that he continues to listen to godly men and open the door to their counsel indicates that something positive could possibly be going on. It also indicates that these godly leaders might be a positive influence on him if he was elected president.

Seventh, although I'm quite aware that a president could do great harm or good to the nation, I'm far more concerned with what we as God's people do with our own lives and witnesses, and for me, the state of the church of America is much more important than the state of the White House. In that context, I echo the words (and warning) of Dr. Martin Luther King, Jr.: "The church must be reminded that it is not the master or the servant of the state, but rather the conscience of the state. It must be the guide and the critic of the state, and never its tool. If the church does not recapture its prophetic zeal, it will become an irrelevant social club without moral or spiritual authority."

So, in sum: 1) my hope is in God, not Donald Trump, and I do recognize that either Hillary or Trump has the potential to do great harm to America; 2) my urgent call is for us as followers of Jesus to get our own act together so we can be the salt and light of the nation; 3) I will continue to urge all believers not to vote for Hillary Clinton, whose policies will certainly do us great harm; 4) ultimately, the most effective way to defeat Hillary is to vote for Trump, while also praying that God will use him for good, not for evil.[3]

In the end, if he gets elected and fails miserably, I will be grieved but not devastated. If he does well, I will rejoice.

Either way, though, my vote is just that—a vote. My greater role is to live a life pleasing to God with the hope of advancing a gospel-based moral and cultural revolution.

November 1, 2016

DONALD TRUMP
WAVES THE GAY FLAG

★ ★ ★ ★ ★

O N October 30, at a rally in Colorado, Donald Trump proudly held up a rainbow-colored, gay flag on which was written "LGBTs for Trump."

As Christian conservatives, what are we to make of this? Is it yet another proof that we must compromise our morals to vote for him? And will he betray us once elected?

Interestingly, major gay websites like Advocate.com were not impressed with his gesture, declaring, "It's an empty gesture from the Republican nominee, who opposes marriage equality and has a proudly homophobic running mate."[1]

The *Washington Blade* was more neutral, stating, "LGBT advocates continue to criticize Donald Trump for the anti-LGBT positions he's laid over the course of his presidential campaign, but they can't say he's never waved a rainbow Pride flag."

The *Blade* also quoted Chris Barron, "a gay conservative activist and founder of LGBT for Trump," who called him "the most pro-LGBT Pres candidate ever nominated by either party." (Spoken with true Trumper hyperbole!)

In contrast, the Advocate noted that, "LGBT advocates have spurned Trump, saying that his gestures amount to little more than pandering—he opposes marriage equality and has wavered on transgender rights and the Equality Act, which would ban anti-LGBT employment and housing discrimination. Besides, his running mate, Mike Pence, has a history of support for anti-LGBT measures, including a law during his time as Indiana's governor that would allow businesses to deny services to LGBT people based on religious reasons."

The Advocate also pointed out that "the Log Cabin Republicans [the primary gay Republican group] refused to endorse Trump" and an "earlier poll shows that almost three-quarters of LGBT voters will choose Clinton in the election."

And it was the influential Human Rights Campaign (HRC) that labelled Trump a "Huge Bigot," stating, "We have seen so much progress for the LGBTQ community under the leadership of President Barack Obama, and it all could be reversed by a Donald Trump presidency." (Here's a scathing attack[2] on Trump from the HRC dated August 25, 2016.)

Overall, then, it would seem that most LGBT Americans will not be impressed by Trump's gesture in Colorado, as he walked around the stage during the singing of "God Bless America" and proudly unfurled the rainbow flag.

But how should we react if we are conservative followers of Jesus who plan to vote for Trump? Doesn't this mean we are forfeiting our integrity and selling our souls?

It all depends on our attitude and expectations: Why are we voting for Trump? (I have written about my reasons for voting for him, with caveats.)

First, Trump's courting of LGBT Americans is nothing new, as the gay websites noted as well. Most notably, Trump had Peter Thiel, the openly gay co-founder of PayPal, speak at the Republican National Convention, and Thiel did so as an out and proud gay man. So, if Trump's proud display of a gay flag at one of his rallies surprises you, then you do not understand who you are voting for.

Second, what Trump was excited about was that LGBT Americans were supporting him, just as he would have been excited about Hispanic Americans or Black Americans or Jewish Americans supporting him, especially since all of these groups largely vote Democrat. So, it was not so much the gay flag he was celebrating as much as the support from LGBT Americans at his rally.

Third, Trump genuinely wants to be a friend of conservative Christians, preserving their liberties, and a friend of gay Americans, persevering their safety, and as far as I can tell, he has not yet come to grips with the inevitable conflicts that will arise between religious rights and gay rights. (Of course, all of us should fight for the safety and fair treatment of every human being, let alone every American.)

So, Trump says that he wants to know where immigrating Muslims stand in terms of gay issues, not wanting to allow radical, gay-hating terrorists to enter our country. But he fails to realize that some of the screening questions that might be asked (such as, "Do you believe gay marriage should be prohibited?" Or, "According to your religious beliefs, is homosexual practice wrong in God's sight?") would also exclude conservative Christians (and Jews) as well.

Of course, the difference between conservative Christian opposition to LGBT activism and radical Islamic opposition to LGBT activism is the difference between day and night, but again, according to everything I know, Trump has not yet worked through the potential conflicts that could arise when gay rights come in conflict with religious rights.

At the same time, I firmly believe that Trump wants to be the champion of religious liberties—he's the first candidate who has challenged the Johnson Amendment—and that he is drawn to conservative Christians like Mike Pence and Ben Carson and the leaders on his Faith Advisory Council. But how, exactly, will he act when push comes to shove and gays feel their rights are being violated by Christian beliefs? That remains to be seen.

Interestingly, friends of mine who have worked with him have told me that he has spent time in poor cities in urban America, not simply because he's courting the voters there but because he feels they have been trashed by the Democrats and he can do a better job for them.

So, he wants to be the champion of hurting Americans everywhere, and he can probably look at his gay friends, like Peter Thiel, his evangelical friends, like Mike Pence, and his black friends who hailed from poor neighborhoods, like Ben Carson, and say, "I'm here to fight for you!"

And again, I believe that he believes that he is the man to fight for all of us.

What, then, are we to do as conservative Christians?

First, if we are voting for Trump, we do so with our eyes wide open, not making him into a larger than life deliverer who will save the day and turn the tide. To do so is to give place to myth rather than reality and to set ourselves up for disappointment.

Second, we do our best to surround him with godly counsel, affirming the value of every human being and applauding Trump's desire to be the president of all Americans, but urging him to prioritize religious freedoms, on which this country was built.

And third, we look beyond the elections to our long-term duty as Christian citizens, committed to loving our neighbors as ourselves while refusing to compromise our biblical convictions. And while our stances will be perceived as hateful by our LGBT neighbors, who are understandably hurt by our rejection of gay "marriage" and our claim that homosexual practice is sinful, we must demonstrate genuine love to them as family members, neighbors, co-workers, and friends.

In short, the dilemma of Donald Trump is a macrocosm of the dilemma that all of us face, and the only way he will get things right is with the help of wise and godly believers.

So, I urge every Christian conservative who plans to vote for Donald Trump not to sell your soul to him as you vote, but rather to commit to pray for him, recognizing his many, serious flaws. And if he is elected, then pray all the more that he will be surrounded in the White House by men like Joseph and Daniel who will bring wise counsel to the Oval Office.

And lest you think this is impossible, I would reply that where we find ourselves today, one week before the elections, would have seemed far more impossible just 18 months ago.

Reality, these days, is far more surprising than fiction.

November 7, 2016

IF HILLARY WINS,
IF TRUMP WINS

★ ★ ★ ★ ★

BARRING some unforeseen scenario, on Wednesday morning, November 9, either Hillary Clinton or Donald Trump will be our president elect. What does this mean for Christian conservatives, and how should we respond?

If Hillary wins:

1. Christians who voted for Trump in the primaries, telling us he was the only one who could defeat Hillary, will only have themselves to blame, since it seems almost certain that virtually any of the other Republican candidates could have handily defeated her. This would mean that these AlwaysTrump Christians chose nationalism over biblical principles and, with all their claims to spiritual insight, saw things after the flesh, not the Spirit, overlooking his serious shortcomings because they wanted an alpha male to fix the nation.

2. We need to pray that what appears to be the massive corruption of the Clintons will still be exposed. It will be difficult with Hillary at the helm, but it can still be done. We should pray for the corruption of the media and the political establishment to be exposed as well. Perhaps a Trump defeat will not signal the end of Trump after all and he will give himself to this task as a private citizen.

3. That being said, our focus for the next four (or eight) years cannot be on the evils of the Clintons and the destructive policies that Hillary will seek to introduce. Instead, our focus must be on revival in the church, on winning the lost and making disciples, on caring for the hurting and the poor in our society, and on calling America to repent, recognizing that we are under divine judgment.

4. But that doesn't mean we ignore Hillary's politics. We need to pray for conservative politicians and judges to show backbone and integrity and for harmful policies to be thwarted, but our *emphasis* cannot be on Hillary. It must be on the Lord and on our responsibilities. A backslidden, compromised Church remains America's greatest problem.

5. We must prepare for civil disobedience (meaning biblical obedience) on a widespread, national scale should our freedoms of religion, speech, and conscience be attacked. *As a Body*, throughout the country, we must refuse to comply with legislation that would seek to silence us, restrict us, or, worse still, force us to engage in practices that violate our sacred, historic beliefs. We must do this peacefully and with respect for authority, but with courage and unshakable faith, regardless of cost or consequences.

6. In short, if Hillary is elected, it is wake-up time for the church.

Conversely, if Trump is elected:

1. We must give credit to those Christians who saw God's hand on Trump through the election season, despite his fleshly flaws, recognizing that there must be a unique, divine purpose in his presidency. There is simply no other way to understand how a man like him could defeat so many fine candidates in the primaries and then bring down the Clinton machine in the general election.

2. That being said, a Trump presidency could do as much harm as good, since his "wrecking ball" methods and his questionable character are so volatile and unpredictable that he could bring us down as easily as he could bring us up. (Imagine what could happen to America if Kanye West and Kim Kardashian were the president and first lady. I know this is a jarring, exaggerated example to use, but you get the point.)

3. We should therefore pray for divine restraint on Trump lest he do or say something rash as president, and we should pray that he will not only surround himself with godly and wise counsel but that he will also listen to his counsellors, doing what is fair and just when it comes to immigration and security and healthcare and the economy.

4. We should also pray that his resolve to do what is right will not waver and that he will not become a compromiser who wants to prove he can work with everyone. (Should Trump's health fail as president and he be succeeded by Mike

Pence, we need to pray the same thing for him, since he infamously caved in to pressure in 2015 with the RFRA bill in his state, and, while still a fine Christian man, betrayed his Christian constituency.) We must encourage Trump to stay true to the Republican platform and to nominate Supreme Court justices in the image of Scalia and to stand up for religious liberty.

5. As God's people, we must work against the deepening divisions in our country, seeking to build bridges and be peacemakers, not troublemakers, also addressing issues of injustice and oppression, be they from the right or the left. And we must pray for revival in the church with the same urgency as if Hillary was president, since we would be making a terrible mistake to look to Trump as some kind of savior figure or to take our foot off the gas because the Clintons, who for many conservatives are the epitome of evil and deception, were kept out of the White House.

6. In short, if Trump is elected, it is still wake-up time for the church.

Either way, things will get very messy in the coming months, with emotions high, news headlines blaring, and our nation being torn and shaken. (I would think that only some kind of national calamity would bring us together, and we certainly hope and pray that will not be the case.)

The bottom line is that the solution to our many problems will not be found in the White House and we must turn the passion and focus and attention we have put on the elections back to where it belongs—on the Lord and on our responsibilities as God's people.

After all, Jesus never said that the President or the Congress or the Supreme Court were the salt of the earth or the light of the world. Instead, He said that to us, His followers (Matt. 5:13-16), and if there is to be a positive, nationwide moral and cultural revolution in America, it must begin with us.

Part Three

Ups and Downs with President Trump

November 9, 2016–August 12, 2018

November 9, 2016

DONALD TRUMP, PRESIDENT OF THE UNITED STATES BY THE SOVEREIGN INTERVENTION OF GOD

★ ★ ★ ★ ★

AS the political pundits weigh in on the many sociological and ideological factors that contributed to Donald Trump's stunning victory, allow me to weigh in on the spiritual side of things.

I believe Trump has been elected president by divine intervention.

I'm aware, of course, that some people believe that everything happens by the will of God, which means that whoever wins the presidency wins by God's express will.

Yet there are times when there are so many odds against something happening, when it so greatly defies logic, that it is easier to recognize God's involvement.

That, I believe, is the case with Donald Trump winning—and remember, this comes from someone who endorsed Ted Cruz and was one of Trump's stronger conservative critics during the primaries.

Just think of the obstacles Trump overcame, including: 1) The massive baggage of his past, including the release of a vulgar video with his tremendously offensive sexual comments along with numerous women accusing him of sexual assault (as reported by no less than the *New York Times*); 2) his myriad campaign errors, with enough misstatements and inappropriate remarks to sink several candidates; 3) a very strong Republican field, including governors like Bush, Christie, Kasich, Huckabee, and Walker, senators like Cruz, Rubio, and Santorum, and outsiders like Carson and Fiorina; 4) the massive power of the Clinton political machine; and 5) the overwhelming collusion of the mainstream media.

To be sure, some will say, "Yes, God has raised up Donald Trump, but it is to judge America, not bless America. He has given us what we deserve, and it is not good."

That is certainly a possibility, and either way, Trump's many negative qualities are still glaring and our nation remains terribly divided.

But if, indeed, God has raised Trump up for certain divine purposes, it behooves us to ask what those purposes are.

First, consider this post from Pastor Jeremiah Johnson, now just 28 years old, dating to July of last year.

Jeremiah knew very little about Trump when he wrote these words:

I was in a time of prayer several weeks ago when God began to speak to me concerning the destiny of Donald Trump in America. The Holy Spirit spoke to me and said, "Trump shall become My trumpet to the American people, for he possesses qualities that are even hard to find in My people these days. Trump does not fear man nor will he allow deception and lies to go unnoticed. I am going to use him to expose darkness and perversion in America like never before, but you must understand that he is like a bull in a china closet. Many will want to throw him away because he will disturb their sense of peace and tranquility, but you must listen through the bantering to discover the truth that I will speak through him. I will use the wealth that I have given him to expose and launch investigations searching for the truth. Just as I raised up Cyrus to fulfill My purposes and plans, so have I raised up Trump to fulfill my purposes and plans prior to the 2016 election. You must listen to the trumpet very closely, for he will sound the alarm and many will be blessed because of his compassion and mercy. Though many see the outward pride and arrogance, I have given him the tender heart of a father that wants to lend a helping hand to the poor and the needy, to the foreigner and the stranger."[1]

Obviously, Trump's policies regarding immigration would seem to contradict the final sentence here, but if the rest of this proclamation is true, then perhaps this part will prove true as well.

Second, consider the perspective of Dr. Lance Wallnau, a Christian speaker and leadership coach who often thinks outside the box. He too felt that God was raising up Trump to be a Cyrus-type leader—someone used by God to help the nation, even though he himself was not a believer—feeling directed to read a passage from Isaiah 45 to Trump (this passage speaks of Cyrus), and say that Trump was called to be the 45th President of the United States.

Wallnau believes that God is using Trump as a "wrecking ball to the spirit of political correctness," claiming, "His emergence is such a destabilizing threat to the vast deal making machinery embedded in both parties that he has the unique distinction of being rejected by both liberal Democrats and establishment Republicans at the same time."

In Wallnau's words, Trump is God's "chaos candidate." (I did a 90-minute interview with Dr. Wallnau on this subject, where he took calls from critics.[2])

But here is the major caveat, even if all (or most) of these things are true: If Trump, indeed, is a divine wrecking ball, then he could do as much as harm as good, and to the extent that he is appealing to the fears and frustrations and anger of a nation, he is channeling some potentially dangerous emotions.

That means that we should pray that: 1) he will continue to surround himself with solid men like Mike Pence, his Vice President, or Rudy Giuliani, possibly his Attorney General; 2) he will listen to the godly leaders who have been speaking into his life, like James Robison and Tony Perkins; 3) he will humble himself, recognizing that the pride that has brought him this far is the pride that could destroy him; 4) he will keep his word about the Supreme Court justices he will nominate; 5) he will not compromise the Republican platform in some misguided effort to prove his moderation; 6) he will do his best not to alienate those who are horrified by his presidency, instead pledging to be the president of all Americans (that would mean, for example, declaring war on radical Islam without declaring war on all Muslims); 7) he will demonstrate that he will ultimately help our nation as a whole (for example, with good economic policies or by proposing something better than Obamacare); 8) he will learn to act presidential (rather than vengeful and impetuous) on both a national and international level.

In short, if Trump indeed is President by divine intervention, we should pray for divine restraint on his life as well, lest this divine wrecking ball wreak havoc on the nation while tearing down what is wrong. May he be a divinely guided wrecking ball!

November 15, 2016

DONALD TRUMP, SAME-SEX "MARRIAGE," AND THE CHURCH

★ ★ ★ ★ ★

I F President Trump does not nominate pro-life justices to the Supreme Court, I will be surprised and disappointed, although not shocked, since I do not put my absolute trust in people, especially political leaders.

If President Trump does not oppose same-sex "marriage," I will be disappointed but not surprised.

That's why his recent comments on *60 Minutes* were disappointing but not surprising.

After all, he had his good friend Peter Thiel speak at the Republican National Convention, and Thiel was warmly received as he proudly proclaimed his gayness. Thiel is also part of the president-elect's transition team, with the potential of a high-level position within his administration.

And Trump (along with Pence) has not made a major point of saying that he wanted to overturn the Obergefell decision, instead putting his emphasis on overturning Roe v. Wade, sending abortion-related decisions back to the states.

Trump has also spoken of a test for immigrants regarding their attitudes toward LGBTs, so he clearly cares about their safety and wellbeing.

It is true, of course, that at various times in the campaign he spoke of his opposition to same-sex "marriage," even saying at least once that he would "strongly consider" appointing justices who would overturn it. But less than one week later, he assured a lesbian reporter that under his administration, there would be great progress for LGBT Americans.

In short, opposition to same-sex "marriage" has never been his mantra, nor he did emphasize this in debates, nor has he ever attempted to offer a clearly articulated answer in terms of what to do when perceived gay rights conflict with perceived religious rights.

I was not surprised, then, when he said to Lesley Stahl on *60 Minutes*, "I'm pro-life. The judges will be pro-life."[1] And I was not surprised when, in reply to Stahl's questioning on same-sex "marriage," he said, "You have these cases that have already gone to the Supreme Court. They've been settled, and I'm fine with that."[2]

Of course, I was disappointed with his answer, and I was not alone in wondering, "Why is Roe v. Wade not settled but Obergefell vs. Hodges is settled? Why should the court overturn the one and not the other?"

At the same time, there's an excellent chance that the pro-life justices President-elect Trump has promised to appoint would also stand *for* religious liberty and *against* the court's redefinition of marriage. Consequently, in the coming years, as cases reach the Supreme Court on these volatile issues, the conservative, pro-life-leaning majority would likely side against many of the goals of LGBT activism.

For me, though, there are three key takeaways from the *60 Minutes* interview. (I'm speaking specifically in terms of the culture wars, not in terms of the interview as a whole.)

First, as bold, strong-willed, and anti-establishment as Trump may be, he is still a human being, and the temptation to "get along with everybody" in Washington is still there. We must strongly encourage him, then, not to compromise his pro-life promises for a single moment of his presidency.

He has made a sacred commitment, and it's one major reason that many Christian conservatives voted for him.

Second, Christian conservatives who voted for him should not suddenly turn on him in light of his same-sex "marriage" comments. Again, we had no reason to expect him to take a strong stand here—although that is certainly something to pray for and work for—and since he knows he owes his election to conservative evangelicals, it would be foolish for us to burn our bridges now.

His door is still open to us, and we need to do our best to walk through that open door.

Third, the president-elect's comments remind us that it is the church's job to change society, not the president's.

As I have said repeatedly in recent months, Jesus never said that the White House was the salt of the earth and the light of the world but that rather that we, His devoted followers, were.

Of course, the president has a tremendous bully pulpit, and his comments on divisive issues influence many, just as President Obama's "evolving" views on same-sex "marriage" influenced many.[3] But did any of us who voted for Donald Trump really think to ourselves, "We're voting for him because we believe he will change the moral climate of the culture and speak out against LGBT activism"? Was this even on our radar? I think not.

Either way, I didn't vote for Trump expecting him to spark a moral and cultural revolution in America.

I voted for him with the hope that he would not do what Hillary Clinton was expected to do and with the prayer that he would keep his word regarding Supreme Court justices and make some healthy decisions for the nation as a whole.

As for transforming the culture, that is the role of the church through the many facets of the gospel.[4]

Are we up to it?

November 16, 2016

Have Evangelicals Lost Their Credibility by Voting for Trump?

★ ★ ★ ★ ★

I find it ironic that the same people who have mocked us for years as hypocrites, bigots, haters, homophobes, transphobes, and worse now tell us that we have lost our moral credibility by voting for Trump.

It is true that there are Christian leaders in other nations[1] who feel that we (meaning, in particular, white evangelicals) have compromised our moral witness by voting for Trump in such overwhelming numbers (81 percent of white evangelicals voted for him). And it is true that it is difficult to reconcile our historic mantra of "character matters" with a vote for Trump, unless we are counting on his imminent moral transformation, which is certainly a risky way to vote.

Considering, then, that Trump would have been the last person on a list of candidates that evangelicals would have drawn up—actually, he would not have made the list at all—it's easy to see how the world could think that we have sold our souls to the devil in some kind of desperate effort to regain power.

But for people to chastise us and say that we have forfeited our moral credibility in the eyes of our critics is to forget that, in the eyes of those critics, we had no moral credibility to lose.

Some of this, no doubt, was our own fault, since much of the evangelical church has, indeed, been hypocritical, with rampant no-fault divorce in our midst, with a plague of pornography in our pews, and with more leadership scandals (both financial and sexual) than we can count. Why should the world take our moral witness seriously?

But that is not the only reason we have been despised. To the contrary, a major reason that the world hates us is *because of* our moral stands and our refusal to capitulate to the culture, as a result of which we are likened to Hitler and the Nazis, to ISIS and the Taliban, to the KKK and other hate groups. This is all because we refuse to celebrate the redefinition of marriage or affirm the latest gender identity fad. (And should I mention what pro-abortion feminists think of evangelicals, especially male evangelicals?)

So, when I hear our critics call us hypocrites for voting for Trump (and again, I speak here primarily of white evangelicals), I have to laugh and say, "I thought we already were hypocrites!"

And I can only wonder what these same critics would have said if we had elected Ted Cruz, a staunch, once-married, Bible-quoting evangelical, as our candidate? They would probably be accusing us of setting up secret internment camps for all non-church attending Americans as we stealthily planned to take over the society. Can you even imagine what their accusations would be?

All that being said, as I have stated before, I do believe that some of us did lose credibility by the way in which we backed Trump, giving him a free pass for the very infractions for which we were ready to condemn Bill Clinton, overlooking his ugly attacks on others, and forgetting that the president and first lady are, in many ways, exemplars for the population.

Writing in 1998, Bill Bennett explained the danger of embracing the pro-Bill Clinton arguments that his private conduct was of no concern to the nation:

These arguments define us down; they assume a lower common denominator of behavior and leadership than we Americans ought to accept. And if we do accept it, we will have committed an unthinking act of moral and intellectual disarmament. In the realm of American ideals and the great tradition of public debate, the high ground will have been lost. And when we need to rely again on this high ground—as surely we will need to—we will find it drained of its compelling moral power. In that sense, then, the arguments invoked by Bill Clinton and his defenders represent an assault on American ideals, even if you assume the president did nothing improper. So the arguments need to be challenged.[2]

Character, then, does matter, and if we evangelicals did sacrifice character on the altar of political expediency, then we have further damaged our witness in the eyes of a watching world, some of which still expects moral goodness from the church.

That being said, it is clear that a large number of evangelicals who voted for Donald Trump did so for highly moral reasons, including protecting the unborn and standing up for religious freedoms. Are these not moral, Christian causes?

As explained by Jonathan Van Maren:

Many of my non-Christian and liberal friends find it bewildering that both evangelicals and Catholics voted overwhelmingly for Donald Trump, a thrice-married casino operator infamous for his vulgar trash talk. I want to take a moment to explain to them directly why most Christians voted for him anyways. It's simple, really: Christians voted for Donald Trump because they felt that the threat a *de facto* third Obama term posed to Christian communities was an *existential* one.

He continued:

The attacks on Christians from the highest levels of government have been relentless now for nearly a decade. Obama wants to force Christian churches and schools to accept the most radical and most recent version of gender ideology, and he is willing to issue executive decrees on the issue to force the less enlightened to get in line. Christian concerns are dismissed out of hand as "transphobia."[3]

And note that Van Maren had not yet mentioned Hillary Clinton, of whom he had much to say.

Where then do we stand today?

With regard to our most hostile critics, as long as we uphold our biblical values, we will be reviled and condemned. That it is to be expected.

With regard to those outside the church who still think that Christians should live moral lives and care for the needy, let us step higher and demonstrate the life-changing power of the gospel.

With regard to our relationship with the president, we must conduct ourselves with integrity and honor, serving as a moral compass to our president rather than his tool. In that way, we will serve both God and the society.

December 12, 2016

WHY MANY AMERICANS TRUST DONALD TRUMP MORE THAN THE CIA

★ ★ ★ ★ ★

WHILE flying home recently from an overseas trip, I watched a movie in which the CIA played a prominent role, and if the movie is anything is close to reality, the CIA knows a lot—and I mean a whole lot, from what's on our computers to what we're talking about on our phones. Yet a healthy percentage of the American population seems to trust President-elect Trump more than our nation's Central Intelligence Agency. How can this be?

I asked my Twitter followers, "When it comes to alleged Russian influence on the elections, do you believe the CIA or Trump?"

Remarkably, only 18 percent said they trusted the CIA while 44 percent said they trusted Trump and 38 percent said they were unsure—and it should be noted that while the vast majority of my Twitter followers are, to my knowledge, Christian conservatives, a good number of them did not support Trump. Why, then, are they so distrusting of the CIA?

To answer that question, we can ask this: "Do you personally trust the federal government?"

As broad as that question is, I think the answer for many Americans would be, "No, I don't."

After all, the federal government is the IRS, the Department of Justice, the FBI—and also the CIA. The federal government is the big bad "them" which is always out to get the vulnerable little "us."

As for Trump, while he is about to become the head of that very federal government, he is perceived by many Americans to be "one of us" rather than part of the system, and the way he is conducting himself thus far as President-elect, with his Twitter account as active as ever, continues to reinforce that perception. He is the champion of "us."

The federal government is also hardly a stranger to corruption or mismanagement, unless you believe the IRS was not guilty of unfair treatment of conservative organizations and the Department of Justice was not guilty of favored treatment of Hillary Clinton, and FBI Director James Comey acted in a completely dispassionate and professional manner. And so it's easy to think that the information leaked from unnamed CIA sources is unreliable. After all, this is President Obama's CIA, is it not?

We also should bear in mind that the source for the Russian hacking claims is the liberal, mainstream media, which has also taken a big credibility hit in recent months.

Consider these striking results from a June, 2016 Gallup poll focused on Americans' "confidence in institutions."[1]

The pollster said to each participant, "I am going to read you a list of institutions in American society. Please tell me how much confidence you, yourself, have in each one—a great deal, quite a lot, some, or very little?"

At the top of the list was the military, with a high mark of 73 percent positive (41 percent responding with "a great deal" of trust and 32 percent with "quite a lot"). At the bottom of the list was Congress, with only a 6 percent positive response (those responding with "a great deal" of trust were too small to number; 6 percent said they had "quite a lot" of trust in Congress). What a staggeringly poor showing for our elected officials, and what a strong showing for our military.

Numbers two and three at the top of the list were small business (68 percent total) and the police (56 percent). Rounding out the bottom of the list were big business (18 percent total), newspapers (20 percent) and television news (21 percent). And despite the constant attacks on religion in America, the church ranked number four on the list, one slot higher than the presidency, which was then followed by the Supreme Court, the public schools, banks, and organized labor.

The offshoot of all this is that the CIA is perceived by many as being part of a larger, untrustworthy system, while those pushing the Russian hacking narrative are part of the untrustworthy media. Added to this is the fact that the Hillary Clinton campaign is supportive of efforts to launch an investigation into the alleged Russian hack, and it's easy to see why many trust Trump more than the CIA right now.[2]

Callers to my radio show also emphasized that, whoever was behind the hack, what was revealed was only damning because it was true. Because of this, there's very little sympathy for the Democratic complaints about the hacking and more concern with the content of the hacked material than the question of who did the hacking.

I personally have no idea whether Russia hacked us or not, and obviously, it will be important for Trump and the CIA to find a place of rapprochement and trust in the days ahead. But right now, Trump continues to represent the views of a fairly significant portion of the populace which is, after all, how he got elected.

December 19, 2016

WHY DONALD TRUMP IS CATCHING HELL FOR PLANNING TO MOVE OUR EMBASSY TO JERUSALEM

★ ★ ★ ★ ★

THERE is no controversy like the controversy that surrounds the city of Jerusalem, the most divided city on the earth and the most coveted city on the earth. The Bible predicted this more than 2,500 years ago, describing the day when Jerusalem would be "a cup that brings dizziness to all the surrounding nations" (Zech. 12:2 NET), even declaring that one day, the whole would be in uproar over Jerusalem.

Stop and think about it for a moment.

Why does the whole world get so upset over Jerusalem? Is there any other city on the planet that evokes such intense emotions and polar views?

And why does every nation put its embassies in the city that the host country identifies as its capital, except for the city of Jerusalem, identified as Israel's capital in 1950? Why do virtually all embassies remain in Tel Aviv?

There is something of spiritual significance to this ancient city that simply cannot be denied.

The Jerusalem Embassy Act of 1995, "passed by overwhelming bipartisan majority in both the House and Senate," states that "Jerusalem should be recognized as the capital of the State of Israel and the United States Embassy in Israel should be established in Jerusalem no later than May 31, 1999."[1]

Then why didn't presidents Bush or Obama move the embassy? As explained by Rabbi Shraga Simmons, "since the congressional act allows the President to implement a waiver at six-month intervals, that's exactly what has happened every six months since 1995."[2]

Now that Donald Trump has insisted that he will, in fact, relocate our embassy—in accordance with the 1995 act—the controversy is hitting the fan. In the words of Sheikh Ekrema Sabri, imam of the al-Aqsa Mosque in Jerusalem, moving the embassy would be as good as a "declaration of war."[3]

Consider the opposition to Trump's appointee for Ambassador to Israel, David Friedman, a strong supporter of Israel who speaks of our embassy's imminent relocation. As he said openly and proudly after his nomination, "I intend to work tirelessly to strengthen the unbreakable bond between our two countries and advance the cause of peace within the region, and look forward to doing this from the US embassy in Israel's eternal capital, Jerusalem."[4]

According to a December 16 email from Rabbi Shmuley Boteach, known as "America's rabbi," Friedman is a "brilliant choice for Ambassador to Israel. One of America's most respected and accomplished attorneys, David is regarded in the highest esteem by the New York Jewish community as an exemplar of the American and Jewish virtues of education, erudition, philanthropy, and communal commitment."

He continued, "David has vast exposure to, and knowledge of, the Jewish State and its history and enjoys the confidence and respect of Israel's leaders. A man of humility and openness, he has a gift for listening, showing respect and deference to all whom he meets."

In sharp contrast, as noted on the Elder of Ziyon website, last Friday's *New York Times* "had *four articles* against Donald Trump's choice to be the US ambassador to Israel. Yes—four articles in one day. Two 'news' articles, one editorial, and one op-ed."[5]

As Noah Pollack reported on The Washington Free Beacon, "The NYT Is Having a Meltdown Over Trump's Israel Nominee." Pollack writes:

David Friedman is a prominent and successful attorney in New York who has spent 20 years representing Donald Trump, among other clients. He is also a proud Jew who holds unapologetic pro-Israel views that are heretical in *Times*-world, and he has also expressed acid disdain for the kind of Jewish anti-Israel activism regularly glorified in the pages of the *Times*.

So he must be destroyed—and to destroy him he must be lied about. Which is what the *Times* did.[6]

Pollack does not specifically mention Friedman's strong support for relocating our embassy, since there are other, controversial pro-Israel positions that Friedman supports, including the building of settlements in territories under Palestinian control and skepticism about a two-state solution. But you can be assured that a big part of the ruckus over Friedman's appointment is his affirmation that the American embassy will be moved.

That's why a headline on the *Independent* discussing Friedman's nomination focused on this issue alone, noting that, "Moving US embassy to Jerusalem would be 'declaration of war.'"

And that's why *New York Times* columnist Thomas Friedman stated to Chris Cuomo on CNN that "moving the American embassy—and this is an evergreen, everyone running for President tosses this out, no one actually does it—moving the embassy to Jerusalem from Tel Aviv, in the absence of an agreed upon solution between Israelis and Palestinians, I would call that the 'Full Employment for Iran Act.'"[7]

Yes, according to Friedman, it would also alienate the Sunni Arab regimes, meaning that this move would provoke the Shiite Muslims in Iran and the Sunni Muslims in countries like Egypt and Saudi Arabia. Jerusalem, the city of controversy indeed!

Thomas Friedman then reiterated to Cuomo and co-host Alisyn Camerota: "This is such madness that it's—it's just—I can't believe we're talking about it."

Yet Kellyanne Conway, Trump's senior adviser, has reiterated that the incoming president really does plan to make this move, calling it a "big priority"[8] for him. And how revealing that Thomas Friedman noted that "everyone running for President tosses this out" but "no one actually does it," whereas Trump is threatening actually to do it. This is the very reason many people voted for him: They expect him to be a doer, not just a talker.

Should President Trump succeed in relocating our embassy to Jerusalem, I predict three things: 1) all hell will break loose against him (expect it in the most shrill tones), with constant, worldwide controversy over the move); 2) God will bless our president for doing it; and 3) God will bless America for doing it.

There's just something about Jerusalem.[9] Watch and see. (And to think that as recently as last month, an article in the *Washington Post* claimed that, "Anti-Semitism is no longer an undertone of Trump's campaign. It's the melody."[10] The irony is exquisite.)

December 20, 2016

"ISLAMIST TERRORISTS CONTINUALLY SLAUGHTER CHRISTIANS": TRUMP SAYS WHAT OBAMA REFUSED TO SAY

★ ★ ★ ★ ★

FOR eight years, we have watched Islamic terrorist attacks take place around the world and on our own shores, with the bloody, gory death toll rising by the day (roughly 30,000 attacks[1] since 9/11). And for eight years, we have listened carefully as our president addressed these horrific acts, studiously avoiding the words that so needed to be spoken: "Islamic terror" or "radical Islam."

Instead, President Obama and his surrogates spoke of "extremism" or "terrorism"—without any reference to Islam—or, worse still, of "workplace violence."

Mr. Obama and his team would not even identify Nidal Malik Hasan, the 2009 Fort Hood mass murderer, as an Islamic terrorist, despite the fact that he identifies as a Soldier of Allah, was mentored by a Muslim terrorist (Anwar Al-Alaki, whom we killed in a drone strike in Yemen), and slaughtered our soldiers in cold blood while shouting out Allah's name.[2] No, this was an instance of workplace violence.[3] (It was not until 2015 that Obama referenced the attack as "terrorist," but still refused to mention the word "Islamic.")

This is not just perverse, it is utterly irresponsible, since it fails to acknowledge that we are not just combatting people, we are combatting an ideology, and if we cannot even name that ideology, let alone describe it, we certainly cannot fight it.

And so yesterday, in the aftermath of the horrific truck attack at the Christmas market in Germany, the Obama administration (not the president himself, who is apparently on his final Christmas break) issued a statement, saying, "The United States condemns in the strongest terms what appears to have been a terrorist attack on a Christmas Market in Berlin, Germany, which has killed and wounded dozens."[4]

In stark contrast, President-elect Trump stated:

Our hearts and prayers are with the loved ones of the victims of today's horrifying terror attack in Berlin.

Innocent civilians were murdered in the streets as they prepared to celebrate the Christmas holiday. ISIS and other Islamist terrorists continually slaughter Christians in their communities and places of worship as part of their global jihad.

These terrorists and their regional and worldwide networks must be eradicated from the face of the earth, a mission we will carry out with all freedom-loving partners.[5]

In one short statement, Trump has done what Obama failed to do in eight years:

1. He identified "Islamist terrorists" by name, directly associating them with ISIS.

2. He specified that their victims have often been Christians, here during the Christmas holiday, and at other times, in their places of worship.

3. He declared war on these terrorists, asking "all freedom-loving partners" to join him in the battle, thereby opening the door to so-called moderate Islamic nations to join us in the battle. (Would Saudi Arabia fit in this category? How about Pakistan? Yemen? Syria?)

4. He used the term "global jihad," again with specific reference to Islamic terror.

The significance of this cannot be exaggerated.

The UK *Mirror* reminds us that "Europe was warned that ISIS planned terror attacks at Christmas markets 25 days before the Berlin atrocity."

Yes, "The attack came after intelligence agencies warned in November that terrorists are planning a wave of Christmas attacks throughout Europe, targeting shopping areas and crowded market-places to maximise casualties.

"The main groups plotting Yuletide blood-letting are Islamic State and al-Qaeda and UK intelligence agencies and counter-terror police are on high-alert."[5]

ISIS has now claimed responsibility[6] for the Berlin massacre, which means that we have: 1) Islamic terrorists stating that they will launch Christmas attacks against Christians in Europe; 2) a terror attack taking place against Christians at a Christmas market in Germany; and 3) ISIS taking responsibility for that attack.

Yet it is Donald Trump, not Barack Obama, who has connected the dots (really, these dots are all but connected for anyone with eyes to see), which is one reason that many Americans said "No" to four (or eight) more years of Obama policies (in the person of Hillary Clinton) and "Yes" to dramatic change in the person of Donald Trump.

It is true that his tweets can be reckless and unpresidential and that not all of his saber-rattling is helpful.

But it is also true that the world needs leaders like Trump who will call out Islamic terror by name, which is why right-leaning, populist movements are growing around the world—and it is not because Americans and Europeans and others are suddenly becoming "Islamophobic."

No, the problem is radical, murderous, terroristic Islam and the failure of these governments to address it head on, appearing to be more concerned with offending "moderate Muslims" than with protecting its own citizens—including unarmed children, women, and men.

The time for that is over.

January 11, 2017

DONALD TRUMP, THE JOHNSON AMENDMENT, AND THE QUESTION OF CHRISTIAN COWARDICE

★ ★ ★ ★ ★

IF President Trump succeeds in removing the oppressive Johnson Amendment, which limits freedom of speech from the pulpits, will Christian leaders be more outspoken on controversial moral, cultural, and political issues? I have my doubts, since I don't believe it is the Johnson Amendment that has muzzled preachers across America.

I believe it is the fear of man that has muzzled us and it is our desire to be affirmed by the world that has silenced us. Until we repent of these sinful, carnal attitudes, our tongues will not be loosed. We have been paralyzed from the inside, not the outside, and the removal of outward hindrances will not set us free within.

Let's be honest about this. The Johnson Amendment, as wrong as it is, is quite limited in its scope, primarily prohibiting "certain tax-exempt organizations from endorsing and opposing political candidates."

It does not prohibit pastors from speaking out against political corruption.

It does not prohibit pastors from speaking out against LGBT activism.

It does not prohibit pastors from speaking out against abortion.

It does not prohibit pastors from speaking out against a host of other moral and cultural issues, yet it is here that we have seriously failed our people—I say "we" because I too am a ministry leader, although not a pastor—since these are the very issues so many of us studiously avoid.

Who needs the controversy? Who wants to be vilified? Why stick in your hand into a hornet's nest? Why ask for trouble?

You might say, "Maybe some pastors think like this, but that's not the real issue for them. The issue is that they don't want to distract from the gospel. They just want to tell people about Jesus."

Unfortunately, this line of reasoning doesn't hold water, since Jesus Himself was tremendously controversial—if memory serves me right, He was actually put to death by His generation—and He said that if we followed Him faithfully, we would be hated just as He was hated (see John 15:18; Matt. 10:24).

Why is it, then, that the same world that hated Him so much loves us so much? Why is it that He offended so many—by being a perfect, shining light, full of grace and truth—yet we offend so few? (Sad to say, when we do offend people, it is often due to us being offensive and obnoxious or hypocritical and self-righteous rather than shining so brightly that people hate our light.)

It is true that Jesus was a friend of sinners—especially the societal outcasts—and we do well to follow His example. But is equally true that He was a threat to all that was wrong in His society—including the religious establishment—while we frequently find ourselves completely at home in this world. How can this be?

In 2014, George Barna discussed the results of his latest poll during an interview on American Family Radio. He explained that, "What we're finding is that when we ask [pastors] about all the key issues of the day, [90 percent of them are] telling us, 'Yes, the Bible speaks to every one of these issues.' Then we ask them: 'Well, are you teaching your people what the Bible says about those issues?' and the numbers drop...to less than 10 percent of pastors who say they will speak to it."[1]

And what, exactly, holds them back from addressing controversial issues from the pulpit, including, "societal, moral and political issues"? According to Barna, "There are five factors that the vast majority of pastors turn to. Attendance, giving, number of programs, number of staff, and square footage."

He continued: "What I'm suggesting is [those pastors] won't probably get involved in politics because it's very controversial. Controversy keeps people from being in the seats, controversy keeps people from giving money, from attending programs."

Yes, at all costs, we must avoid the controversy that will stop us leaders from fulfilling the Christian version of the American dream: Great success and popularity, and a happy, financially prosperous congregation, all made possible by preaching a watered-down gospel.

This mindset has nothing whatsoever to do with the New Testament faith.

Fired up by the results of the Barna poll, pastor and radio host Chuck Baldwin wrote:

> Please understand this: America's malaise is directly due to the deliberate disobedience of America's pastors—and the willingness of the Christians in the pews to tolerate the disobedience of their pastor. Nothing more! Nothing less! When Paul wrote his own epitaph, it read, "I have fought a good fight, I have finished my course, I have kept the faith." (II Timothy 4:7) He didn't say, "I had a large congregation, we had big offerings, we had a lot of programs, I had a large staff, and we had large facilities."[2]

Are his accusations too harsh? In many cases, yes, since there are sincere shepherds who simply feel ill-equipped to address the hot-button issues of the day, instead finding their gifting in the systematic teaching of the Scriptures and caring for their flocks. It is not fear that holds them back as much as a sense of calling to minister in a different way.

But in all too many cases, Baldwin's accusations are right on target: We have compromised for the sake of comfort and convenience. We have found a way to bypass the cross and its shame. We have created a no-cost, pop-gospel, forgetting that a gospel that costs nothing saves no one and is not a gospel at all.

The irony of all this is that Barna's survey also indicated that the vast majority of Christians surveyed—around 90 percent—wanted their pastors to address these difficult moral and cultural issues, since this is the world they live in and these are the problems they confront, right down to their kids in nursery school.

They are expecting their pastors and leaders to help them sort these things out based on Scripture, and they are frustrated and grieved when the men and women they look to are not there when they need them. Shouldn't the shepherds care more about the well-being of their flocks than their own popularity? Shouldn't the pastors care more about the health of their congregation than the wealth of their congregation?

To be clear, I have preached in wealthy, large mega-churches that are not afraid to tackle the controversies and I have preached in poor, small churches that are afraid to tackle these issues. The fear of man comes in many shapes and sizes, but the expression of it will always be the same: You will not do what you know is right because you fear the negative consequences.

That is a fear that must be broken, and it is only the Lord—not Donald Trump—who can help us break it.

Will we rise to the occasion when society needs us the most, or we will cower behind our cheap excuses?

It's time for the lion to roar.

January 13, 2017

WILL THE "TRUMP EFFECT" TRICKLE DOWN TO CHRISTIAN CONSERVATIVES?

★ ★ ★ ★ ★

LIKE no one before him, Donald Trump has shaken our nation, and love him or loathe him, he has done what no one else has ever done. On his journey to the presidency, he has broken (and rewritten) the rules, he has defied the establishment, he has challenged the status quo, he has played both the bully and the victim, he has proved the pundits wrong, and he has emerged from every storm stronger than before.

Not only so, but the climate of the nation has changed (some say for better and some say for worse), to the point that what seemed inevitable just three months ago no longer seems so inevitable. Could it be that America is about to make a massive change in direction, a radical course correction?

This, to me, this an important aspect of what some are calling the "Trump effect" (often in pejorative terms; a Google search on January 12 yielded 1,160,000 results for "Trump effect" in quotes): The inevitable can be challenged; the status quo can be changed; the bullies can be conquered.

Again, I'm aware that for many, President-elect Trump is the ultimate bully, hardly a model to follow, especially for followers of Jesus, and my goal here is not to call pastors and believers to emulate his tone or his style. Instead, I'm encouraging us to learn from his example that America's course has not been inexorably set, that the seemingly impossible is very possible, that history is full of surprises, and that now is the time for fresh courage and commitment.

For several years now, we conservatives have been told that we have lost the culture wars, that we should throw in the towel and concede, that we should consolidate our losses and move on to non-controversial, spiritual issues, that the tide of history is set against us. And those of us who refused to go along with this narrative were mocked and ridiculed, told that we represented a dying breed that was about to be replaced by an enlightened generation, mocked as unfortunate relics of a bygone age, ridiculed as an endangered species soon to be obsolete.

Now, the tide of history has shifted suddenly, with the real possibility of a complete reversal in the expected makeup of the Supreme Court (under Hillary) and the equally real possibility of a wholesale repudiation of radical liberalism. And to think that on election day, even into early election evening, this was the exact opposite of what was widely expected to be. The direction of the nation literally turned on a dime, and with it, the sense that anything is possible. The very rules of engagement have changed.

Who says that we have to cower before the cultural bullies? Who says that we have to apologize for our convictions? Who says that the mainstream media sets the agenda and establishes the talking points? Who says that the defeat of conservative values is inevitable?

Again, I am not saying that we emulate the style of our president-elect (in terms of the negative aspects of his style) or that we take on the posture of bullies. Instead, I'm urging us to learn from what he has accomplished, to change our way of thinking, and to seize the day and take back the ground that has been pulled from under our feet.

Just three months ago, it appeared that Planned Parenthood would be firmly ensconced and generously funded for a generation or more. Now, the abortion giant stands on the verge of national defunding.

Just three months ago, it appeared that Roe v. Wade would not be overturned in our lifetimes or perhaps even in the lifetimes of our children. Now, talk of its possible reversal is anything but fantasy.

Just three months ago, it appeared that LGBT rights would push religious rights into the closet. Now, an unlikely champion of religious rights has arisen (and oddly enough, he fashions himself a friend of LGBT rights as well).

This is not just the tables turning. This is the floor becoming the ceiling and the ceiling becoming the floor. This is nothing less than upheaval.

Of course, we have no way of knowing how President Trump will govern and how far the Republican-led Congress will go in terms of making positive, necessary changes.

But what's clear is this: Donald Trump, in the past more famous for hedonism than for heroics, has declared war on a sacrosanct, PC world, and it's high time for others who call themselves overcomers and world changers and who fashion themselves to be countercultural Christians—I'm speaking about the born-again Church of America—to rise up, stand tall, and speak the truth in love.

After all, if a thrice-married, former-playboy, billionaire businessman can shake the nation, why can't we as the Lord's people—in the power of the Spirit and in the footsteps of Jesus, overcoming evil with good.

Enough with our compromise and cowardice. It's time for courage and conviction. It's time we led the way.

January 20, 2017

AN OPEN LETTER TO CRITICS OF PRESIDENT TRUMP

★ ★ ★ ★ ★

A S one who issued numerous warnings about candidate Donald Trump during the Republican primaries, on radio, in writing, and on video, I'm sympathetic to your concerns.

You see him as an incredibly dangerous loose cannon, as someone who could start a world war with his tweets, as a mean-spirited man unfit for the presidency, as a divider not a uniter. You might even see him as a potential dictator, rising up like a new Hitler in an increasingly xenophobic, angry, and fearful America.

How on earth, you wonder, did Donald Trump become the President of the United States? How did this narcissistic, playboy businessman become the most powerful leader in the world?

To repeat: I'm sympathetic to your concerns and I understand why you feel like this, and even as someone who voted for Trump, I never dissed the Never Trumpers.

But now that Donald Trump will be our 45th president—yes, get used to hearing "President Trump"—may I have a word with you?

The first issue is one of attitude.

During the 2008 Democratic primaries, I warned my radio listeners that Barack Obama would be the most radical pro-abortion, pro-gay-agenda president in our nation's history. Over the subsequent months, I also questioned where he stood with Israel.

More than eight years later, I'm sad to say—not happy to say—that I was right. (Honestly, it didn't take a rocket scientist to figure out what kind of president he would be.)

During his presidency, I often told my listeners, "I'm praying that he will be the greatest president we've ever had, but right now, I don't see that at all. I have grave concerns."

So, I'm encouraging you to have a godly attitude toward our new president. I'm encouraging you to pray for him with the heartfelt desire that God will make him into a great president rather than for you to stand on the sidelines, rooting for his fall. According to the Scriptures, the former attitude is godly; the latter is not.

Let your attitude, then, as a past critic be: "I have grave concerns about President Trump, but I'm hoping that I'm wrong about my concerns."

If you really care about America and are a person of prayer, that should be your mindset.

The second issue is one of expectation.

Could it be that Trump is not quite the man you think he is? Could it be that he has more going for him than you realize? Could it be that many Americans had solid reasons to vote for him and that he could get a lot done for the good of our nation? Could it be that, despite his very rough edges and non-presidential tweets, God is already working in his heart?

From all that we can see, he is very serious about:

- Appointing strong conservatives to the Supreme Court
- Standing for life, beginning in the womb
- Moving our embassy to Jerusalem and standing up to radical Islam
- Fighting for our religious liberties
- Rebuilding our inner cities
- Taking on the political establishment
- Strengthening our security and our economy
- Exposing the biased media

I also believe he really wants to be the president of all Americans, despite his divisive words, and I truly believe he wants to recapture many of the things that have made our nation great over the decades. And, as a biblically based conservative, I believe he has already made a number of excellent personnel choices, in particular in his cabinet picks, and he continues to keep his door open to evangelical Christian leaders. In my book, these are encouraging signs.

And so, while it is true that we have no guarantee of what will happen once he begins to govern, I believe we have ample reason to expect the best rather than the worst. Perhaps you can find it in your heart to be at least a little positive?

Perhaps you can ask yourself, "What if I was a pro-Trumper rather than an anti-Trumper? What good would I see in him? What potential would I see in him?" Perhaps you can tweak your attitude just a little?

We tend to defend the weaknesses of those we like and attack the weaknesses of those we don't like, meaning that we use different standards on different people. This is unrighteous and unethical, also obscuring the clarity of our vision.

Why not ask God how He wants to you view President Trump, and then, with full awareness of his potential failings and still-glaring faults, why not pray for him with hope and root for his success rather than his failure?

Once Donald Trump became the Republican candidate, I said, "I hope I get to eat my negative words about Trump," rather than, "I can't wait to say, 'I told you so!'"

I'm urging you to do the same. After all, four or eight years from now, wouldn't it far better to say, "I'm so glad I was wrong about President Trump," than to say, "I told you he was not fit to be president"?

Please join me in praying for and hoping for the success of our 45th president and new Commander in Chief.

January 23, 2017

An Attempted Impartial Reading of President Trump's Inaugural Speech

★ ★ ★ ★ ★

IS it possible to read President Trump's inaugural speech in a dispassionate manner? With his devotees fawning over every word and his critics branding the speech "Hitlerian,"[1] it can be challenging to stand above the fray and give it an impartial reading. But, it certainly can be done. As Ben Shapiro recently tweeted, "This is not hard. When Trump does good things, praise him. When Trump does bad things, condemn him. Basic decency is not tough."[2]

First, a tweet-worthy summary of the speech: It's time to give power back to the people and make America great again by putting America first.

One journalist pointed out how few times Trump said "I" and how frequently he said "we" in contrast, it was alleged, with President Obama who was famous for his I-centric speeches.[3] But that is a superficial analysis, since, in his 2009 inaugural speech, incoming President Obama's I/we percentage was even better than Trump's, and it was common for other presidents to do the same in their opening addresses.

More to the point, does anyone really think that we will not be hearing a lot of "I" and "me" from our president in the days ahead? The power of Donald Trump is directly tied to his personality, for better or for worse.

As for the content of his speech, he began by addressing "Chief Justice Roberts, President Carter, President Clinton, President Bush, President Obama, fellow Americans, and people of the world," stating that, "We, the citizens of America, are now joined in a great national effort to rebuild our country and to restore its promise for all of our people."

On the one hand, other incoming presidents have described their vision using terms like "renewal" (as did JFK in 1961), as if there had been decay and ruin before them. But for Trump to speak of the "great national effort to rebuild our country and to restore its promise for all of our people" is to say something very specific and clear: America was collapsing under Barack Obama; America had lost its way under Barack Obama; now is the time to rebuild and restore.

Can you imagine how it felt to be the outgoing POTUS and FLOTUS as those words were spoken? To paraphrase, "Your administration has made a total mess of things and destroyed what made our country great. It's time to fix the mess you made."

Is there any other interpretation to put on Trump's words? I think not. The fact that he immediately commended the former president and first lady, saying that "They have been magnificent" during the transition did not remove the sting.

But it was not just President Obama who failed America, according to President Trump. No, it was all of Washington, and our new president, a Washington outsider, made a formal declaration of war: It's time to take the power away from the political establishment and give "it back to you, the American people."

Indeed, "For too long, a small group in our nation's Capital has reaped the rewards of government while the people have borne the cost. Washington flourished—but the people did not share in its wealth. Politicians prospered—but the jobs left, and the factories closed."

Yes, "The establishment protected itself, but not the citizens of our country. Their victories have not been your victories; their triumphs have not been your triumphs; and while they celebrated in our nation's capital, there was little to celebrate for struggling families all across our land."

Who are the members of that "small group" in Washington, the ones who make up "the establishment"? What are the names of those politicians who are prospering at the expense of their constituents? Does the list include Democrats like Nancy Pelosi and Chuck Schumer who participated in the inauguration or perhaps their Democratic colleagues who boycotted the event? Does it include

Republicans like Paul Ryan, also involved with the inauguration, or other Republicans who are part of the establishment?

Without further specificity, all of Washington is guilty right now, and Trump is the Robin Hood who will take from the unlawfully rich and redistribute the funds to the hurting citizens of our nation. As he said, "That all changes—starting right here, and right now, because this moment is your moment: it belongs to you."

And his promise was bold: "January 20th 2017 will be remembered as the day the people became the rulers of this nation again. The forgotten men and women of our country will be forgotten no longer."

This is why many Americans voted for him, and this was a centerpiece of his speech, including this audacious claim: "You came by the tens of millions to become part of a historic movement the likes of which the world has never seen before. At the center of this movement is a crucial conviction: that a nation exists to serve its citizens."

Worldwide history was being made, and the power of self-serving government was being broken.

Can Trump deliver on even a fraction of this promise? Can he dismantle the power of the very establishment whose votes he needs to accomplish his goals? In my view, he can only do it by: 1) effectively exposing and then cutting through Washington bureaucracy, using his public platforms to embarrass those who play political games; 2) aggressively pare down the size of the government; and 3) empower his appointees (like Betty DeVos) to offer non-centralized, non-Washington-run alternatives (like school choice).

And although Trump didn't use the word "indignant," this is clearly what he meant when he spoke of "the just and reasonable demands of a righteous public." They want America back!

Surprisingly, he focused on the bleak condition of our inner cities—in graphic detail, at that—from poverty to broken homes to a failed education system to no jobs to gangs, but this was followed by his Trumpian promise: "This American carnage stops right here and stops right now."

Apparently, he is genuinely concerned with (or, at the least, bothered by) the state of our inner cities (as friends connected to him have privately reported to me), and he did well by making this a problem for all Americans to solve: "We are one nation—and their pain is our pain. Their dreams are our dreams; and their success will be our success. We share one heart, one home, and one glorious destiny."

How can this be done? Obviously, not through Washington, DC, which can only play a small role in rebuilding our broken nation. Instead, there must be empowerment of the people, and if former football great Ray Lewis has reportedly things accurately, Trump was very impressed with the work of football legend Jim Brown, devoted to making gang members into solid citizens.[4]

What role is the church to play? Hopefully, Trump will looks to grassroots agents of change, starting with his solid Christian connections, rather than lean on welfare politics, which increase, rather than decrease, the real needs of the inner cities.

But the focus on fixing the inner cities prepared the way for Trump's gradual crescendo, with the emphasis on one concept—America first. To paraphrase again: "We've helped the rest of the world at the expense of our own nation. This stops here today, and I'm shouting that out for the whole world to hear."

In his exact words: "We assembled here today are issuing a new decree to be heard in every city, in every foreign capital, and in every hall of power." From here on, every decision that is made—from jobs to security to immigration to infrastructure—"will follow two simple rules: Buy American and hire American."

Is this a hyper-nationalistic, über-populist, xenophobic vision, one that could be compared to Germany during the rise of Adolph Hitler? Is it perhaps not quite so dangerous but still narrow-minded and selfish, echoing Pat Buchanan's "America first" cry from 2000? Or is it the logical and right strategy for every nation on the planet, as Trump said, "We will seek friendship and goodwill with the nations of the world—but we do so with the understanding that it is the right of all nations to put their own interests first."

Yes, every nation should put its own interests first—a slap in the face to the globalist mentality—and if America is healthier, the world will be healthier. But for Trump, this does not mean dominating the rest of the world. Instead, "We do not seek to impose our way of life on anyone, but rather to let it shine as an example for everyone to follow."

In my view, this is the most ambiguous part of his speech: What exactly does "America first" mean? How exactly will it play out? Obviously, this remains to be seen.

To his credit, though, in his very first speech as President, Trump said three words that Barack Obama has refused to say for eight years and which Hillary Clinton would have surely refused to say if elected: "radical Islamic terrorism." This he pledged to "eradicate completely from the face of the earth" with the cooperation of like-minded nations.

Coming back to his vision for America itself, he stated that "through our loyalty to our country, we will rediscover our loyalty to each other," also claiming that, "When you open your heart to patriotism, there is no room for prejudice" (with a nod to Psalm 133:1).

And it was this call to unity amid our disagreements that undergirded the climax of his speech, because, "When America is united, America is totally unstoppable."

The obvious problem, however, is that Trump's whole style of campaigning and leading has been as unifying as it has been dividing—have we had a more polarizing figure in memory?—and it appears that the only way he will succeed in rallying us together is by dropping the unnecessary attacks on others, toning down the rhetoric, and fulfilling some of his promises.

After all, the average American is more moved by a healthy economy and a feeling of security than by all kinds of political bantering. Indeed, he proclaimed, "A new national pride will stir our souls, lift our sights, and heal our divisions."

The idea is certainly right; making it happen is a very tall order, barring a national catastrophe (God forbid) that would bring us together by default.

Moving toward his conclusion, he stated that military and law enforcement will protect us—an obvious word of solidarity in contrast with some of the negative sentiments of the previous administration—and with Americans feeling safe and secure, "we must think big and dream even bigger."

Americans must not stop striving to be great, and if anyone stands in our way, including, "politicians who are all talk and no action—constantly complaining but never doing anything about it"—they will be removed: "The time for empty talk is over. Now arrives the hour of action."

And then, his final inspirational words, which in my judgment, represented his best teleprompter delivery to date, climaxing with the emphasis on "you," the people of America, before ending with a resounding "we."

"Together, we will make America strong again.

"We will make America wealthy again.

"We will make America proud again.

"We will make America safe again.

"And yes, together, we will make America great again. Thank you. God bless you. And God bless America."

What are we to make of this? I am convinced that President Trump will work tirelessly and that he and his team will be doers and not just talkers; I have no doubt that he must become more of a statesman if America is to unite around him on any serious level; and I do believe that putting America first in a healthy way will benefit the whole world.

The dangers are that his attack on the establishment (which, indeed, must be confronted) will lead to governmental paralysis; that he will become more contentious, not less contentious, thereby deepening our divides; and that his America-first emphasis will appeal to our baser instincts, thereby making us anything but truly great.

Have the possibilities for good or bad ever been more stark and more real at one and the same time?

I'd say now is a good time to pray for our president like never before. The stakes have never been higher.

January 30, 2017

FIVE THINGS BOTHERING ME ABOUT THE RESPONSE TO TRUMP'S EXECUTIVE ORDER ON REFUGEES

★ ★ ★ ★ ★

HAVE you ever seen America so ablaze with controversy? Protests in the streets, hysteria in the news rooms, chaos and weeping at the airports, cries for impeachment among political leaders—all because of President Trump's executive order concerning refugees.

Some have openly called for the president's murder,[1] drawing swift rebuke from others:

A well-educated Christian professor in Canada has dubbed Trump the antichrist:

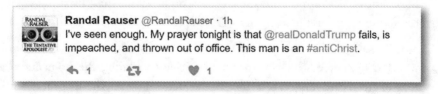

A progressive Christian leader argues that supporting Trump and following Jesus are incompatible:

Benjamin L Corey @BenjaminLCorey · 27m

If you wondered if it were possible to follow Jesus and support Trump, that question should be loudly answered for you by now.

↩ 2   ⟳ 39   ♥ 96

The leftwing media elite are indignant, with the *New York Times* branding Trump's order a "cowardly and dangerous" act of "unrighteousness," with a host of others echoing similar claims.[2]

On the flip side, rightwing conservative sites like Breitbart feature bold headlines declaring, "Terror-Tied Group CAIR [The Council on American-Islamic Relations] Causing Chaos, Promoting Protests & Lawsuits as Trump Protects Nation."[3]

On Twitter, I asked my followers, "Is Trump's executive order on the refugees fundamentally unChristian, or is it being misreported by the media?"

In response, 74 percent answered "misreported by the media," 16 percent said it was "fundamentally anti-Christian," and 10 percent chose "Other."

How do we sort this out?

In response to the national (actually, international) outcry, President Trump issued a statement Sunday afternoon, restating the rationale behind his order and defending its particulars. In the statement he emphasized that, "America is a proud nation of immigrants and we will continue to show compassion to those fleeing oppression, but we will do so while protecting our own citizens and border." And, he stated, "To be clear, this is not a Muslim ban, as the media is falsely reporting. This is not about religion—this is about terror and keeping our country safe."[4]

Others, far too numerous to cite here, have disputed his words, and the din on both sides is rising in intensity by the hour. So, rather than try to sort out all the controversies surrounding the executive order, let me share five things that are bothering me about the reaction to Trump's order.

To be clear, though, we need to separate the executive order itself from the way it was executed, which led to even more chaos, including the momentary banning of green card holders returning to the States and even the alleged[5] detention of a newborn and an 18-month old baby, both American citizens, at Chicago's O'Hare airport. One can be upset over the initial implementation of the order while still defending the order itself.

Here, then, is what is sticking in my craw.

First, I have a hard time believing that suddenly, across America, countless thousands of Americans are upset that Muslim refugees from seven countries will be temporarily banned from entering our country while "extreme vetting" measures are put in place.

Muslims make up about one percent of our population, and many of the Muslims who live here are not from the countries on Trump's list. Yet suddenly, all across the nation, Americans are outraged that Muslims from countries like Libya and Yemen will be temporarily prohibited from immigrating here.

In my opinion, while some of the outrage is legitimate, much of it is more of an expression of hatred toward Trump than an expression of solidarity with, say, Somali refugees. As to the degree that Islamic groups like CAIR are behind some of the protests, others can decide.

Second, this massive, loud, national expression of compassion for Muslim refugees strikes me as quite hypocritical when we remember that there have been very few words spoken about the decades-long genocide of Middle Eastern Christians at the hands of radical Muslims. As I tweeted out Saturday night, "Where were all the protests across America as millions of Christians overseas were being slaughtered or sold into slavery or exiled?"

Yet now, we Americans are in a state of frenzy because of the temporary halt on some refugees entering our country. Something is not lining up here.

Third, I don't understand why some Christian leaders are upset with putting a priority on resettling Christian refugees.[6] (I suggested prioritizing Christian refugees back in November 2015.) This is the right thing to do scripturally and legally, for at least three reasons:

1. Christians are called to do good to all people, but especially to fellow believers (see Gal. 6:10); so, we continue to help Muslim and other refugees, but as a majority Christian country, we prioritize Christian refugees.

2. Christian refugees really are "the least of these My brethren" in

the classic words of Jesus in Matthew 25:31-46, being trapped as a tiny, persecuted minority in the midst of Islamic civil wars and surrounded by Islamic countries, with very few making it to our shores.[7] Sadly, as I noted in 2015, "A friend of mine who pastors a large church in Tennessee traveled to Jordan and spoke with Christian refugees there. Their perception was that American Christians had completely abandoned them."

3. Legally, the issue is not one of Islamophobia but rather, to quote the executive order directly, a call "to prioritize refugee claims made by individuals on the basis of religious-based persecution, provided that the religion of the individual is a minority religion in the individual's country of nationality." This could apply to groups like the Yazidis too, and rightly so. (See: a talk of Safe Zones[8] in countries like Saudi Arabia aiming at helping Muslim refugees.)

Fourth, I have no tolerance for the media's hysteria and their use of inflammatory phrases like "the Muslim ban." As David French explained on the *National Review* (note that French was a well-known Never Trumper), "You can read the entire executive order from start to finish, reread it, then read it again, and you *will not* find a Muslim ban. It's not there. Nowhere. At its most draconian, it temporarily halts entry from jihadist regions. In other words, Trump's executive order is a dramatic climb-down from his worst campaign rhetoric."[9]

Again, French is hardly a defender of Trump, writing that "the ban *is* deeply problematic as applied to legal residents of the U.S. and to interpreters and other allies seeking refuge in the United States after demonstrated (and courageous) service to the United States." But he is quite correct in labelling much of the media's reporting of the order as "false, false, false."

Similarly, Dan McLaughlin, also posting on the *National Review*, penned an article titled, "Refugee Madness: Trump Is Wrong, But His Liberal Critics Are Crazy," stating that the anger at Trump's new policy "is seriously misplaced."[10]

I would go as far as saying that some major media players are being downright irresponsible, engaging in the worst type of partisan politics, possibly even endangering lives in the process. I say that because the immigration crisis is volatile enough in itself, as is the presidency of Donald Trump, and some of the media's irresponsible and inflammatory reporting could easily provoke acts of wanton violence.

Fifth and finally, I don't understand why evangelicals who voted for Trump feel the need to defend everything he does and even how he does it (and I am one who voted for him and who at times has defended him). Not only does this give further fuel to the fire of those critics who claim that we are hurting our Christian witness by supporting him, but it eliminates our high calling to be the president's "loyal opposition" at times (to borrow a phrased coined by biblical scholar Yochanan Muffs regarding Israel's prophets). If we truly care for and support the president, we should demonstrate that by lovingly opposing him when we feel he has done wrong.

In this case, I'm *not* saying that he has acted wrongly (although, as is self-evident, the implementation of his order was terribly messy and unnecessarily confusing). I'm saying that we can't simply have a gut-level reaction of defending the president against all criticism, even if, in some (many?) cases, he is being unjustly accused.

Let's put our faith before our politics, lest we make the mistake the religious right made in generations before and become an appendage of the Republican Party.

With that being said, if you know how to pray, now's a good time to put those prayers to work. We desperately need God's gracious intervention to heal our broken land.

February 3, 2017

FOUR MAJOR TAKEAWAYS FROM PRESIDENT TRUMP'S NOMINATION OF JUSTICE GORSUCH

★ ★ ★ ★ ★

NOW that the dust has settled in the aftermath of the president's nomination of Justice Neil Gorsuch and the battle lines are being drawn, here are four major takeaways.

First, more than any president in memory, Trump is acting swiftly on his campaign promises, and when he said to the American people the night of the Gorsuch announcement that "I am a man of my word,"[1] you had to say to yourself, "Like him or not, he's doing exactly what he said he would do." This is incredibly significant.

In February 2016, in the heat of the Republican primaries, I wrote an article titled "Donald Trump, Vacillator-in-Chief," starting with this: "If Donald Trump ends up being our next president, I will pray that he will be the greatest president we have ever had and I will fervently hope that I'm absolutely wrong about all of my concerns. Until then (or at least until we decide on the Republican nominee), I will sound the alarm and raise my voice as loudly and clearly as I can. Do not be duped by Donald Trump!"

Among other examples in the article, I stated that Trump "vacillated wildly when asked whether his sister (of pro-partial birth abortion fame) should be nominated as a Supreme Court justice including: yes, no, I was joking, I wasn't joking, I have no idea what she believes. (This is a partial, very rough summary.) Then add to the mix that, in 2000 he said there should be no abortion litmus test for federal judges."

I also pointed out that, "During Thursday night's debate, Leon Wolf tweeted this quote from Trump: 'I have great respect for Justice Scalia,' followed by, 'Trump Less than five months ago...slammed Scalia for not supporting affirmative action.'"

As the campaign wore on, Trump's positions became more and more consistent, to the point that he convinced me that he was serious about nominating a pro-life justice in the mold of Scalia.

That he did the very thing he promised he would do—and quite swiftly[2] at that, given the turmoil surrounding his first weeks in office—is something to commend.

So, let it sink in. Donald Trump is keeping his word. (And, as noted about in the quote from my February article, I'm glad I was proven wrong. My hope now is that our president will weigh his words even more carefully so that what he promises to do is what he should do.)

Second, the ideological divide in our country between left and right has never been more stark. (The horrifically costly divisions during the time of the Civil War were along other lines.)

The conservative praise for Gorsuch is off the charts, and I could fill this entire article with links to quotes from well-placed individuals (like Senator Ted Cruz) to influential organizations (like the Family Research Council) to conservative websites (like the National Review Online) all praising Gorsuch as someone truly in the mold of Scalia, a real Constitutionalist, a worthy pro-life nominee.

The reaction against Gorsuch from the left has been at least as strident—if not far more—than the reaction from the right, and it can truly be called hysterical.

An op-ed headline on *USA Today* announced, "Time for outrageous obstruction against Gorsuch: Jason Sattler,"[3] while Nancy Pelosi said at a CNN Townhall meeting, "If you breathe air, drink water, eat food, take medicine, or in any other way interact with the courts, this is a very bad decision," labelling Gorsuch a "very hostile appointment."[4] Could you make yourself a little clearer, Ms. Minority Leader?

It is true that there is a history[5] of hysterical reactions to Supreme Court picks in the past, but the reactions to Gorsuch are but the very sharp, quite obvious tip of the iceberg of massive social divide. Or did a former aide to President George

W. Bush suggest the military overthrow of President Obama, as a former aide to Obama just did to Trump?[6] Or did conservative entertainers call for a violent coup against the newly installed President Obama, as Sarah Silverman just did to Trump?[7] (And let's not forget Madonna's expressed desire to blow up the White House.)

The opposition to Gorsuch simply illustrates the intensity and depth of the chasm between right and left.

Third, there will be no appeasing the Democratic Party.

As much as Trump may want to be a team player (I do believe he'd like to be seen as someone who can bridge divides) and as much as he is a master negotiator, there will be no appeasing the current Democrat leadership, which is simply dead-set against him.

Forget about common political courtesies.

Forget about building a consensus.

Right now, there's as much chance of that happening with the Democrats as there is of Cecille Richards of Planned Parenthood being nominated pro-life champion of the year.

Of course, Trump's style of campaigning and leadership has certainly contributed to the conflict, but the Democratic response to Trump's pick so far—namely, oppose him at all costs, and use every tactic in the book to do it—should be strong reminder to Trump that a friendly, let's meet in the middle attitude will be totally counterproductive right now.

The simple fact that the some of the same Democrats[8] who voted for Gorsuch in 2006 are now firmly pledged to vote against him says it all.

Fourth, believers who pray regularly for our president should also pray for the members of the Supreme Court, especially for Gorsuch, should he be appointed as seems highly likely.

I say that because nothing can be taken for granted with our justices, and hardly anyone would have imagined that Justice Kennedy, appointed by Ronald Reagan, would one day be the swing vote in redefining marriage (really now, who would have imagined during Reagan's presidency that the Supreme Court would one day sanction homosexual "marriage"?), nor would many have guessed that

Chief Justice Roberts, appointed by George W. Bush, would have been the swing vote in favor of Obamacare.

It is true that neither Kennedy nor Roberts have the pedigree of Gorsuch, but the significant failings of these two justices should put a cautionary damper on our enthusiasm, at the least, reminding us to pray for Justice Gorsuch to judge righteously if appointed.

The late Justice Scalia famously wrote that, "A system of government that makes the People subordinate to a committee of nine unelected lawyers does not deserve to be called a democracy."[9]

Unfortunately, that is the system of government which we currently have, and with Neil Gorsuch having the real potential to serve our nation well past the year of 2050, an investment of prayer on his behalf makes good sense.

And while we're at it, we should pray for God's mercy on our land. If ever we needed it, it is now. (If I sound like a broken record here, it is quite intentional. America needs the mercy of God!)

February 5, 2017

THE ELECTION OF DONALD TRUMP TELS US THAT ANYTHING IS POSSIBLE

★ ★ ★ ★ ★

W E are often too rational for our own good, not willing to believe in the seemingly impossible because, well, after all, it seems to be impossible. But are some of the things we're afraid to dream about any more unlikely than the election of Donald Trump to the presidency of the United States?

In the morning prayer service the day of the inauguration, evangelical leader James Robison said after addressing Trump, "We believe, dear God, that the stage is set for the next great spiritual awakening, and I believe with all my heart it is absolutely essential."[1]

Yes, of course, an awakening "is absolutely essential" to our nation, but are we really supposed to believe that "the stage is set for the next great spiritual awakening"? Are we really supposed to believe that the moral climate of our nation can be changed? Absolutely.

History tells us it is possible and the unlikely events we're witnessing before our eyes remind us that anything is possible.

From the perspective of history, if you'll study past awakenings, you'll see that they all came after a season of steep spiritual decline, often leading to hopelessness, with many feeling as if "things will only go downhill from here."

But if God awakened us before, He can do it again and, from the perspective of current events, is it really any harder to believe that God can send another great awakening than it is to believe that a man like Donald Trump could become our president?

Just think about it.

Let's say I asked you this two years ago: Which is more likely to occur? There will be a spiritual awakening in America or Donald Trump will win the Republican nomination, defeating senators and governors along the way, and then will defeat Hillary Clinton in the general election, getting 81 percent of the white evangelical vote. What would your answer have been? Which would have seemed more likely?

Let's take it one step further. What if I asked you two years ago, which is more likely to occur? There will be a spiritual awakening in America or Donald Trump will become the darling of the pro-life movement, nominating a solid pro-life conservative to replace Antonin Scalia within two weeks in office?

Certainly a spiritual awakening would have seemed far more believable than what has happened already with President Trump. What stops us, then, from believing for the former if the latter is happening before our eyes?

In an interview in the *Star-Telegram*, Robison said, "I do believe if [Trump] remains wise—as preposterous as this might sound to some—...he can prove to be as great a president as this nation has ever had."[2]

For some, this does sound preposterous, but is it any more preposterous that these words came from the mouth of Robison?

After all, during the primaries, Robison had very strong reservations about Trump, urging Dr. Ben Carson not to endorse him. In fact, Robison shared on my radio show that to the very last moment, even as Carson was on stage, about to endorse Trump, the two were talking by phone, with Robison urging him not to give his endorsement.

Ironically, Carson gave his endorsement on the condition that Trump would meet privately with Robison, which he did, for 90 minutes. Afterward, Robison joked to Trump that it was "the longest you've been quiet in your entire life."

Who would have thought that this staunch opponent of Trump would have become of one of his most trusted spiritual advisors?

John Zmirak, a conservative Catholic columnist who holds a Ph.D. in English from Louisiana State University and is a senior editor of The Stream, told me that when he was a student at Yale, his professors uniformly praised communism, making clear that it was communism, not capitalism, that was the key to the world's future success.[3] They were quite confident that this socialist system was here to stay, with its sphere of influence growing by the decade.

Who would have imagined how dramatically and quickly it would collapse around the globe? And, Zmirak asked, who would have believed that the principal players who would help topple communism would be a former Hollywood actor (Reagan!); a female Prime Minister in England, the daughter of a lay preacher and grocer (Thatcher!); a shipyard worker who became the head of a Polish trade union (Walesa!); and a Polish pope (John Paul II!).

Today, it is a wealthy, former-playboy, real estate tycoon and reality TV star who is shaking up the political scene and exposing the biases of the mainstream media.

If this, then, is actually happening, why is it so hard to imagine that God will send a massive spiritual awakening to our nation?

Why not?

February 15, 2017

MY RESPONSE TO A HUFFINGTON POST CONTRIBUTOR WANTING TO TALK WITH A WHITE, CHRISTIAN SUPPORTER OF TRUMP

★ ★ ★ ★ ★

THIS article is written in response to Susan M. Shaw's February 11 article in the Huffington Post, "Dear White, Christian Trump Supporters: We Need To Talk."[1] (Shaw is Professor of Women, Gender, and Sexuality Studies at Oregon State University.)

Dear Professor Shaw,

Thanks so much for opening the door to dialogue in such a candid and gracious way, and thanks for admitting that you're having a hard time relating to many conservative American Christians today.

You say explicitly, "I don't think I know how to understand you at all," and, "We need to talk, and I don't know how to talk to you anymore."

Hopefully, I can help bridge that gap, clearing up some areas of confusion for you and, at the least, helping you to understand why many compassionate, God-honoring, and neighbor-loving Christians voted for Trump.

But allow me to say this first: I am a registered Independent, not Republican, and I opposed Mr. Trump during the primaries before ultimately voting for him as our president. Now that he is our president, I do support him, and I believe that he has the potential for doing much good for our nation, despite his many evident flaws.

With that, let's get to the heart of your issues.

Speaking of your upbringing, being raised by a Southern Baptist father who did not to go college, you wrote, "My white, conservative Christian upbringing had told me that was the American Dream—to work hard and succeed. I did, and I feel you're holding it against me now that I no longer share your views."

Actually, it wouldn't dawn on me to hold it against you for not sharing my views. My father was the senior lawyer serving in the New York Supreme Court, and he was extremely liberal politically and socially. And all my studies, through my Ph.D. in Semitic languages at New York University, were in secular schools, so I never once studied under a professor who shared my spiritual or biblical beliefs.

I recognize that over the course of years people's views do change, for better or for worse, and one reason I write articles and books and do radio and TV shows is to seek to be a positive influence on others. If I can I help you to see your views need adjustment at some point, great. If not, I respect your right to differ with me and to seek to influence me.

You say, "Along the way, a lot of us developed progressive ideas, not out of our privilege, but out of our own experiences of discrimination, struggle and oppression."

Again, I respect that, but can you understand that many of us—meaning, the conservative American Christians whom you address—came to opposite conclusions out of our own experiences of caring for the poor and hurting and rejected, out of our own experiences of raising families and building relationships, out of our own learning and study and encounter with God, and that our convictions are as far from bigotry and hatred as the east is from the west? And do you understand that many of us used to be "liberal and progressive," but we have concluded that these ideas and ideologies are not in the best interests of society? (Take for example the welfare system. We see that as doing far more societal harm than good, as conservative intellectuals like Thomas Sowell have explained.)

I also must take issue with the way you describe the university environment as one in which ideas are rigorously debated and subjected to peer review. To one extent, that is true. To another extent, it is quite misleading, since today's secular universities skew hard left in many ways, and it is well-documented that conservative views are often suppressed on campuses.

I assume you're familiar with books like Alan Bloom's classic *The Closing of the American Mind*, or Roger Kimball's important work *Tenured Radicals: How Politics Has Corrupted Our Higher Education*. Or perhaps you've read *So Many Christians, So Few Lions: Is There Christianophobia in the United States?* by professors George Yancey and David A. Williamson (they answer the question of the subtitle in the affirmative).

Often, the secular academia serves as a liberal echo chamber rather than as a true proving ground for different ideas, and while I recognize that there are many fine scholars at the so-called elite schools in our nation, I would encourage you to make efforts to interact with conservative scholars at top Christian universities and seminaries. My guess is that it would be a fruitful learning experience for all involved.

But now we get to the real issues for you. You simply cannot understand how conservative Christians who prize morality and family life and biblical values could vote for Donald Trump, better known in the past as a playboy businessman than as a serious political candidate.

In short, that's one reason many of us did not back him at first. We had real concerns about his character, and character does matter to us. Over time, however, we voted for him because: 1) we were convinced that a Hillary Clinton presidency could be disastrous for America; 2) we saw that he was surrounding himself with fine Christian leaders, people of character and conviction who were speaking into his life and who had his ear; 3) we felt that God could use someone who was entirely politically incorrect, having lost our faith in the political establishment (on both sides of the aisle) long ago; and 4) we looked at him as a Cyrus-type figure (referring to an idol-worshiping, non-Israelite king whom God raised up to help the Jewish people 2,500 years ago; see Isaiah 45).

You wonder aloud how we could vote for him if we prize truth, and you view him as a serial liar—perhaps as a man out of touch with reality—pointing to his claims about the size of the crowd at his inauguration.

Frankly, many of us wish he would have never brought up the issue of the crowd size (really, who cares?), but we see other issues as being much more important, and so we keep advocating for those issues while encouraging him to step higher and act more presidentially.

But there is another side to this story. Senator Obama campaigned as a Christian who believed that marriage was the union of one man and woman (something "sacred"), yet he was previously on record as affirming same-sex "marriage," and it was David Axelrod who stated plainly that Obama lied to his conservative voters (specifically, his fellow-black voters) to get their trust, thereby misleading the nation.[2] In your eyes, which is worse, pushing a false narrative about the size of the inaugural crowd or deceiving your voters about a foundationally important moral issue?

And what of Hillary Clinton? How many lies did she tell about Benghazi? How many lies about her emails? Where do we start?

Again, I'm not minimizing lies that Trump may have told. I'm simply putting them in a larger context of political chicanery, and if you condemn one, you condemn the other.

You write, "You say you want progressives to listen to you. Then prioritize truth. This election was filled with 'fake news,' shared widely on Facebook, and this administration already has begun to create a language of 'alternative facts' to misinform and mislead. If you want to talk, offer evidence, real evidence based on verifiable data and reliable sources, not wishful imaginings or fabricated Breitbart stories."

With all respect, Professor Shaw, I see at least as much "fake news" on the left as on the right, and a glance at the daily headlines at the Huffington Post tells me that the publication for which you write is at least as biased as, if not more biased than, Breitbart. And how much "fake news" has been reported by CNN, MSNBC, the *Washington Post*, and the *New York Times* in recent months?

What troubles me is that you seem to feel that the right has a monopoly on bias and mendacity and the left on dispassionate truth-seeking. Far from it. Can you not see the faults on both sides?

I personally believe I could stand up publicly and make a powerful presentation of your worldview and core convictions before explaining why I differ with you. Could you do the same for me? If not, then please keep reading and let me help you.

You write, "Help me understand how you align your Christian perspective with [Trump's] racism, misogyny, homophobia, Islamophobia, and antisemitism."

Frankly, there are things he said that have disturbed us and there are other things we believe are false charges (to mention one in particular, President Trump is not an anti-Semite[3]). Perhaps you're listening to some fake news here?

In any event, we see him as far from perfect and in need of much growth, but we also see him moving in the right direction and taking a stand for many things that are important to us socially and politically and even morally.

You explain that you have a hard time simply "getting over" the fact that Trump is our president, noting that this election is a matter of life and death, and writing, "Perhaps you can tell me to get over it because you do not have to worry that Trump will appoint a Supreme Court justice that could play a role in invalidating your marriage. If Congress passes and Trump signs the First Amendment Defense Act, you probably won't have to worry that a bakery, restaurant, or hotel might legally deny you service. You don't have to worry about being stranded at an airport and refused admission to the U.S. because of the country you're from or the religion you practice. You don't have to worry about having your family divided across the world with a simple signature on an executive order."

Truly, this paragraph startles me.

How do you think we felt when Barack Obama was elected—which means that he was our president (and my president) for the last eight years? How do you think we felt when he appointed Supreme Court justices who helped to fundamentally redefine marriage, an absolute horror to us for many reasons? How do you think we felt about the prospect of Hillary Clinton deepening America's ties with Planned Parenthood, in our view the number-one slaughterer of babies in the womb?

And since you mention bakeries, restaurants, and hotels—none of which, by the way, have refused to serve a gay person simply because he or she was gay—how do you think we felt when friends of ours lost their jobs or were put out of schools or suffered serious professional recriminations because they were forced to violate their religious beliefs, bullied by LGBT activists and their allies? Are you not aware of the two-way nature of this street?

And how do you think we felt when President Obama and the Department of Justice launched an aggressive campaign designed to punish all states that took issue with, say, a 16-year-old boy who identifies as a girl playing on the girls' basketball team and sharing her locker room and showers? Twenty-three states took the administration to court over this, yet Barack Obama remained our president throughout, just as Donald Trump is now your president.

That's what we mean by "get over" it. We didn't riot in the streets after Obama was elected and reelected, nor did we plan to riot and demonstrate if Hillary was elected.

You ask how we could use a "pagan" (my word) like Trump over "a woman who is a Christian, a lifelong Methodist and who, from the heart, quotes the Bible and John Wesley," yet you then write, "I'm afraid that what you want is a nation that conforms to your interpretation of the Bible."

Well, doesn't Hillary want that? Don't "progressive Christians" want that? Don't gay clergy want that? (As for Hillary's Christian views, that's what galls us all the more. Some of her beliefs are in direct contradiction with the teachings of the Bible, let alone those of Wesley. To us, this is a matter of religious hypocrisy and of Bible-twisting, neither of which are light matters.)

In reality, in this democratic republic in which we live, we all do our best to see our values prevail, and we do so by persuasion and by voting and by influencing and by educating. We believe God's ways, as understood by traditional Jewish and Christian morality, are wonderful and in the best interests of any country. Liberal Christians and Jews differ with us, as do many agnostics and atheists.

So be it. May the best position win! That's what we advocate for.

That being said, I do believe you mischaracterize the intent of our founding fathers, writing, "You say you want a Christian nation, but our founders were clear that was never their goal. In fact, the Constitution goes to great lengths to protect the government from religion and religion from government."

I agree that our founders were not trying to establish a Christian nation, but they presupposed that Christian beliefs and values would lie at the foundation of the nation, with John Adams famously stating that, "Our Constitution was made only for a moral and religious people," and, "It is wholly inadequate to the government of any other." And do you actually believe that our founders could have countenanced the day when a Christian who could not in conscience participate in the "marriage" of two men would be punished—rather than the two men being punished?

In any case, we advocate strongly for our beliefs, and oddly enough, we find President Trump to be a recent champion of our religious liberties. In that vein, I answer in the affirmative these questions of yours: "Can't we agree that all people should be free to practice their religion or practice no religion and should be safe from coercion based on religion? Can't we agree that we share values of love, kindness, respect, and community and then try to live those with each other?" Of course we can!

As for the knotty question of immigration, you ask, "Do you really think a Christian, especially a biblical literalist, can want a wall built?" And, you note, "The Bible is clear about how we are to treat foreigners among us—no matter how they got here."

First, many of us who voted for Trump are actively involved in helping the needy and poor worldwide, and my own family was part of a church that sponsored Vietnamese refugees during the Boat People crisis in the late '70s and early '80s, welcoming these dear people into our homes for years at a time. So, we are hardly a monolithic, xenophobic group of angry populists.

We simply recognize that there's a problem with those illegal aliens who drain and damage our society. (In the words of President Obama in 2015, "What we should be doing is setting up a smart legal immigration system that doesn't separate families but does focus on making sure that people who are dangerous, people who are gangbangers or criminals, that we're deporting them as quickly as possible."[4]) We also recognize that radical Islam presents a serious security issue for America (and the world), and therefore we need to improve our vetting.

As for a Christian building a wall, do Christians lock their doors at night? That's what this is about, although plenty of Christians do take issue[5] with the president's proposed immigration policies, and that is a healthy debate we must have.

As for the Bible's teaching on how we treat foreigners, remember that the same Old Testament to which you allude called for the killing of hostile foreigners (the Canaanites and others), so I would encourage you to give that subject further reflection so you might gain a more holistic view of the subject.

Finally, regarding your call for us to work together to reduce abortions, you state, "We can lower abortion rates together but not by denying women choices over their own bodies. We can be effective together by listening to the data and working together to ensure all women have access to contraception, education, and social and economic resources. Are you willing to have that conversation?"

Professor Shaw, we cannot work together unless you begin by at least understanding our viewpoint: A woman does not have the choice over someone else's life—namely, the little baby living in her womb. Or do you think the words, "It's a child, not a choice" are just some catchy slogan to us? In our view, we are witnessing a black genocide (among other things), with staggeringly high rates of abortion among blacks in particular and among the poor in general, and we're not looking for some kind of middle ground here.

We are all for education and social and economic resources to help lower these rates, but not if it means partnering with those who believe that the child in the womb is merely an appendage of the mother's body, just a clump of cells or a mass of tissue. Would you at least reflect on these truths?

You close your article with a series of questions, and, to answer, I assure you that we're more interested in doing good than winning, that we're open to building coalitions where lives can truly be changed for the better, open to real science and factual evidence as it pertains to choices we make, and 100 percent committed to "live the love of God we claim."

Are you committed to the same? And do you really want to dialogue? Let's start with our two articles here, and hopefully, you'll back up your call for interaction by joining me on my radio show to talk—not fight.

Deal?

(For the record, Professor Shaw never responded to me, despite our efforts to reach out to her.)

March 1, 2017

PLEASE DON'T TELL ME TRUMP'S SPEECH TO CONGRESS WAS RACIST

★ ★ ★ ★ ★

DURING the Republican primaries, when I was most critical of candidate Trump, I still didn't believe he was a racist (in general) or an anti-Semite (in particular), yet charges of racism and even anti-Semitism persist against him to this day. After his speech last night, it seems to me that only his most cynical critics can lodge such charges against him. Will you really say that his address to Congress was racist?

Let's start with black Americans.

He began his speech by saying, "Tonight, as we mark the conclusion of our celebration of Black History Month, we are reminded of our Nation's path toward civil rights and the work that still remains."

Was he seeking to get a message across? Quite obviously, he was.

Several minutes later (but still early in his speech), he said, "We've financed and built one global project after another, but ignored the fates of our children in the inner cities of Chicago, Baltimore, Detroit—and so many other places throughout our land."

It is no secret that a disproportionately high percentage of black Americans live in these inner cities, and so here too, he appeared to be sending a message, including this line, a few minutes later, as well: "And our neglected inner cities will see a rebirth of hope, safety, and opportunity."

And since black Americans suffer disproportionately from poverty and joblessness, were these lines directed their way as well? "Ninety-four million Americans are out of the labor force." And, "Over 43 million people are now living in poverty, and over 43 million Americans are on food stamps."

More overtly, he singled out a black American woman, Denisha Merriweather, as an example of the merit of private schools, calling her a "remarkable woman," noting that she was the first in her family to graduate from college (soon to get her Master's degree), and stating, "We want all children to be able to break the cycle of poverty just like Denisha."

Even the reference that followed to breaking the cycle of violence, using Chicago as an example, probably spoke to black Americans as well. In fact, his first example of an American killed by an illegal immigrant was a 17-year-old black man, Jamiel Shaw, Jr., "an incredible young man, with unlimited potential who was getting ready to go to college where he would have excelled as a great quarterback. But he never got the chance. His father, who is in the audience tonight, has become a good friend of mine." (Note also that Trump honored Susan Oliver, a black woman, whose husband Danny, a white man, was a policeman killed by an illegal immigrant.)

Of course, the critics blast Trump as being a hypocritical opportunist, using these individuals to advance his own cause. But for anyone listening with an open heart and mind, the overall impression would be clear: President Trump is reaching out to the African American community and saying, "We are in this together, and I want to help."

As for the Jewish people, also in his very first lines, Trump referenced "Recent threats targeting Jewish Community Centers and vandalism of Jewish cemeteries," while later stating, "I have also imposed new sanctions on entities and individuals who support Iran's ballistic missile program, and reaffirmed our unbreakable alliance with the State of Israel."

Could you imagine an anti-Semite speaking in these ways, mentioning the vandalism of the Jewish cemeteries in his first paragraph, and in the context of civil rights at that?

He also referenced at the outset "last week's shooting in Kanas City," where a gunman who allegedly yelled "get out my country" before killing one Indian man and wounded another, also wounding a white American who tried to stop him.

In other words, nationalism for Trump does not mean war on immigrants.

As for the immigrants whom he is deporting, Trump said, "we are removing gang members, drug dealers and criminals that threaten our communities and prey on our citizens. Bad ones are going out as I speak tonight and as I have promised."

Do even the most "progressive" Democrats really want to keep such dangerous people in our country, especially when they are here illegally? And can the president really be accused of being anti-immigrant or, more broadly, anti-Hispanic for saying that such criminals should be deported? For that matter, was President Obama an anti-Hispanic, anti-immigrant racist when he deported 43,000 illegals in 2015?

As for Islam, Trump could not have been more specific, saying, "We are also taking strong measures to protect our nation from radical Islamic terrorism," then proclaiming, "As promised, I directed the Department of Defense to develop a plan to demolish and destroy ISIS—a network of lawless savages that have slaughtered Muslims and Christians, and men, women, and children of all faiths and beliefs. We will work with our allies, including our friends and allies in the Muslim world, to extinguish this vile enemy from our planet."

Here he made clear that radical Muslim terrorists are "lawless savages" (rather than model Muslims) who "have slaughtered Muslims and Christians, and men, women, and children of all faiths and beliefs," significantly putting Muslims at the top of this list.

In other words, even though Christians in Islamic lands suffer most acutely at the hands of radical Muslims, while Christians in other countries are often targeted by radical Muslims, the greatest number of casualties of radical Muslims are themselves Muslims. That's why the president pledged to work with "our friends and allies in the Muslim world, to extinguish this vile enemy from our planet."

Can you genuinely say that Trump is anti-Muslim (rather than anti-radical Muslim) based on these carefully delivered words?

He even reached out to women, stating, "With the help of Prime Minister Justin Trudeau, we have formed a Council with our neighbors in Canada to help ensure that women entrepreneurs have access to the networks, markets and capital they need to start a business and live out their financial dreams." (I'm not saying this removes charges of misogyny or undoes his past, inexcusable comments; I'm simply noting the statement and its purpose.)

Of course, critics like the extreme-left, Islamic congressman Keith Ellison will disparage Trump's speech, claiming that Trump will say whatever he needs to say to sway public opinion but will not act accordingly.[1] And, obviously, this was just a speech.

But a speech is designed to accomplish certain goals and to send a certain message, and as far as a speech goes, the goals were clear and the message was clear.

Perhaps some of you who remain implacably opposed to the president will find room for at least a little hope?

Perhaps some of you who have accused him of racism (and worse) might be willing to take a second look, give him some benefit of the doubt, and see if his actions match his words?

Personally, I think it's the least you can do.

For supporters of the president, his speech lived up to your expectations and proved that Donald Trump can truly act presidentially.

In the words of John Podhoretz, "In the first 38 days of his presidency, Donald Trump seemed to struggle to find his footing. On his 39th, he found it unexpectedly in a strong, direct and—surprise of surprises—beautifully modulated and spectacularly delivered address before Congress."[3]

March 2, 2017

WHEN TRUMP IS PRESIDENTIAL, HIS CRITICS ARE LEFT OUT IN THE RAIN

★ ★ ★ ★ ★

I T was an altogether fitting, albeit pathetic, picture. Shortly before Donald Trump delivered the greatest speech of his life, a speech some pundits called historic in its own right,[1] Rosie O'Donnell "addressed a rain-soaked crowd outside the White House...during the 'Resistance Address,' an event countering President Trump's speech to a joint session of Congress later that evening. She criticized Trump on his foreign policy, stance towards race, and women's rights, while urging *the 100 or so gathered* to resist Trump (and the weather) through the night" (my emphasis).[2]

And so, as Trump spoke to tens of millions of Americans (and probably millions of others watching around the world), O'Donnell spoke to roughly 100 protesters, doubtless chilled to the bone in the rain.

And as Trump called for unity and reached out to African Americans and Jews and Muslims and immigrants—and Democrats—O'Donnell exclaimed, "This is not Russia. To Donald Trump and his pathetic band of white, privileged criminal businessmen, I would like to say to him, 'nyet, sir.'"[3]

In reality, the "nyet" is to her, not to him, and her words and actions only underscore that fact.

This was a night when CNN's Van Jones had the sense to praise Trump for his speech, especially the moment he honored the widow of the slain Navy Seal, saying, "He became President of the United States in that moment, period," adding, "That was one of the most extraordinary moments you have ever seen in American politics."[4]

It was a night when Wolf Blitzer said that Trump delivered "an important, powerful speech";[5] when Anderson Cooper said that, "This was probably, without a doubt, one of his best speeches that I've ever heard";[6] and when even NPR's Scott Detrow could say, "This is far and away Trump's most presidential moment to-date, and the most broadly-framed argument for his agenda. All relative, but notable."[7]

And remember: This is the voice of the left (and many more quotes could be cited), the voice of the Trump critics, of those characterized by the president as enemies of the people. Yet they were largely in agreement in recognizing the importance of the moment.

But on the Democratic side of the aisle, a little-known, former governor was tasked with responding to Trump, but his presentation was so underwhelming that even Rachel Maddow described it as "stunty and small"[8]—which actually describes the state of the Democratic Party at this point in time. (We could also add the adjective "leaderless.")

And so, we will remember the Democrats who would not stand with and for the president when he called for war against radical Islam or, worse still, who would not stand with and for the widow of a slain Navy Seal.

And we will remember the comment of the new DNC Chair Tom Perez who described Trump's epic speech by saying, "This was Steve Bannon on steroids with a smile."[9] Did I just say "stunty and small"?

We will also remember the celebrities who railed[10] on Trump in the most vulgar and immature of terms, like Charlie Sheen (who really does seem to need help), addressing the president as, "you FASCIST, legally retarded, DESPOTIC IMBECILE!" (Yes, a grown man wrote this; he also labelled Trump a "simpleton" and a "Ho-a— piglet fraud.")

George Takei responded to Trump's statement that, "We cannot allow a beachhead of terrorism form inside America," by tweeting, "Yes. And let's start by putting a stop to Radical White Supremacist Terror." And Joshua Malina tweeted, "That was the worst speech I ever didn't have to watch to know that it was terrible."

Of course, Trump has many hurdles to overcome, many difficult decisions to make, many storms to navigate, much work to be done, and perhaps even some crises to endure.

But the formula for his resounding success—which means the even more resounding defeat of his opponents—is to step into the fullness of his role as the President of the United States of America, with all the awe and responsibility that position evokes, and to do his best to keep his most important campaign promises.

If he will do that, his critics will end up all wet, perhaps literally as well as figuratively.

To quote Van Jones again, "For people who have been hoping that maybe he would remain a divisive cartoon, which he often finds a way to do, they should be a little bit worried tonight. Because that thing you just saw him do, if he finds a way to do that over and over again, he's going to be there for eight years."[11]

Well said.

April 19, 2017

"AMERICA FIRST" DOES NOT MEAN "AMERICA ONLY"

★ ★ ★ ★ ★

DURING the presidential campaign, when Donald Trump spoke of putting "America first," I never thought he meant "America only." It appears, however, that others understood him quite differently, and they are not happy with his overseas actions. As summed up by Ann Coulter, "We want the 'president of America' back—not 'the president of the world.'"[1]

Of course, Coulter, along with other Trump loyalists like Paul Joseph Watson, Laura Ingraham, and Mike Cernovich[2] were not upset because the president bombed another country. They were upset because he bombed Syria after saying for years that we should stay out of there.

They felt betrayed and double-crossed.

They also felt that any American intervention in Syria was unwise, especially if it led to an attempt to remove Assad.

But we did not only bomb Syria. We sent warships to North Korea, warning the demented dictator of that country to behave, or else.

For Coulter, this means that Trump has already become a pawn of the Washington establishment. As she wrote, "Looking for some upside to this fiasco, desperate Trump supporters bleated that bombing Assad had sent a message to North Korea. Yes, the message is: The Washington establishment is determined to manipulate the president into launching counterproductive military strikes. Our enemies—both foreign and domestic—would be delighted to see our broken country further weaken itself with pointless wars."

What, then, are we to make of this? Has Trump caved in to the establishment already? Has he abandoned his pledge to put "America first"?

As to the larger question of President Trump and the Washington establishment, time will tell. The same can be said regarding which direction the president will go. Will it be the way of Jared Kushner or will it be the way of Steve Bannon (to oversimply things dramatically)? Only time will tell.

But when it comes to Trump's bombing of Syria and standing up to North Korea, I see no contradiction between these actions and him being the president of "America first."

To begin with, there is nothing exceptional with the elected leader of a country saying that they intend to put the interests of their country first. But of course!

Would the Israelis be shocked if Prime Minister Netanyahu said, "We must put Israel first!" How about the Canadians if Prime Minister Trudeau said, "It's Canada first!"? What about the Russians if President Putin said, "It's time to put Russia first!"?

Obviously, it's the role of the leader of a country to put that country first, just as it's the role of the head of the household to pay his or her family's bills before helping a neighbor (or stranger) with their bills. Even the New Testament, with all its calls for altruism, addresses this. In the words of Paul, "If anyone does not provide for his relatives, and especially for members of his household, he has denied the faith and is worse than an unbeliever" (1 Tim. 5:8).

So, to repeat, I find nothing exceptional about the "America first" mentality, especially the way Trump articulated it in his inaugural speech:

> From this moment on, it's going to be America First.
>
> Every decision on trade, on taxes, on immigration, on foreign affairs, will be made to benefit American workers and American families.
>
> We must protect our borders from the ravages of other countries making our products, stealing our companies, and destroying our jobs. Protection will lead to great prosperity and strength.[3]

Can anyone really call this "xenophobic"?

He also said, "We will follow two simple rules: Buy American and Hire American." In keeping with that pledge, he signed a bill to that effect yesterday. As CNN reported, "President Donald Trump signed an executive order Tuesday directing federal agencies to implement the 'Buy American, Hire American' rhetoric of his campaign." In the president's words, "It's America first, you better believe it. It's time. It's time, right?"[4]

But during his inaugural speech, Trump also said this:

> We will seek friendship and goodwill with the nations of the world—but we do so with the understanding that it is the right of all nations to put their own interests first.
>
> We do not seek to impose our way of life on anyone, but rather to let it shine as an example for everyone to follow.
>
> We will reinforce old alliances and form new ones—and unite the civilized world against Radical Islamic Terrorism, which we will eradicate completely from the face of the Earth.

What happens, then, when one of our allies faces potential danger from a reckless regime, as South Korea could be facing from the North? Do we abandon them because we put "America first"? And when North Korea threatens us directly, do we simply laugh it off, because we put "America first"? Of course not.

And when it appears that another ruthless dictator crosses a bright red line, do we sit back and do nothing—following the example of President Obama—or do we send a message, loud and clear?

It would be one thing to provoke North Korea into a nuclear conflict, just as it would be one thing to put American troops on the ground in order to oust Assad. And it would be one thing if we fashioned ourselves to be the world's moral judge, jury, and police force, acting unilaterally whenever we felt it was right.

But it's another thing to send a message (that's what our warships are doing and that's what our bombing did), reminding the tyrants of this world that they cannot act with impunity.

The reality is that the world needs a strong America, and for us to be strong, we must put our own interests first. In doing so, we will be able to help the rest of the world.

April 27, 2017

DONALD TRUMP DISAPPOINTS THE ANTI-SEMITES

★ ★ ★ ★ ★

SO, Donald Trump delivers a speech in honor of Holocaust Remembrance Day, and the anti-Semites are up in arms. He is not the man they thought he was.

In reality, he never was that man, which was more a projection of their own ideology than a right assessment of his. As Sam Kestenbaum reported on the Jewish *Forward*, "Trump Gives A Holocaust Speech—And The 'Alt Right' Screams 'Betrayal.'"[1]

How, exactly, did Trump betray the "alt-right"?

In his speech, he said, "The State of Israel is an eternal monument to the undying strength of the Jewish people. The fervent dream that burned in the hearts of the oppressed is now filled with the breath of life, and the Star of David waves atop a great nation arisen from the desert."[2]

This was certainly in keeping with his campaign speeches, in which he pledged to be a great friend of Israel and guaranteed that he would move the American embassy in Israel to Jerusalem.

Trump commended the late Elie Wiesel, perhaps the most famous Holocaust survivor, affirming his call that "we must bear witness." Trump spoke to the survivors who were there, people who witnessed "the Nazi genocide of the Jewish people."

And he denounced Holocaust denial, saying, "Denying the Holocaust is only one of many forms of dangerous anti-Semitism that continues all around the world. We've seen anti-Semitism on university campuses, in the public square, and in threats against Jewish citizens. Even worse, it's been on display in the most sinister manner when terrorists attack Jewish communities, or when aggressors threaten Israel with total and complete destruction."

He pledged to confront anti-Semitism, and said, "As President of the United States, I will always stand with the Jewish people—and I will always stand with our great friend and partner, the State of Israel."

Then he closed with some moving, personal stories of courage and hope.

All in all, a fine and fitting speech, and one that I would have expected from President Trump, since at no point in his campaign did I think he was an anti-Semite (despite the many other reservations I had about him).

But words like these from Trump's speech are fighting words for the anti-Semites of this world. As Kestenbaum reported:

"You can never appease the Jews," wrote Benjamin Garland at the neo-Nazi website the Daily Stormer. "Give them an inch and they want a mile. The only way to deal with them is to ignore them and/or tell them to shut their filthy mouths."

Garland bemoaned what he saw as a turnaround for Trump. Months ago he was "a man who knew how the Jews operate and as a man with enough self-respect to not be publicly humiliated by them by bowing to their every whim and demand."

But Jews "have their ratlike claws deep in him now," Garland wrote.

What in the world he is talking about? The Trump who gave the Holocaust remembrance speech is the same man as the Trump whom Garland supported.

It's the same Trump whose daughter Ivanka converted to Judaism. The same Trump who remains very close to his Jewish son-in-law Jared. The same Trump whose grandchildren through Ivanka are considered Jewish. The same Trump who has had many Jewish colleagues and friends. The same Trump of whom Israeli Prime Minister Benjamin Netanyahu said, "I've known the President and I've known his family and his team for a long time, and there is no greater supporter of the Jewish people and the Jewish state than President Donald Trump. I think we should put that to rest."[4]

This is who Trump has been for many years. Why the shock from the alt-right now?

David Duke, a leading anti-Semitic, white supremacist (and former KKK leader), tweeted, "Why is the so called Holocaust the only atrocity to receive its very own 'Remembrance Proclamation'? Jewish privilege."[5]

Is Duke unaware that Trump also gave a speech in memory of the Armenian genocide this week (although he didn't use the word "genocide" in his speech)?[6] For the record, it's officially called Armenian Remembrance Day, and it's recognized by the White House. Shall we call this "Armenian privilege"?

Getting back to Duke, he challenged Trump directly, asking, "Do you not have any power? Why are you surrounding yourself with the enemies of the American people?"

And who are these "enemies of the American people"? Obviously, the Jewish people and their allies, to whom Trump has now sold out.

The reality is that Trump is simply carrying out his campaign promises and being true to who he has been for many years—a friend of the Jewish people.

As my colleague Rabbi Shmuley Boteach wrote in February, "Trump as anti-Semite is not implausible, but it is absurd and libelous. It would also suggest that his strong support for Israel is inauthentic, when it's something he has worn on his sleeve for his entire adult life."[7]

Shmuley even said this: "He has surrounded himself with Jews—they are his business colleagues, employees and friends. I know orthodox Jews who have long worked for Trump and say that his respect for the Jewish faith has been exemplary."

Did you hear that, Mr. Duke? Are you listening, Mr. Garland? Trump "has surrounded himself with Jews" for decades, so it's nothing new if he's doing so today.

We can certainly debate whether Jared Kushner has too much influence or whether Kushner's views represent those of Trump's major supporters. But we can't debate Trump's historic relationship with Israel and the Jewish people. That's not new at all.

What's new is that he has also surrounded himself with conservative Christians in recent years. And what's new is that his populist, pro-America message helped catapult him to the White House.

Apparently, these anti-Semites misunderstood Trump's words and pledges, finding confirmation for their white-supremacist, Jew hatred, thereby projecting their views on his.

It looks like they're in for a rude awakening.

May 10, 2017

FIVE THINGS ANN COULTER GOT WRONG ABOUT DONALD TRUMP

★ ★ ★ ★ ★

IS Ann Counter about to dump Trump? Is the outspoken author of *In Trump We Trust* about to take a giant step in the opposite direction?

Coulter was certainly ahead of most pundits in putting her money on the winning horse (she was way ahead of me in that respect), and she identified many of Trump's strongest qualities. She also understood why his message resonated with many Americans. But she made a big mistake when she put so much trust in him, as if he could singlehandedly fix the nation. No human being can do that, not even the man who wrote *Art of the Deal*.

As the *Daily Caller* noted, "She wrote *In Trump We Trust* and proclaimed that she worships him like the 'people of North Korea worship their Dear Leader—blind loyalty.'"

Putting Coulter's evident hyperbole aside, and understanding her penchant for the provocative, it seems that she did, in fact, put way too much trust in a frail human leader. Now she's feeling let down and even betrayed, and Coulter's worship could soon become Coulter's wrath.

What did she get wrong along the way? Here are some suggestions.

First, it appears that she got caught up in the Trump hype, as if he alone of all the candidates could deliver on all his promises, as if he alone of all the candidates was not a consummate salesman as well.

To be sure, there are some values on which the president stands, and he is certainly a true patriot. But as to his guiding, non-negotiable principles, the political and moral hills on which he is prepared to die, some of that remains to be seen. In that regard, he is still a work in progress.

Second, it appears that Coulter failed to realize that Trump's bombastic style would create a never-ending cycle of media distractions, taking the president's eyes off the prize.

It's one thing to have the mainstream media against you, which Trump seems to thrive on. It's another to create an unnecessary cycle of firestorms that obscures your message and mission.

Third, it appears that she underestimated the influence of Ivanka and Jared.

In oversimplified terms, they are pulling Trump to the left while he was elected by voters leaning to the right. But this is hardly a new revelation. The dueling viewpoints in the Trump camp were evident long before he was elected, along with his deep family loyalty. Perhaps Coulter underestimated just how impactful Ivanka and Jared would be?

She said, "I have from the beginning been opposed to Trump hiring any of his relatives. Americans don't like that, I don't like that. That's the one fascist thing he's done. Hiring his kids."

Did she not see this coming?

Fourth, it appears she underestimated the degree of compromise in Washington—in other words, the depth and density of the swamp.

On the one hand, she is indicting Congress directly, saying, "I do, of course, blame Congress most of all. They are swine. They only care about their own careers. Who knows how much of it is corruption and how much of it is pure stupidity? ...They are the opposition party to Donald Trump. This is really something we've never seen before. The president stands alone, it's his own political party, he's Gary Cooper. All we have is millions of Americans behind him, but he doesn't have anybody in Washington behind him."

But is this such a new revelation (even if somewhat overstated)? Was she unaware of this too when she effused about what Trump would do? And could it be that the president's divisive style has hindered his ability to get more of Washington behind him?

I too fault Congress for many of the bumps in the road so far, and I also hoped (and still hope) that Trump would be able to take on the Washington establishment. But it's possible that a more experienced, less controversial, deeply conservative president could have been more successful to this point.

Fifth, and most importantly, it appears that Coulter made Trump bigger than life. (Let's give him credit for selling himself as well as any person in our time. The Trump name now adorns the White House.)

She said to the *Daily Caller*, "I got to tell you when I wrote *Adios America* I thought there was a 10 percent chance of saving the country. On the evening of November 8, I thought, 'Wow we have a 90 percent chance now, this is a chance that comes a long [*sic*] once every thousand years, we can save America now.'"

Really? Someone like Trump comes along once in a thousand years? With him at the helm, America's chances for survival went from 10 percent to 90 percent? This is completely unrealistic, almost guaranteeing disappointment and, worse still, bitterness and anger.

Only God can turn around a nation like that, and that's why America's greatest need is a great revival in the Church that will become a great awakening in the society. As I argue in *Saving a Sick America*, due out later this year, the darkening state of the nation affords an incredible backdrop against which God's people can rise and shine. We are certainly very sick, but with the Lord's help, radical change can come.

That's also why President Trump needs our prayers and support and encouragement. He is a flawed human being, like the rest of us, with the weight of the world on his shoulders, surrounded by sharks and serpents (metaphorically speaking), with genuine intentions to do good.

We do him a disservice by putting disproportionate trust in him.

May 19, 2017

The Importance of Trump's Saudi Arabia Speech Denouncing Islamic Terrorism

★ ★ ★ ★ ★

ALTHOUGH President Trump's speech before 50 Muslim leaders in Saudi Arabia did not break new ground in terms of America's Middle Eastern policy, it was highly significant for at least four reasons.

First, Trump mentioned "terror" or "terrorism" 30 times. In stark contrast, during President Obama's (in)famous Cairo speech in 2009, he did not mention terrorism at all.[1] More importantly, President Trump spoke directly of "the crisis of Islamist extremism and the Islamist terror groups it inspires."[2]

To fight against this, Trump urged, "means standing together against the murder of innocent Muslims, the oppression of women, the persecution of Jews, and the slaughter of Christians."

And remember: Trump said this in the heart of Islamic holy land, Saudi Arabia.

The president called on these Muslim leaders to drive out the terrorists from "your places of worship...your communities...your holy land, and this earth."

Yes, these terrorists are currently in some of your mosques, and you need to drive them out.

To say that, in that setting, required chutzpah.

Trump also announced the founding of "a new Global Center for Combating Extremist Ideology, located right here, in this central part of the Islamic World.

"This groundbreaking new center represents a clear declaration that Muslim-majority countries must take the lead in combatting radicalization."

It's about time that Muslim leaders were urged to combat this deadly ideology.

Second, Trump identified Iran as the enemy, linking Iran directly and repeatedly to Islamic terrorism.

He called it "the government that gives terrorists...safe harbor, financial backing, and the social standing needed for recruitment."

He labeled it "a regime that is responsible for so much instability in the region."

He stated that, "From Lebanon to Iraq to Yemen, Iran funds, arms, and trains terrorists, militias, and other extremist groups that spread destruction and chaos across the region. For decades, Iran has fueled the fires of sectarian conflict and terror."

He said, "It is a government that speaks openly of mass murder, vowing the destruction of Israel, death to America, and ruin for many leaders and nations in this room."

This had to sting Iran. And this had to be unprecedented for an American president speaking in such a setting. (Note also that some of the Muslim leaders there presumably want to see Israel destroyed, yet Trump spoke of this as evil.) Elsewhere in his speech, Trump mentioned Shias and Sunnis together. So he was stating that his issue was with terrorism, not Islamic sectarianism.

Not surprisingly, in a critical article on Trump's speech, CNN cited a professor from Iran's Tehran University who was skeptical of the president's outreach to the Muslim world. The professor, Hamed Mousavi, said, "It will be met with deep skepticism in the Muslim world because Trump has been hostile and offensive to Muslims—with his Muslim travel ban, for example. All they've seen so far from Donald Trump is a lot of hostility."[3]

But what else should we have expected from an Iranian professor? His country was just slammed as a major agent of terror by the president of the United States before dozens of Muslim leaders. Should we have expected him to greet Trump's words warmly?

Professor Mousavi also spoke against our new arms deal with the Saudis. He did raise a legitimate point regarding our inability to combat Wahhabism, the fundamentalist expression of Islam that dominates Saudi Arabia and has helped spurn radical Islamic terrorism. But his critical comments should be expected, since Saudi Arabia and Iran are arch-enemies.

CNN provided no context to Mousavi's critique, which must now be read with a big grain of salt.

Note also that Trump (as president) never proposed a generic "Muslim travel ban" (as claimed by the professor). That was the exaggeration of a hostile media and Trump's political opponents, presumably traced back to some of his campaign rhetoric.

Third, the president put Hamas and Hezbollah in the same category as ISIS and al-Qaeda. This means that opposition to Israel is not a justification for terrorism. He said, "The true toll of ISIS, Al Qaeda, Hezbollah, Hamas, and so many others, must be counted not only in the number of dead. It must also be counted in generations of vanished dreams."

The significance of this was not missed by a Lebanese professor, who, CNN reports, "pointed out that Trump equated Hezbollah, a Lebanese political and military group made up mostly of Shia Muslims, with ISIS and al Qaeda. Hezbollah was conceived in the early 1980s primarily to fight against Israeli occupation in southern Lebanon."

The professor, Karam Makdisi, claimed that, "This is irresponsible on many levels. With Israeli rhetoric increasing against Lebanon, this does not bode well. The Lebanese will not put much stock in yet another grand speech, but they will keep an eye out for Trump's position towards Israel's threats against Lebanon, and any shift in US policy towards Syria."[4]

I'm sure that Professor Makdisi was not the only Muslim intellectual who got Trump's point loudly and clearly. To paraphrase: "You may call Hamas and Hezbollah freedom fighters against the Israeli occupation. We call them terrorists."

Fourth, Trump rejected the theology of martyrdom by suicide bombing, saying, "Terrorists do not worship God, they worship death."

He said, "This is not a battle between different faiths, different sects, or different civilizations.

"This is a battle between barbaric criminals who seek to obliterate human life, and decent people of all religions who seek to protect it.

"This is a battle between Good and Evil."

Trump also made clear that the victims of this terror are primarily Muslims. He said that "in sheer numbers, the deadliest toll has been exacted on the innocent people of Arab, Muslim and Middle Eastern nations. They have borne the brunt of the killings and the worst of the destruction in this wave of fanatical violence. Some estimates hold that more than 95 percent of the victims of terrorism are themselves Muslim."

Somehow, another critic cited by CNN missed this emphatic statement.

Former Jordanian Justice Minister Ibrahim Aljazy said, "Referencing 'Islamic' terrorist organizations only will not be appreciated by the vast majority of people in the region when other forces are carrying out acts of aggression, especially as Arabs and Muslims are the prime victims of these organizations."

Did Mr. Aljazy not hear Trump's words?

Perhaps CNN needs to vet its Trump-critics more carefully. At the least, they should have qualified some of the quotes. But again, is anyone surprised?

Turning back to President Trump, we can certainly debate his policies, actions, and words at home. (I am not Trump's defender-in-chief. Not anywhere near it.)

We can question the propriety of the massive arms deal with Saudi Arabia. (Will this be used to finance terror? Will it lead to more bloodshed in the region? Is this good for Israel too?)

But we should not question the landmark nature of Trump's speech, which also referenced the oppression of women and called on these Muslim nations to lead the way in repatriating Muslim refugees.

In short, an American president stood on holy Islamic ground and called on 50 Islamic leaders to fight against Islamic terrorism. This is highly significant.

June 1, 2017

Kathy Griffin Is Not the Only One Guilty of Anti-Trump Hysteria

★ ★ ★ ★ ★

WITHOUT a doubt, Kathy Griffin crossed a dark and ugly line when she posted her instantly infamous beheading picture. And she is suffering the consequences for her foolish actions. But is she alone to blame? Have not others contributed to the toxic atmosphere that provided the backdrop for her misdeed?

Certainly, she alone is responsible for her decisions, and she took responsibility for those decisions in her apology. No one made her do what she did. No one pressured her or coerced her. She made a choice, and she'll have to live with it.

But she is not alone in terms of the unhealthy anti-Trump hysteria that has rocked the nation, and without that hysterical backdrop, I don't think she would have had the audacity to go as far as she did.

In January of this year, Madonna stirred up an anti-Trump women's march, saying, "Yes, I'm angry. Yes, I'm outraged. Yes, I have thought an awful lot about blowing up the White House, but I know that this won't change anything."[1]

And how did the women respond? With shock or with delight?

She said, "It took this horrific moment of darkness to wake us the f— up." And she led the women in chanting to the newly elected president, "I'm not your b—."

Naturally, she had to walk back some of her comments, saying they were taken out of context, leading to ridiculous headlines like this on CNN: "Madonna: 'Blowing up White House' taken out of context."[2]

In reality, her comments only made sense in context, and it was a context that these angry women devoured with glee.

Just a few weeks before Madonna's rant, Charlie Sheen tweeted out his prayer request that Trump be the next famous person to die in 2016: "Dear God; Trump next, please! Trump next, please! Trump next, please! Trump next, please! Trump next, please! Trump next, please!"[3]

Kathy Griffin's sin was to articulate what these other celebrities wished for and longed for. The murderous hatred was already there.

But it's not just singers and actors and comedians who have stirred up anti-Trump hysteria in America. Politicians have done it too.

Naturally, their words are more measured than those of entertainers like Madonna and Charlie Sheen. But their constant talk of impeachment and their over-the-top criticisms of the president give the impression that there is a ticking bomb in the White House, ready to explode at any time. Put another way, Donald Trump is a real threat to our nation and the world.

To be sure, I agree with Senator Ted Cruz that some of the president's problems are self-inflicted.[4] During the campaign, he made his own over-the-top statements, and he was hurt by very vulgar comments from his past. Since elected, every time he has behaved in an unpresidential manner, he has made himself a bigger target for his critics.

But none of that justifies the sustained political attack he is experiencing, to the point that Rep. Maxine Waters could even claim that the public is "getting weary"[5] with the Democrats for not impeaching Trump.

And impeaching him for what? Having two scoops of ice cream at dinner while his guests only got one? Or is he worthy of impeachment because he has been *accused* of stealing the election from Hillary Clinton with the help of Russia? Since when do you impeach someone based on unsubstantiated accusations?[6]

Also contributing to the anti-Trump hysteria is the mainstream media with its incessant Trump-bashing, excoriating him for virtually everything he says and does, always looking to find fault, to embarrass, to hamstring him at every turn.

Watching some news reports, you get the feeling that there is almost an immature fixation on the president, and these experienced news commentators suddenly sound like chattering children.

As far as their reaction to the Kathy Griffin photo, while there was widespread media condemnation of her actions, in some circles, the criticism was muted.

For example, when Jake Tapper introduced the photo during a CNN panel discussion, he gave a warning to viewers, especially those with kids, saying, "You might find what we're about to show you a little bit graphic."

A little bit graphic? Really? Would he have introduced the picture the same way if it had been the severed, bloodied head of President Obama? Would CNN have even shown it?

He further described it as "pretty disgusting," laughingly wondering how anyone would think it was appropriate. But again, would his tone have been the same had, say, Tim Allen done to Obama what Kathy Griffin did to Trump?

But once the panel starting talking, things got worse—much worse. Molly Ball, a political writer with *The Atlantic,* said she had a hard time even bringing herself to care about this, claiming it was just another case of Trump playing the always-persecuted victim card.

As for Griffin's actions, Ball said, "Of course, like, comedians and celebrities say dumb stuff and do dumb stuff. And, and violence is not appropriate. But I just don't think that's the source of President Trump's problems."

CNN contributor David Urban was then asked for his opinion. His response: "I think we've got much bigger issues to focus on than Kathy Griffin."

Tapper then asked former White House communications director Jen Psaki for her view of the matter, and she simply affirmed Urban's assessment, saying, "Agreed."

So, not only do major media outlets like CNN help fan the flames of anti-Trump hysteria, but they also engage in the worst kind of self-righteous hypocrisy, downplaying the ugliness of a photo of the severed head of the President of the United States. No big deal! Just comedians being dumb. There are bigger fish to fry.

As for the image itself? It's a "little bit graphic" and "pretty disgusting." Nothing more.

In incredibly stark contrast, as pointed out by the *Daily Wire*'s John Nolte, CNN expressed outrage when a rodeo clown wore a Barack Obama mask during his act in 2013: "It should also be noted that in the past this same rodeo clown had worn a mask of presidents' Reagan and Bush. Nevertheless, until he was properly banished from society and lost all hope of future employment, CNN pushed and pushed and pushed the story; toxified this poor guy as an example in never mocking The Precious."[7]

Coming back to 2017, even though CNN decided to release Griffin from her New Year's Eve job, and even though Tapper and others have since weighed in with stronger condemnation of the photo, that initial panel discussion said it all and reminded us that Griffin did not act in a vacuum.

For those on the left who would say, "Yeah, but the right-wing media savage President Obama," I would certainly agree. There's hypocrisy on the right as well.

I would simply argue that the major players in right-wing media did not incite the same kind of anti-Obama hysteria that the left has against Trump (although I don't justify the sins of the right any more than the sins of the left).

Lastly, though, there's one more player that helped create the toxic platform for Griffin's actions, but this one is somewhat nameless and faceless. It is made up of millions of people posting the most horrific comments on social media and composing the vilest graphics and videos. It is a savagery let loose by the Internet, and it makes people think they can get away with feigned murder. Or even murder.

It's time with take a deep breath, get a grip on our emotions, and ask ourselves what kind of world we want to bequeath to our children and grandchildren.

A little dose of civility, anyone?

June 2, 2017

Trump Not Moving Our Embassy to Jerusalem—Yet

★ ★ ★ ★ ★

I'M not the least bit surprised that President Trump signed the waiver to delay moving our embassy in Israel to Jerusalem, as each of our presidents has done since 1995. I'm disappointed, because he made such a point of this during the campaign, assuring us that he would be the man to make this momentous move. But I'm not surprised.

We've had indications that he was waffling on this for several weeks now. Plus, a move like this is easier said than done.

Still, there's reason for hope in the midst of the disappointment.

First, as a White House official emphasized, "It's a question of when, not if."[1]

Yes, "President Trump made this decision to maximize the chances of successfully negotiating a deal between Israel and the Palestinians, fulfilling his solemn obligation to defend America's national security interests. But, as he has repeatedly stated his intention to move the embassy, the question is not if that move happens, but only when."

This is certainly positive. I don't recall past presidents making this point so emphatically. We *will* move the embassy, just not yet.

Second, sources indicate that Trump actually yelled at Palestinian President Abbas when they during the president's Middle East trip. This led to several minutes of stunned silence on the Palestinian side. "You tricked me in DC!" Trump is reported to have said. "You talked there about your commitment to peace, but the Israelis showed me your involvement in incitement [against Israel]."[2]

This too would indicate that President Trump is striking a very different tone than his predecessors.

Third, there was no indication that the president put heavy pressure on Prime Minister Netanyahu when they met, telling him he would have to make major sacrifices, or else. Certainly, there was talk of making concessions for peace. But again, we have no indication that Trump tried to force Netanyahu's hand on any major issues.

That could explain why Israel's official response to the announcement that relocating the embassy had been postponed was muted: "Though Israel is disappointed that the embassy will not move at this time, we appreciate today's expression of President Trump's friendship to Israel and his commitment to moving the embassy in the future."[3]

Of course, Israel reiterated that "the American embassy, like the embassies of all countries with whom we have diplomatic relations, should be in Jerusalem, our eternal capital." But the statement itself expresses only mild disappointment, given Trump's clear commitment to Israel's well-being.

The real problem, however, is this. A White House official explained that, "In timing such a move, [the president] will seek to maximize the chances of successfully negotiating a deal between Israel and the Palestinians."[4]

Unfortunately, moving the embassy to Jerusalem will always be a point of contention with the Palestinians and the larger Muslim world. As noted in Israel's statement, "Maintaining embassies outside the capital drives peace further away by helping keep alive the Palestinian fantasy that the Jewish people and the Jewish state have no connection to Jerusalem."

Why keep this fantasy alive? The Palestinians are totally dependent on America to help broker peace negotiations. And at some point, they will have to accept that our embassy will be in Jerusalem. Why not make the move now, while also affirming to the Palestinians our commitment to work for their best interests as well?

As I (along with others) suggested previously, nothing is stopping us from moving the embassy to West Jerusalem. Even Russia recognizes this as Israel's capital (while claiming that East Jerusalem should be the capital of a Palestinian state). We can make this move without making a final determination about a Palestinian capital in East Jerusalem. (Obviously, I don't believe there is any historic Palestinian claim to East Jerusalem. But again, that can be a subject for later talks.)

The Camp David Accords are almost 40 years old (signed in September, 1978). The Oslo Accords are nearly 25 years old (signed September, 1993). Does President Trump really think that by not moving our embassy to Jerusalem now, we will be able to move the peace process forward? And can he really imagine that there will be some magic, opportune time to make the move in the future?

I'm thankful that President Trump is showing himself to be a true friend of Israel. He is holding the Palestinians' feet to the fire over terrorism and he has reaffirmed his commitment to stand with the Jewish State. I would just urge him once again to do what no other president has done.

Mr. Trump, be the man who made the move.

As I wrote last month, I'll write again: History will smile on you for it.

June 26, 2017

PRESIDENT TRUMP, THIS ADVICE COULD REALLY HELP YOU

★ ★ ★ ★ ★

Dear President Trump,

ALTHOUGH I was a strong critic of yours during the presidential primaries, I did vote for you in the general election, and I'm praying for you and I am rooting for you. So, the advice I want to offer has one intent only: I want to help remove some unnecessary burdens from you so you can focus on the goals of your presidency.

Obviously, the whole Russia investigation has been a major distraction, and like many other Americans, I don't believe there's anything to it.

I also believe that if another Republican candidate was elected president (say, Senator Ted Cruz), the mainstream media would be all over him, virtually day and night. After all, the Democrats were already launching outlandish attacks against Mitt Romney back in 2012—including Joe Biden's infamous claim that as president, Romney would put blacks "back in chains"[1]—so who can imagine what they would be doing to a President Cruz?

So, yes, even if you did everything right, as a conservative and a Republican, you'd be attacked by the liberal media and by leftwing elites day and night. But there's one big difference here. You started a lot of the fights—and I say that with the utmost respect for you as our president.

I was reading a very hostile article about you this week, but the writer made one charge that carried some weight, namely, that you created the atmosphere in which you now have to live. Sadly, there's some truth to this.

Let's say that you did not mock a disabled reporter (I initially thought you did but saw video evidence that refutes that, plus you have denied it repeatedly). What about saying that if one of your supporters roughed up a protestor in the crowd that you would pay for their legal fees? What about mocking those you defeated or making fun of the appearance of others or denigrating people in different, ugly ways?

Some of this is water under the bridge, but it still colors you to this day, especially when you revert to some of your old, pre-presidential (and, frankly, non-presidential) habits. And then, when your critics pile on mercilessly, even undeservedly, the perception for many is that, "Trump deserves this. After all, he started it."

What then can you do?

Do you remember when you apologized last August in what CNN called "an astonishing act of contrition"? (Yes, that's how CNN reported it.) You said, "Sometimes, in the heat of debate and speaking on a multitude of issues, you don't choose the right words or you say the wrong thing. I have done that." And, you added, "And believe it or not, I regret it."

Wasn't that a fruitful thing to do back then? Well, here is the simple principle for today.

It takes two to fight, and if you will humble yourself again—but this time even more clearly—and apologize to the American people, then the perception of many will change.

If you say, "During the campaign, and since being elected, I've said many things that inflamed tensions and provoked anger, and I truly regret those remarks. And I now see more clearly than ever how powerful this office is. So, I ask you to forgive me for my shortcomings.

"I'm totally committed to helping each of you, but I've made some mistakes and hurt lots of people—the truth is, I'm new at this and I'm not a professional politician. From here on, I want to focus on being your president and making America proud. Thank you for your prayers and your support."

Then, you go on from there, taking the high road rather than the low road, not flinging mud back if someone flings it on you.

And if you'll do that, even though your political opponents and your media adversaries will continue their attacks, if they don't moderate their tone, they will only look worse. And if they attack and you don't retaliate, they will look ugly. You can still expose fake news and you can continue to get your message out through social media and other means. That's not the problem. But it's the way in which you do it that will be critical from here on in.

There's a wonderful verse in the Book of Proverbs that says, "A gentle answer turns away wrath, but a harsh word stirs up anger" (Prov. 15:1 NIV). You can defuse an argument or you can provoke a fight. Which do you want it to be?

On the one hand, if you weren't a natural fighter, you wouldn't have made it this far, and on a certain level you must fight for what is right every day of your life. But there's a fighting that's destructive, not constructive, a fighting based on personality and emotion and pride. That kind of fighting will blow up in your face.

You are the most powerful elected official on the planet. Surely that should be enough for your sense of self-worth, no matter what the press says. After all, would you rather be the President of the United States or a journalist writing an op-ed about the president? And which would be better for the fruitfulness of your presidential term(s), not to mention your legacy—being a peacemaker or a troublemaker?

Please give prayerful consideration to what I've written here, sir, and see if this resonates with the counsel of your wisest advisors. It could be the difference between success and failure in the years ahead.

June 30, 2017

DON'T SELL YOUR SOUL IN DEFENSE OF PRESIDENT TRUMP

★ ★ ★ ★ ★

I'M all for defending our president when he's the subject of unjust attacks. And as a follower of Jesus, I voted for him, despite my misgivings. I'm also very happy to point out the many good things he has already done as president. But I will not sacrifice my ethics and demean my faith to defend his wrongful words. To do that is to lose all credibility before a watching world.

Plenty of Christians and non-Christians had a hard time understanding how so many of us evangelicals could vote for a candidate who seemed to be so thoroughly un-evangelical. But when we explained that we were voting against Hillary, that Supreme Court appointees were important to us, and that Trump seemed to care about religious liberties, many of them understood our vote. They see we're not whitewashing him or denying his faults. Some dissenters can even respect our choice.

But when we find it necessary to defend his every word, we discredit ourselves and tarnish our witness.

What prompted me to pen this article was the recent series of Trump tweets regarding MSNBC's Joe Scarborough and Mika Brzezinski. The president wrote:

Donald J. Trump ✔ @realDonaldTrump · 14h
I heard poorly rated @Morning_Joe speaks badly of me (don't watch anymore). Then how come low I.Q. Crazy Mika, along with Psycho Joe, came..

💬 36K   ⟲ 19K   ♡ 68K   ✉

Donald J. Trump ● @realDonaldTrump · 14h

...to Mar-a-Lago 3 nights in a row around New Year's Eve, and insisted on joining me. She was bleeding badly from a face-lift. I said no!

💬 82K ⟲ 18K ♡ 65K ✉

In response to this, I tweeted:

Dr. Michael L. Brown @DrMichaelLBrown · 5h

If you're a Christian who supports Trump, you should still be ashamed of his Twitter attacks on MSNBC hosts today. Beneath the POTUS!

💬 33 ⟲ 31 ♡ 98

Really now, for the most powerful elected official on the planet to call liberal newscasters "Psycho Joe" and "low I.Q. Crazy Mika" is indefensible. (Let's not even discuss the "bleeding" reference and where that leads.) And to defend him—I mean for us to defend him as Christian conservatives—is even less defensible.

We can be loyal to the president and still be ashamed of such language. We can support him and still say, "Mr. President, you demean yourself with such behavior, and you'll never get the respect you desire if you sink so low." In fact, that's what real loyalty and support looks like.

But when we find it necessary to stand up for him, as if he's the weak little victim being attacked by these terrible giants, we also demean ourselves. And what if it was your son or daughter or spouse or parent who the president was attacking with such language? How would you feel? When he does this, he ultimately hurts himself.

One man responded to my tweet saying, "This perfect Savior had a very blue collar flavor which we try to scrub away with our sensibilities. Newscasters need accountability too."

First, no one is denying that newscasters need accountability, and there are a slew of conservative newscasters blasting the liberals day and night (and vice versa). Second, and more importantly, it is ridiculous and almost obscene to compare our perfect Savior's rebukes of sinners with the president calling TV journalists *psycho* and *crazy*.

But this man who tweeted to me was not the only one to make the Trump-Jesus comparison. At least two ministers defended Trump on my Twitter account, with one also comparing Trump's words to those of Jesus and Paul. (I'm just referencing them here rather than posting their tweets here; perhaps they've had a change of heart. You know things are really bad when ministers of the gospel compare Trump's words to those of Jesus.)

One Christian woman was indignant with me: "You've gone too far! You Sir, are not God Almighty and do not speak for Him!"

I've gone too far by saying we ought not defend the president's childlike words? I've gone too far in suggesting that the president would do well to read what Proverbs says about the conduct of kings? (I tweeted that out the Proverbs reference during the interaction.) I've gone too far in saying that we, as followers of Jesus, should find these tweets embarrassing?

Another wrote, "No need to be ashamed, hope he keeps it up." Yes, I hope that the president keeps disparaging people in the crudest, most immature manner. I'm cheering you on!

Still another added: "Christians don't look at the faults of a person just the answer to them. Not ashamed of a person who doesn't hide their emotions."

I wonder what these Christians would be saying if Hillary Clinton were our president and she was the one ridiculing conservative newscasters in such crass terms?

Then there were those who felt sorry for Mr. Trump. They tweeted that the media is not fair to him and that he gets death threats all the time. Surely he has to protect himself!

Once again, such responses boggle the mind. He is the most protected man on the planet, and to my knowledge these newscasters are not trying to kill him. And how, pray tell, is he defending himself by calling them ugly names? If they misrepresent him, he can set the record straight, but he need not throw mud in their faces. The mud he throws will only splatter back. And the best way to push back against his critics is to push forward with the agenda they hate.

But for us to defend his every tweet is to make ourselves into stooges more than supporters, helping no one in the end.

This week, Ann Coulter attacked Sean Hannity, writing, "Sean Hannity, bless his heart, has the zeal of the late Trump convert. He would endorse communism if Trump decided to implement the policies of 'The Communist Manifesto.' (Which the GOP's health care bill actually does!)"[1]

I will leave that battle to them, but the reminder for us is that loyalty does not require blind allegiance.

So, if you're a Christian conservative, put the shoe on the other foot, and ask yourself how you'd be feeling had President Obama gone after, say, Rush Limbaugh and Laura Ingraham like this. Would you be defending him?

July 18, 2017

IS IT "THEOLOGICAL MALPRACTICE" FOR MINISTERS TO PRAY FOR TRUMP?

★ ★ ★ ★ ★

ACCORDING to NAACP board member Rev. Dr. William Barber, when evangelical ministers prayed over President Trump in the Oval Office last week, it was "a form of theological malpractice that borders on heresy."[1] Really? What could be wrong with praying for the president? Why was Rev. Barber so upset?

Speaking on MSNBC's "AM Joy," Rev. Barber stated, "When you can p-r-a-y for a president and others while they are p-r-e-y, preying on the most vulnerable, you're violating the sacred principles of religion. You know, there is a text in Amos Chapter 2 that says religious and moral hypocrisy looks like when a nation of political leaders will buy and sell upstanding people when they will do anything to make money, when they will sell the poor for a pair of shoes, when they will grind the penniless into the dirt and shove the luckless into the ditch and extort from the poor. That is an actual text."

While I appreciate Rev. Barber's heart for social justice, and while I share his antipathy for religious hypocrisy, his criticism is completely off base, if not hypocritical itself.

First, we are called to pray for our leaders, be they good or bad. As Paul instructed Timothy, "I urge that supplications, prayers, intercessions, and thanksgivings be made for all people, for kings and all who are in high positions, that we may lead a peaceful and quiet life, godly and dignified in every way. This is good, and it is pleasing in the sight of God our Savior, who desires all people to be saved and to come to the knowledge of the truth" (1 Tim. 2:1-4).

At the time Paul wrote this, the Roman emperor was Nero, an exceedingly wicked and even deranged man, a man who ultimately had Paul beheaded, according to church tradition. Yet Paul urged Timothy to have the believers pray for Nero.

If it was appropriate to pray for Nero, it is certainly appropriate to pray for Donald Trump, even if you are a Never Trumper. Prayer for our leader's wellbeing is prayer for our nation's wellbeing.

Second, prayer is not the same thing as political endorsement or personal approval. In fact, some of the leaders on the president's Faith Advisory Council did not endorse him for office, since they have a non-endorsement policy.

As expressed by Pastor Jack Graham, one of the men who prayed for Trump last week, "We as followers of Jesus have always believed that we are to be politically incorrect. 'Political correctness' is the mantra of the media and the world at large and *Christians are always against an anti-God or anti-biblical worldview*. Jesus stood against the prevailing worldview in His day. So we have always been a voice speaking to the culture or the government leaders. And the great opportunity we have in America is the freedom to speak, and leaders like our President want to hear from us."[2]

This is part of the prophetic calling of the church—to speak truth to power, regardless of cost or consequences. How much better it is when those leaders welcome our input.

Third, while Rev. Barber accused those who prayed for the president of "preying on the most vulnerable," apparently with reference to the president's attempt to repeal and replace Obamacare, he was an outspoken supporter of Hillary Clinton, a radically pro-abortion candidate.

Speaking at the Democratic National Convention in July, Rev. Barber said, "When I hear Hillary's voice and her positions, I hear and I know that she is working to embrace our deepest moral values—and we should embrace her."[3]

Really? Our deepest moral values as followers of Jesus include slaughtering babies in the womb right through the ninth month of pregnancy? Our deepest moral values include terminating more than 55 million innocent lives before they could see the light of day?

Rev. Barber describes himself as "a theologically conservative liberal evangelical biblicist," yet he supported the Democratic Platform, which was in many ways an anti-life platform. Based on what passages in Scripture, we might ask?

I genuinely believe that Rev. Barber cares for the poor and the oppressed, that he recognizes many injustices in America and the nations, and that he sees himself as fighting for God's cause. And I believe he sees his support of President Obama and Hillary Clinton as part of that struggle for justice. I can even agree with him that the Republican Party and President Trump fall short of God's ideals in many ways.

But it is the height of hypocrisy to fault other ministers for praying for the president when he himself supported Hillary Clinton. And, to use Rev. Barber's own words, it is "a form of theological malpractice that borders on heresy" to claim that a radically pro-abortion candidate shares our "deepest moral values."

That is absolutely, categorically false. Almighty God forbid.

(Once again, I extend an invitation to Rev. Barber to discuss these issues on my radio broadcast. Previous attempts to reach out failed.)

July 26, 2017

WAS I WRONG ABOUT
DONALD TRUMP?

★ ★ ★ ★ ★

A few days ago, I came across an article I wrote in April 2016 titled, "Donald Trump Is Not Your Protector: A Warning to Conservative Christians." Was I wrong to issue this warning? Hasn't President Trump proven himself to be a friend and protector of conservative Christians?

Without a doubt, I want my warning to be wrong, since I'm far more concerned with our religious freedoms than with being right. In fact, as soon as it became clear that Trump would be the Republican candidate, I wrote an article titled, "Why I'm Actually Rooting for Donald Trump," making clear that I hoped to be wrong in my many warnings.

That's also why I voted for him on Election Day, albeit with trepidation; I was not only voting *against* Hillary Clinton, I was voting *for* Donald Trump, with the hope that my fellow-evangelicals who knew him and spoke well of him were right. I wanted my warnings to be wrong then, and I want them to be wrong now, for the good of the country and the world.

In the April 2016 article, I wrote that, "when the rubber meets the road, [Trump] is anything but the defender of conservative Christians and their values."

Just the day before, on the *Today* show, he had said without hesitation that he wanted to change the Republican Platform on abortion, adding in three exceptions. He had also been critical of North Carolina's HB2, and he had said that Bruce (Caitlyn) Jenner would be free to use the ladies' room in one of his buildings.

Since I didn't trust his character or his track record or his promises (especially in contrast with the positions of Senator Ted Cruz, whom I had endorsed), I cautioned my fellow Christian conservatives against putting their trust in him.

Indeed, regarding Trump's criticism of HB2, Cruz had said:

Donald Trump is no different from politically correct leftist elites. Today, he joined them in calling for grown men to be allowed to use little girls' public restrooms. As the dad of young daughters, I dread what this will mean for our daughters—and for our sisters and our wives. It is a reckless policy that will endanger our loved ones.

Yet Donald stands up for this irresponsible policy while at the same time caving in on defending individual freedoms and religious liberty. He has succumbed to the Left's agenda, which is to force Americans to leave God out of public life while paying lip service to false tolerance.

That's why I closed my article with a strong warning:

Please don't look to him to be a defender of conservative Christian values or a protector of religious freedoms.

Barring dramatic divine intervention in his life, you will be sadly disappointed.

Be forewarned.

How wrong was I in penning these words? Or has there been, in fact, divine intervention in his life?

Obviously, there are many things I (and others) were concerned about, and I continue to have some of those concerns.

I sincerely wish that he would not launch twitter attacks against a good man like Jeff Sessions, his attorney general. I sincerely wish that he would not stoop to the name-calling of hostile journalists. I sincerely wish that he did not issue an executive order reinforcing President Obama's transgender guidelines for federal employees.[1] (The list could easily be multiplied.)

At the same time, it seems clear that President Trump greatly esteems the conservative Christian leaders who have become close to him, that he realizes that he was elected with the help of conservative evangelicals, that he wants to defend our liberties, and that he has become a strong pro-life ally. (Need I say more than "Neil Gorsuch"?) Could it be that he even has a growing fear of the Lord?

On my radio show this week, Dr. Richard Land, who has been to the White House with other evangelical leaders, told me that on a number of occasions, President Trump has prayed with Vice President Pence before making major decisions. This is a far cry from the Trump of just a year or two ago.

Lifesite News reported on April 28 that, "U.S. Vice President Mike Pence along with eight other members of President Trump's cabinet are gathering every week to pray and to study the Bible."[2] Surely Trump knows of this, and I assume he has positive feelings about it, which also speaks well of him.

This means that, while we always make a mistake when we put our trust in a person—even the President of the United States—and while Trump's shortcomings are there for the world to see, it does appear that God has been working in his life.

Was I wrong, then, about Donald Trump? The jury is still out, but there's evidence that there has been "dramatic divine intervention" in his life, which is all the more reason for us to pray that God will get hold of him even more powerfully and profoundly in the days to come.

I, for one, am ready for more surprises.

July 29, 2017

WHAT THE HIRING OF ANTHONY SCARAMUCCI TELLS US ABOUT PRESIDENT TRUMP

★ ★ ★ ★ ★

WHO is the real Donald Trump? If you talk with evangelical leaders who have met with him, they will tell you how humble and gracious he is and how deeply he embraces their values. If you look at some of his public statements or judge him based on his hiring of Anthony Scaramucci, you might come to a very different conclusion. How do we sort this out?

There was nothing enigmatic about President Barack Obama.

Raised in the Muslim world as a child, he was sympathetic to the religion and saw its best side. As a community organizer, identity politics was part of his mind-set. And influenced by radical leftists and gay professors, he took on their cause as his own. His religious environment in America supported these stances as well, from liberal Christianity in general to the Rev. Jeremiah Wright.

Not so when it comes to President Trump.

On the one hand, it's not hard to understand how the same man who ran casinos with strip clubs and boasted about his infidelities would settle down later in life. There's nothing inconsistent in that. And it's not hard to understand how some of his positions became more conservative over the years, galvanizing once he began to campaign.

But how do we understand the man today? How can he be such a pro-life champion, such an advocate for religious freedoms, such a friend of the evangelical church, while saying and doing some of the things that he does?

Earlier this month, when Trump learned that some evangelical leaders were working nearby with other White House staffers, he invited them to the Oval Office and was glad to have them lay hands on him in prayer.

Two weeks later, he hired Scaramucci, who previously described himself as pro-choice, for "gay marriage," and even "a gay rights activist." (This was as recently as 2016.) And as we learned through his unhinged and vulgar interview with a *New Yorker* reporter, he is hardly a model Christian.[1] How do we reconcile all this?

The more I think about it, the clearer it becomes to me.

First, as a businessman the president hires people he thinks will get the job done. Period. That's the same reason many Americans (including Christian conservatives) voted for him. They believed he would get the important things done, and his perceived character issues were secondary. As I heard endlessly during the campaign, "We're not electing a pastor in chief; we're electing a Commander in Chief."

So, just as a soldier risking his life on the front lines would rather have a brilliant general who was profane and slept around than a polite, faithfully married, but ineffective general, so many voters chose Trump as the most effective person for the job.

It would appear to be Trump's perspective when it comes to Scaramucci, hired to plug up a very leaky White House. The leakers must go and the mess must be cleaned up. Better to come with thunder than with a whisper at times like this.

As for Scaramucci himself, he announced on Twitter, "Full transparency: I'm deleting old tweets. Past views evolved & shouldn't be a distraction. I serve @ POTUS agenda & that's all that matters."[2] Let the past, then, be the past.

Second, as for the Trump the man, consider looking at him through different eyes.

Here's something we can easily wrap our minds around, although the example is extreme. Imagine an old-world mafia leader, ruthless in his business dealings and murderous in his methods, but with a deep love for his mother, his wife, and his daughters. He would sacrifice anything for their wellbeing, and with them he is as tender as a child, the ultimate gentleman.

Now let's take it one step farther. Let's say that this same man has a great respect for the Catholic Church, even though he himself is not that observant. He hears that the local parish is in trouble, and so he secretly donates money, not wanting to take any credit. And when he hears that the local priest has been threatened by thugs, he sends them a strong warning: You threaten him again, and you'll find yourself at the bottom of the river.

Again, these are exaggerated examples, but you can see where I'm going with this.

In the past, Trump seemed to have some respect for the Christian faith, even in his partying days. Now, as an older man who has become more conservative, that respect has deepened greatly. More importantly, as he has spent hours with godly Christian leaders, and as he has people like Mike Pence close to his side, he has been positively impacted by their faith, their character, and their influence.

He genuinely wants to stand up for their rights. He genuinely espouses their causes—which include social justice and care for the poor along with pro-life, pro-family, and pro-Israel stances.

He genuinely believes that preserving our religious freedoms is key to our nation's success. And he knows that likeminded people helped get him elected, so he feels indebted to them as well.

At the same time, he is a 70-year-old, rough and tumble New York business-man, more cutthroat than compassionate when it comes to getting things done.

He is a man who can communicate impulsively and say unsavory things, a world-famous celebrity and a self-marking expert.

Put another way, he is far from a model Christian himself.

But he is definitely a work in progress, he truly wants to be a champion of many good, Christian causes, and his door remains wide open to committed people of faith.

Viewed from this perspective, he's not really that much of an enigma after all. It does make sense, and when you factor in that God often uses unlikely vessels to carry out His plan, it's not that hard to understand. Do you agree?

August 2, 2017

THE OLD LADY, THE DEVIL, AND DONALD TRUMP

★ ★ ★ ★ ★

WHENEVER I write an article on Donald Trump, I'm sure to get a flood of responses asking me, "So, when are you going to admit you were wrong about him?"

This, however, means two very different things, depending on who is asking the question. For one group, it means, "Are you going to admit that you were wrong not to see him as God's man for the job?" For the other group, it means the exact opposite: "Are you going to admit that you are wrong to see him as God's man for the job?"

To be clear, then, I'm neither a defender nor an accuser of our president, neither his champion nor his critic. My goal is to be objective and redemptive, analyzing everything through the lens of Scripture, and doing my best to understand what God is doing in the midst of our chaotic world.

With that goal in view, let me tell you a story about a saintly old woman, totally destitute and dependent on her Lord. The application to President Trump should be apparent immediately.

As the story goes, this woman was out of money, had no credit, and was without anything to eat in her little house. So she cried out to God in prayer, "Lord, You know that I trust You, and You know that I love You, but I need a miracle now! I'm going to take a walk into town, and when I come back, I'm believing there will be groceries sitting right here on my kitchen table."

With that, she got up and left for her walk, trudging her way into town.

It happened to be summer time, and this old woman kept the windows open to create a small breeze. Little did she know that a teenage boy from her neighborhood, an irreligious prankster, was standing outside her house and heard every word she prayed.

He decided that this was a perfect opportunity to make fun of this old woman's faith, so he rode into town on his bike, bought a few bags of groceries, hurried back to her house, and climbed in through one of the open windows. Then he neatly placed the groceries on her kitchen table and waited outside to watch her response.

A few minutes later, the old lady returned home. To her joyful shock, just as she prayed, there were bags of groceries on her table. God had worked a miracle!

With tears in her eyes, she began to thank Him, almost shouting as she prayed: "Lord, You are so faithful! You never let me down! You didn't let me go hungry! Thank You so much for sending me this food!"

The moment she stopped praying, the boy outside shouted back to her through the window, "Lady, God didn't bring you that food. I did!"

She replied, "I don't care if the devil brought it. God sent it!"

I trust you get the point.

If you are a pro-family, pro-life, pro-Israel conservative like me, you have to be pleased with some of the things President Trump has done, even if you don't like his method.

Not only did he appoint Neil Gorsuch to the Supreme Court, but he has nominated other fine justices, similar in pedigree to Gorsuch, for district and appeals court appointments. This alone is quite major.

The president continues to work toward defunding Planned Parenthood, in total contrast with what Hillary Clinton would have done.

Through Attorney General Sessions, the president did not continue President Obama's radical transgender policy in our children's schools, and just last week, the Department of Justice filed a friend of the court brief that has LGBT activists up in arms.[1]

In the words of one critic, "Trump has given all of his anti-LGBTQ lieutenants—from Betsy DeVos and Tom Price to Ben Carson and Mike Pence—free rein to assault LGBTQ rights and, just as profoundly, he has listened to their counsel on the issue. That's why we've seen protections for transgender and gay students threatened, elimination of data collection on LGBTQ seniors and a devastating attack, via Twitter, on transgender people serving in the military."[2]

Of course, I would frame these decisions in positive terms, opposite to the perspective of LGBT activists. But their attacks on the president only underscore the extent that he has followed a conservative family agenda. And did anyone notice that, after eight years of gay pride in June, there was a very conspicuous silence this past June?

Trump has also showed much stronger support for Israel than his predecessor, with reports indicating that he rebuked Palestinian President Mahmoud Abbas to his face, allegedly yelling at him, "You tricked me in DC!"

Now, you might say to me, "You still don't get it. Trump doesn't give a flip about any of these issues. He's a con man playing to his base, and when he's done with them, he'll spit them out and move on to whoever suits his purposes best. He can't be trusted! The guy doesn't have a moral bone in his body."

That's why I shared the story of the old woman. Whether the devil brought the groceries or whether an angel brought them, God sent them.

In the same way, whether you see President Trump as the devil or an angel or a mixture of the two, it seems clear that God is sending many answers to prayer through him. Shouldn't we be glad for this? And even if we feel he's doing damage in other ways, can't we be thankful for these major, positive strides?

Let's not be so focused on the latest sensational news that we miss some of what's happening behind the scenes. And, to repeat, I write this neither to defend the president nor to accuse him.

I'm just making some observations, as objectively as I can.

August 13, 2017

CHARLOTTESVILLE, WHITE SUPREMACISTS, EVANGELICALS, RACISTS, AND TRUMP

★ ★ ★ ★ ★

THE alt-right. White supremacists. Nationalists. Trump supporters. Racists. Evangelical Christians. Is this a list of unrelated, widely disparate groups that overlap only on the fringes? Or does this describe the inter-connected spokes of the same wheel, different in emphasis but not in kind? The tragedy in Charlottesville, which has heightened tensions and exacerbated divisions in our country, calls for clarification.

If you listen to some secular media, you'd get the impression that Donald Trump is responsible for Charlottesville and that those who voted for him are culpable as well. You'd also get the impression that unless you denounce Trump, you are guilty of racism and are likely a white supremacist. And since Trump has support from many evangelical Christian leaders, you'd be led to believe that they are part of the alt-right, all of them racists and hyper-nationalists.

Because I was out speaking Saturday afternoon and evening, I did not post anything on social media about Charlottesville until late that night. By that time, my Twitter feed was lit up with calls for me renounce racism and distance myself from Trump. Quite out of the blue, I was judged to be implicit in a racist cause because I did not speak out against a white supremacist rally quickly enough. And because I had voted for Trump, I was now an accomplice in racism and, by default, a member of the alt-right.

Many of you reading this have had the same experience, as if there was an explicit connection between Charlottesville and Trump voters, between racism and evangelical Christians. But is there a connection?

When I was finally got around to posting on Facebook on Saturday night, I wrote: "There is nothing American about White Supremacism—nothing heroic, nothing praiseworthy, nothing patriotic. It is a rotten, ugly mindset full of hatred, bigotry, and pride, and every person of conscience should denounce it. It degrades others who are also created in the image of God and takes His name in vain to further its cause. Whatever our political or racial or ethnic background, as Americans, we need to stand together against it."

All this seems self-evident, and every friend and co-worker I have would agree with this. What is there to argue with?

The response to the comment was excellent, with strong support for what was shared. Others, however, chimed in negatively, criticizing blacks (since I was criticizing white supremacists), asking me why I never renounced Black Lives Matter extremism (which, of course, I had), and claiming that anyone who voted for Trump was complicit in the Charlottesville riot.

In response to some of these comments, I wrote: "The bottom line is simple: I don't care what color your skin is and what your ethnic background is. When Neo Nazis rally, you condemn it. When the KKK rallies, you condemn it. When Black Supremacists rally, you condemn it. And when a man plows his car into a crowd, killing one person and injuring 19, you condemn it. If you can't do that, you shouldn't be on this page. I trust we share the same heart here."

Again, this seems straightforward, yet even this comment drew negative responses, which makes one thing very clear: There are dangerous extremes on the right and on the left, and there is racism on the right and on the left. All of this is wrong and contemptible.

What about connecting all the dots on the right and drawing a coherent circle with Trump in the center? I believe that would be inaccurate for the following reasons:

1. Although there were certainly divisive aspects to Trump's campaign there's little hard evidence that he is a racist. And from the reports I hear from people close to him, he has a genuine

burden to help the inner cities, which are largely minority.

2. Although right-leaning, white nationalists overwhelmingly voted for Trump, they still make up a small part of his overall base and do not reflect the sentiments of the vast majority of his voters.

3. It is a *non sequitur* to argue that, because the KKK supported Trump, others who voted for Trump support the KKK. I'm sure the New Black Panthers overwhelmingly voted for Barack Obama (and Hillary Clinton), but that doesn't mean that a white California Jew who voted for Obama and Hillary supports the New Black Panthers. Let's be realistic.

4. The vast majority of evangelical Christians denounce racism and have no connection with the alt-right or with white supremacists. The fact that some white racists use Christianity as a cloak tells us one thing only—they are hypocrites.

5. Identity politics can be just as dangerous as outright racism. Both are divisive, both demean the value of others, and both make judgments based on skin color or ethnicity.

6. We should distance ourselves from the extremism of groups like Black Lives Matter and Antifa just as we distance ourselves from the extremism of white nationalism, exposing the hateful rhetoric, rejecting the violent acts, and saying with one loud voice, "As Americans, this is not who we are."

Right now, across the country, there is massive distrust, polarization, misunderstanding, and misrepresentation. And rather than bringing us together, much of the media is fanning the flames of division and fear, often in grossly hypocritical ways (in other words, finding fault with one side only when there is fault on both sides).

At volatile times like this when our blind spots only become bigger, we must determine to be part of the solution and not the problem. That means listening before speaking, understanding before opining, and caring before criticizing.

Will we be peacemakers or troublemakers, ones who build bridges or blow up bridges, those who reach out or those who push away?

Whether we like it or not, with our deep differences and strong convictions, we are one nation under God, and united we stand, divided we fall. Which will it be?

August 20, 2017

Should Trump's Evangelical Advisors Abandon Him?

★ ★ ★ ★ ★

IN the aftermath of the President's comments about Charlottesville, some Republican leaders have distanced themselves from him, while a number of major business leaders have stopped supporting him. Why are the evangelical leaders on his faith advisory council still standing with him?

As reported[1] by NPR, "President Trump's belated and halfhearted denunciation of the hate groups that marched in Charlottesville, Virginia, has cost him the support of numerous business leaders and fellow Republicans and prompted at least a half-dozen nonprofit organizations to cancel planned fundraising events at his Mar-a-Lago resort.

"By contrast, Trump's religious advisers have been mostly silent"—with the notable exception of Pastor A.R. Bernard of New York City. This respected megachurch pastor said, "It became obvious that there was a deepening conflict in values between myself and the administration."

Before Rev. Bernard announced his resignation, Matthew Dowd, a "proud independent" and the Chief Political Analyst for ABC News tweeted, "Not a single member of Trump's Evangelical Council has resigned. We have learned corporate America has a greater moral compass. So so sad."[2] The tweet has since gone viral.

How is it, then, that political leaders and business leaders feel the need to distance themselves from the President while these other spiritual leaders do not? Are these Christian leaders lacking in integrity? Have they sold their reputation, not to mention their souls, for a seat at the President's table?

Of course not. Now is when President Trump needs them most, and it is very wrong to assume that their public silence reflects their private silence.

To the contrary, they are doing what faith leaders are supposed to do—praying for the President and doing their best to speak into his life, calling him to do what is right in God's sight and is best for the nation.

To be clear, I'm not speaking officially for the faith advisory council, although I'm close to several of the men serving on that council. But I do believe that most (or all) of them will affirm what I've written here. It is for times like this that the council exists.

First, let's remember that some of the men on this council did not endorse Trump for president, and at least one told him that he was their last choice of all the Republican candidates. Why, then, do we equate their presence on a faith-based council with a sign of endorsement or approval?

Second, it is wrong to assume that these men are simply yes men who never differ with Trump or risk their good standing with him. One of these leaders has shared on my radio show that on more than one occasion he has respectfully rebuked Mr. Trump in strong and clear terms.

In fact, this evangelical leader once took the president to task so strongly that minutes later, he called back to apologize for being so forceful. At no point, though, has the President rebuffed their words or shut them out of his life.

Isn't it good to know that these solid, godly leaders are still doing their best to speak truth to the president? Wouldn't you want people like that having access to him? Why would they abandon him now?

Third, as a colleague said to me last week, we Christians are so quick to divorce one another the moment conflict arises. Why don't we get in the trenches and say, "I don't like what you said and how you said it, but I'm here to help. How can we fix this and move forward?" Why must we immediately abandon one another the moment conflict arises?

Fourth, it is ridiculous to think that ministry leaders should dance to the media's tune. Remember: They are ministers, not politicians.

Just because the media is in a panic doesn't mean everyone else has to be. Just because they want everyone to write Trump off as a Nazi sympathizer doesn't mean that's the truth.

When it comes to the massive controversy concerning the President's statements about Charlottesville, I think we all agree that he should have been more clear and specific in his first statement, which pointed to violence "on many sides."

He sought to correct this two days later when he said, "Racism is evil. And those who cause violence in its name are criminals and thugs, including KKK, Neo-Nazis, White Supremacists, and other hate groups are repugnant to everything we hold dear as Americans. Those who spread violence in the name of bigotry strike at the very core of America."[3]

Although some critics felt he was being insincere and others said it was too little too late, he did make himself perfectly clear: All these white supremacist groups are evil and he rejects them as utterly un-American.

Unfortunately, the President made another statement the next day when speaking with the press, with some clearly unscripted comments, including: "I think there is blame on both sides. You look at both sides. I think there is blame on both sides. You had some very bad people in that group. You also had some very fine people on both sides."[4]

This is when all hell broke loose, and it was after this that more and more leaders began to distance themselves from him.

On the one hand, having categorically denounced the Neo-Nazis and their ilk the day before, he was right to draw attention to the problems on both sides, since there certainly was blame to spread around.

On the other hand, he was quite wrong to say that there were "some very fine people on both sides." Really? Some "very fine" Neo-Nazis and KKK members?

But is that what he meant? I personally thought he was referring to people who simply objected to the removal of General Lee's statue *in distinction from* the white supremacist groups, while on the "alt-left" side, he was referring to peaceful protestors who rightly objected to the "Unite the Right" rally.

This is something he needs to clarify, and I hope that these faith leaders can help him to do so.

If, in fact, he simply expressed himself in an ambiguous and confusing manner, then he can easily correct the matter, apologize, and move on, not giving further fuel for the critics' fire.

But if he meant that there are "some very fine" Neo-Nazis, white supremacists, and KKK members, then I would expect the rest of the faith leaders to follow in A.R. Bernard's footsteps, telling the President they can no longer be associated with him.

Right now, I'm glad they're still together, I'm glad they're still doing their best to give him strong counsel, and I'm glad that, in his moment of greatest need so far in his presidency, there are still servants of God ready to speak truth to power.

Pray that the Lord would give them wisdom and clarity and that President Trump will have ears to ear. It truly is a critical time for our country.

*Note: I fully respect Rev. Bernard's decision and do not want to imply in any way that he forsook the President in a time of need. He has his own race to run and he answers to God on this, not you or me.

September 19, 2017

PRESIDENT TRUMP CALLS OUT NORTH KOREA'S "ROCKET MAN" BEFORE THE UN

★ ★ ★ ★ ★

PRESIDENT Trump's first speech before the UN was vintage Trump, for better or for worse. One line in particular epitomized why some people love him and others loathe him: "Rocket Man is on a suicide mission for himself."[1] Accordingly, his speech drew enthusiastic praise as well as breathless condemnation.

Prime Minister Benjamin Netanyahu tweeted, "In over 30 years in my experience with the UN, I never heard a bolder or more courageous speech."[2]

In stark contrast, the leftwing Israeli standard-bearer, *HaAretz* exclaimed, "Trump Delights Netanyahu With Belligerent and Nationalist Right-wing UN Speech."[3]

According to former UN Ambassador John Bolton, the speech was "the best of the Trump presidency."[4]

On the opposite side of the spectrum, Hillary Clinton told Stephen Colbert, "I thought it was very dark, dangerous, not the kind of message that the leader of the greatest country in the world should be delivering."[5]

To repeat: This was vintage Trump, for better or for worse.

Others have already analyzed the perceived strengths and weaknesses of the president's speech as a whole. Here, we'll focus on his comments regarding North Korea.

Not surprisingly, these comments drew the sharpest rebuke from his critics, including Chemi Shalev of *HaAretz*.

The subtitle to his article announced, "In threatening to 'totally destroy' North Korea, Trump resorted to rhetoric once reserved for half-crazed despots from semi-developed countries." As for calling Kim Jong-un "Rocket Man," Shalev suggested that "Pyongyang could very well respond with another Elton John song, 'Madman Across the Water.'"[6]

Shalev even accused Trump of committing a war crime: "According to the laws of war and judgments rendered by the International Court of Justice in The Hague, the threat of total annihilation is a war crime in and of itself. It will be welcomed in retrospect if it somehow succeeds in getting Kim to climb down from the ballistic missiles on which he is currently cruising towards confrontation. It will be seen as reckless and possibly cited in an indictment if it spurs Kim to further escalate his clash with Trump, as he's done in the past."

Hillary Clinton wished that the president had been more diplomatic, "And not call him Rocket Man, the Elton John song, but to say clearly 'we will not tolerate any attacks on our friends or ourselves.'"[7]

But had the president been more diplomatic, we wouldn't be talking about his speech so passionately, nor would he have been true to himself (again, for better or worse). On the other hand, one can only wonder what Secretary of State Rex Tillerson and Ambassador Nikki Haley were thinking as they heard their Commander in Chief read his "Rocket Man" line. (As of 11:33 P.M., EDT, September 19, the night of the speech, a Google search for "Trump 'Rocket Man' UN" yielded 1.3 million hits.)

What, then, should we make of this historic speech, focusing on Trump's North Korea remarks?

First, he did well to call out the evils of this godless regime for the entire world to hear. "No one," he said, "has shown more contempt for other nations and for the well-being of their own people than the depraved regime in North Korea. It is responsible for the starvation deaths of millions of North Koreans. And for the imprisonment, torture, killing, and oppression of countless more."

And this was just the beginning of his scorching and well-deserved rebuke.

How typical is this kind of talk before the UN? According to Rabbi Shmuley Boteach, it is all too rare.

As he wrote in an email, "While it would seem to be self-evident, it is so rare to see denunciations of these rogue regimes [referring also to Iran and Venezuela] and those like them from the podium of the UN. The United Nations has embarrassed itself as it has repeatedly morally equivocated on brutal governments and terrorists. But today President Trump, as leader of the Free World, upended the entire UN institution, demanding and delivering moral clarity."

Second, Trump called the bully's bluff on the most public, international platform available, warning the North Korean dictator of dire consequences should he dare go to war with America or our allies. He also called on the UN to do the right thing and denuclearize this rogue regime.

The president said, "No nation on Earth has an interest in seeing this band of criminals arm itself with nuclear weapons and missiles. The United States has great strength and patience, but if it is forced to defend itself or its allies, we will have no choice but to totally destroy North Korea.... The United States is ready, willing, and able, but hopefully this will not be necessary. That's what the United Nations is all about. That's what the United Nations is for. Let's see how they do."

Obviously, the goal is to liberate North Korea, not destroy it, and we must view the people of that nation as victims more than criminals. They have been brainwashed, beaten down, starved, deprived, and deceived, and our enemy there is an evil dictator, supported by other evil people.

Yet President Trump wanted to reiterate a message he has been getting out for some weeks now on social media: Don't mess with us, son. You're in over your head. You're out of your league. Best to go back to your fantasy world while you have a chance.

Is this the best way to deal with an unhinged, almost unaccountable dictator? Perhaps it is. I hope, at the least, that the generals and advisors counseling the president have told him this is the best way to go.

Third and last, we return to where we started, citing the most memorable words of the speech: "Rocket Man is on a suicide mission for himself and for his regime."

To my knowledge, Kim Jong-un is not known to be a fan of Elton John. (See a fascinating article[8] about Jong-un's alleged favorite songs, including Andrew WK's "She Is Beautiful," which I just heard myself for the first time. Wild.)

So, the "Rocket Man" reference was no deeper than what it appeared to be on the surface—a demeaning and derogatory reference to Kim Jong-un as if he were a little boy playing with rockets, not to be taken seriously in the least.

Will this further provoke this unpredictable leader? Or will the public scorn, which would likely embarrass him, cause him to back off?

Only time will tell.

What we know today is that Donald Trump continues to be Donald Trump, this time on a unique world stage.

This is how he got to be president, and this is why he is so loved and so hated.

This was vintage Trump, for better or for worse.

September 25, 2017

What Do We Make of the Battle Between President Trump and the NFL?

★ ★ ★ ★ ★

O N Sunday evening, the lead story on the Huffington Post announced, "FOOTBALL TAKES THE KNEE" while the lead story on the Drudge Report proclaimed, "NFL TAKES KNEE." Left and right both agreed on the major news of the day. Beyond that, there was little agreement to be found.

NFL owners expressed their solidarity with the protestors and their disappointment with President Trump.

In the words of NFL team owner (and previous Trump supporter) Robert Kraft, "Our players are intelligent, thoughtful and care deeply about our community and I support their right to peacefully affect social change and raise awareness in a manner that they feel is most impactful."[1]

In contrast, NASCAR owners made clear that such protests had no place in their sport.

And so, when NASCAR team owner Richard Childress was asked "what he would do if one of his employees protested during the anthem," he replied, "Get you a ride on a Greyhound bus when the national anthem is over. I told them anyone who works for me should respect the country we live in. So many people have gave their lives for it. This is America."[2]

Earlier in the week, the president had referred to NFL players who knelt in protest during the national anthem as "SOBs"[3] who should be fired, also disinviting the NBA's Golden State Warriors to the White House. In response, LeBron James called President Trump a "bum."[4]

Is there a right and wrong in all this? How do we sort things out?

Kevin Durant commended the NFL players for bringing a unified and unifying message, writing, "I think our NFL players are doing a great job of sending a great message, and we stand behind them as athletes, and we support them as well."[5]

In contrast, conservative Joel Pollack wrote, "President Donald Trump called out former 49ers quarterback Colin Kapernick and other NFL players on Friday for protesting the national anthem, expressing what millions of football fans have already registered by tuning out.

"But NFL officialdom, Hollywood, the mainstream media, and left-wingers in all quarters have distorted what he said, to the point where entire teams felt obligated to protest—something."[6]

How, then, do we sort things out? Is there really a right side and a wrong side?

Here are six points to consider (with the hope of bringing some clarity and with the risk of getting everyone mad at me):

1. The American flag is associated with sacrifices made for our national freedom, and it represents the best of our nation. Therefore, protesting during the national anthem should be avoided since it is perceived as unpatriotic.

In this light, it would have been better if Colin Kaepernick had found a better way to express his concerns about alleged social injustice.

It's true that he launched a national movement of sorts, but his actions (and those of others in past weeks) drew more attention to the man than to the message, bringing more division than awareness.

2. If we want to celebrate America's greatness, we can't ignore America's faults.

I agree with those who blame President Obama's identity politics for much of the racial division in our country today, but I also agree with those who say that there are systemic problems in our justice system, with rich and poor not being treated equally (and, in many cases, blacks and whites not receiving equal treatment).

We can stand for patriotism and justice together. Don't they go hand in hand? Don't they support and complement each other?

3. The debate about the protests is not a debate about race.

It's true that most NFL players are black and that most of Trump's Alabama crowd was white. And it's true that most of the Golden State Warriors, who are *not* going to the White House, are black, while most of the NHL's Pittsburgh Penguins, who *are* going to the White House, are white.

But the ultimate issues here are not black and white issues, unless we want to claim that no blacks are patriotic or that no whites care about social justice. To make this into a race debate is to play into the hands of the race baiters.

4. Incendiary rhetoric begets more incendiary rhetoric.

Speaking to a conservative crowd in Alabama, President Trump knew he was on solid ground when he ripped into protesting NFL players, calling them "sons of b—s" who should be fired.

To paraphrase, "How dare these spoiled brats despise the blood that was shed for their freedom!"

But as president, his role is not only to appeal to his base. He must also rally the nation around important causes. Comments like this have the opposite effect.

And when America's Commander in Chief derides others in such terms, he only stokes the fires of division, also opening the doors to outrageous comments like LeBron's "bum" remark.

Can you imagine what the liberal response would have been if a famous white athlete had called President Obama a bum? Conversely, can you imagine what the conservative response would have been if President Obama had referred to MLB's Albert Pujols and Tony LaRussa as "SOBs" for attending a Glenn Beck rally in DC?[7]

5. Most Americans want sports to be sports.

It's likely that ratings will continue to drop as games continue to be politicized and Americans feel our flag is being disrespected. Must everything be politicized?

Why can't athletes entertain their loyal fans while finding ways to raise awareness of important causes outside the playing field? They have instant media audiences and, with their large followings, they could recruit rather than alienate.

6. Once again, this is about President Trump.

No political figure in memory has been able to drive the news like Donald Trump drives the news, shifting our attention from North Korea to the NFL in the blink of an eye. He even sets the parameters for debate and discussion, virtually setting up the talking points for both sides in advance.

And so, what was a fairly minor issue in the NFL (in terms of numbers of players protesting) became a massive issue overnight, with several hundred players involved in making a statement one way or another. The response even trickled into a Major League Baseball game.[8]

As one professional athlete commented to me in private, the protest on Sunday was a response to the president's attack more than it was a statement about social justice issues.

Mr. Trump now has a fresh set of enemies, and, unfortunately, the race card is being played against him.

But there's a silver lining to all this. If our president recognizes the sacred entrustment that has been given to him—he has been elected to lead the entire nation—he can use his marketing genius to unite, rather than divide.

Let's pray that he'll find a way to tweet constructively rather than destructively (I know that's a tall order, but that's why we pray!) and that those who oppose him would take the olive branch and put their own weapons down.

I honestly believe that those standing for patriotism and those standing for justice are seeking one and the same thing—an America that is truly great. And in the end, what everyone desires is the same—to be treated with dignity and respect.

If each of us acted that way today, treating with dignity and respect even those we differ with, we could start a movement of our own. Shall we?

October 2, 2017

Donald Trump Wins Again
★ ★ ★ ★ ★

N FL players are standing for the anthem, and team owners are urging them to stand. The NHL is asking everyone to stand. The NBA has said its players will stand. NASCAR owners have said team members will stand or be fired. As a headline last week on Breitbart declared, "Trump Wins Bigly as Every NFL Player Stands for Thursday Night Anthem."[1]

Is this another example of President Trump's marketing genius? Is this a classic proof that he is playing proverbial 4-D chess, always several steps ahead of his detractors? Did he intentionally bait NFL players and owners with his provocative remarks in Alabama, knowing how they would respond and knowing what the backlash would be?

If that's the case, we have to assume that: 1) Trump knew that his over the top, "fire the SOB" comments would provoke a negative response from the NFL, even from supportive owners and players; 2) he knew that there would be a mass protest *against him* by these players and owners; 3) he knew that the mass protest would further alienate and exasperate football fans across the nation, who would now turn against these players and teams; 4) he knew that, although many Americans hate him, they do not like our flag being disrespected, and so by standing with the flag it would feel as if they were also standing with him; 5) he knew that major league sports owners, for whom revenue is everything, could not take a major hit on their product, and with NFL ratings in freefall, these leaders would say, "We better stand!" 6) he also knew that these owners (and players) would not want to be perceived as anti-American and unpatriotic, which we assume they are not. This would give them further incentive to say, "We'll all stand!"

So, in typical Trumpian fashion, what begins as a loss for him as the nation decries his Alabama remarks—from leftwing media to some of his friends in the NFL—ends up as a big win. And what begins as a small protest by a few players against perceived social injustice becomes a large protest against Trump, then reverses itself and becomes a referendum on standing for our flag. As John Nolte said in the aforementioned Breitbart column, "Trump Wins Bigly."

After all, wasn't Trump's goal to call out a perceived lack of patriotism? Wasn't he appealing to nationalism? Wasn't he trying to isolate players who would not stand for our flag?

In the immediate aftermath of his remarks, it appeared that he lost badly (rather than won bigly). First, he was blasted as being racist (white Alabama crowd; black NFL players). Second, he was criticized by former supporters. Third, it seemed the whole league rose up as one to say to the president, "You will not divide us! We are united! We will protest *you* together."

But, to repeat, in typical Trumpian fashion, the whole thing turned around on a dime and now, across the world of professional sports, there is a fresh emphasis on standing for our flag. Not only so, but in last Thursday's game in Green Bay, many in the crowd chanted, "USA! USA!" when it was time for the anthem. When's the last time something like that happened?

And who is the perceived winner in this whole episode? Certainly not the NFL. Certainly not the protesting players (although I do believe that, if they demonstrate their patriotism, the nation will hear their concerns[2]). Certainly not critics of the president.

No, the perceived winner is our national anthem along with our president, the man who stood for the flag, the man who called out the dissenters, the man who rallied the nation.

Did he foresee all this when preparing his comments (or launching into them) in Alabama?

I personally doubt it—unless he really is playing multi-dimensional chess and is that far ahead of the rest of us.

Was he willing to speak his mind and take whatever hits came next? Absolutely.

Was he determined to keep making his point even when there was a national outcry against him? Without a doubt.

Was he pleased when, rather than the debate being about players and the flag, it was now about him? I would expect so, since the standard marketing philosophy is that any news about you is better than no news about you.

Did he realize that he hit a positive nerve with his constituency? Certainly, he knew that from the start, hence his well-received initial comments at the Alabama rally. (If you recall, his NFL comments were much stronger than his endorsement of the losing candidate, Luther Strange.)

Did he understand that the mass anti-Trump protest hurt the NFL and that the owners and players would feel stung by it? Once it happened, of course, and that's another reason he upped his rhetoric rather than backed down.

And will he now commend the players and teams for standing and seem conciliatory and positive? I would assume so, since he knows how to be a good winner.

But, as my wife Nancy asked me when we were discussing all this, if he was brilliant enough to foresee all this before he made his comments, why then does he make so many other comments that only hurt him in the long run?

What I personally believe is that he understands his base and knows how to hit the right notes, and by doing do, the ripple effect turns out well for him. Either that, or he's an incredible marketing genius or God is with him in the strangest ways or he's just plain lucky.

Whatever the case may be, for those wanting him to change and telling him that his strategy won't work, his answer, I'm sure, is the same: "This is how I became president. It looks like it's working for me."

October 16, 2017

HAVE EVANGELICAL LEADERS BECOME DISCIPLES OF DONALD TRUMP?

★ ★ ★ ★ ★

A headline on the conservative, RedState website announces, "Trump's Cheap 'Merry Christmas' Christianity Continues to Sway Evangelicals."[1] Is this true?

According to Kimberly Ross, "Last year, congregants at the Church of Trump stormed into polling places nationwide and voted a godless reality star into the highest office in the land."

But that was only the beginning. Since then, Ross claims, "It's been crystal clear that too many Evangelical Trump supporters have not only placed their political faith in the real estate magnate; they have become sold-out disciples for him. It seems as if, in their eyes, the GOP and Christianity are interchangeable."

What prompted Ross to pen this article now, in October 2017? It was President Trump's appearance at FRC's Values Voter's Summit. He was the first sitting president to speak at this annual D.C. summit, and he received a thunderous response when he made clear that we would be saying, "Merry Christmas" again. In the words of Ross, "Home run! And the crowd...goes...wild."

Yes, "The proud, starry-eyed Evangelicals who cast their ballot for the Christian-in-Chief believe Trump has miraculously brought faith back to the nation.

"And that is all that matters."

Is Ross being fair? Yes and no—and that is a very big no.

On the "yes" side, it is true that we evangelicals can be guilty of making "Merry Christmas" into a big deal, no doubt the result of what we perceive to be the constant attack on our faith. So, when the president pushes the right button and uses the right line in the right setting, he's sure to get a response.

Overall, saying "Merry Christmas" is the least of our concerns, and Ross's criticisms here are fair.

It's also true that some evangelicals have been guilty of turning Trump into Saint Donald. He is presented (by a precious few) as a truly Christian man who can do no wrong, a selfless champion of the people whose most unbecoming tweets are justified because of the fierceness of the battle. He is one of us, and he is our hero!

I addressed this concern during the campaign, and since the election I have urged my fellow evangelical leaders not to sell their souls in defense of our president. We only discredit ourselves when we ignore his shortcomings.

Worse still, we hurt our witness. People are less likely to hear our message about Jesus when we seem oblivious to the president's clay feet.

Having said this, I believe that in other, more serious ways, Ross has missed the boat.

In my experience, most evangelical leaders do not turn a blind eye when Trump speaks or acts in a way that we find objectionable. And I know very few leaders who voted for him without reservation, as if we had no reason to be concerned.

Instead, we were voting against Hillary, we were voting for someone who would take on the system (including the Republican establishment), and we were voting for a man whom we hoped God could use despite there being no evidence that he was an evangelical Christian. In other words, we voted with our eyes wide open, and we continue to have our eyes wide open.

But were we unjustified in some of our expectations? Were we wrong in thinking that he would stand for religious liberties? Were we wrong in thinking that he would nominate pro-life, conservative justices to the Supreme Court and federal courts? Were we wrong in thinking that he would stand against radical LGBT activism? Were we wrong in thinking that he would be a friend of Israel?

Even Ross admits that "some of Trump's presidential actions have indeed been worthy of praise by communities of faith (see his recent protection of religious liberty)." But, she continues in the same sentence, "it is his cheap brand of convenient, crowd-pleasing, substance-free Christianity that is truly loathsome."

I concur that this brand of "Christianity" is loathsome, but it's not the brand I'm embracing, nor is it the brand my evangelical colleagues are embracing. Instead, we see our biblically based, sacred, evangelical faith for what it is, and we see the president for who he is: An ally and friend; a fearless, strong-headed leader; a rough and tumble, often impetuous, sometimes unwise, even divisive Commander in Chief.

But he is not the representative of our faith, nor do we look to him to be a Christian leader, let alone the "Christian in chief." To repeat: Our eyes are wide open.

At the same time, we will be quick to thank him for doing good, we will stand with him against unfair criticism, and we will pray that he will truly know and walk with the Lord.

In my opinion, Ross is reading far too much into the president's speech at the Values Voter Summit, as if the audience should not have appreciated his presence there—again, he was the first sitting president to address this convention—and as if they should have booed, rather than cheered, when he made his "Merry Christmas" comments.

Most evangelicals I know grimace when he sends out a "Psycho Joe" tweet but rejoice when he appoints a Neil Gorsuch to the Supreme Court. They're willing to put up with the former for the sake of the latter, although they wish the former would finally stop. And you can be assured they are not mistaking Donald Trump for the apostle Paul. Trust me on that.

October 30, 2017

What Martin Luther and Donald Trump Have in Common

★ ★ ★ ★ ★

THE differences between Martin Luther, the 16th century reformer, and Donald Trump, the 45th President of the United States, are countless. Yet, in some significant ways, they are very similar, and understanding the one helps us to understand the other.

Again, to be clear, the differences between these two men are countless.

Luther spent years as a celibate monk; Trump spent years as a philandering playboy.

Luther was a theologian turned reformer; Trump is a businessman turned politician.

Luther translated the entire Bible into German, word for word; Trump, at best, has a superficial knowledge of parts of the Bible.

Luther literally changed world history; Trump's impact on history remains to be seen.

And yet these two men bear striking similarities that are worth exploring.

Now, had I not been speaking in Germany this past weekend, I probably would not have thought of comparing Luther to Trump. But while conversing with some leaders about the strengths and weaknesses of Luther, I immediately thought of the strengths and weaknesses of Trump.

Luther was a courageous, even bull-headed leader, a man who took on the establishment of his day, both religiously and politically. Indeed, in terms of its breadth and scope and power, the establishment Luther faced down was far greater than anything Trump will ever face.

Yet almost singlehandedly, Luther took on the Church of his day, an entity that spanned continents and had immense power and wealth and influence. This required a forehead of steel and a courage that was as stubborn as it was fearless. This required the mindset of a wrecking ball.

But Luther's strengths were also his weaknesses, and just as he was responsible for much good—really, an immeasurable amount of good—he was also responsible for much bad.

His words often got him in trouble—shall I quote here some of his worst sayings regarding the Jewish people, the peasants, or the Anabaptists?—and his bullheaded style of leadership made for him many unneeded enemies. Can you see why I liken him to Trump? (For those in the know, Luther's *Table Talk* can be compared to Trump's Twitter account.)

Clearly, I'm not trying to make a detailed comparison between their personalities, which from what I can tell were quite dissimilar. But when one thinks of the strengths and weaknesses of Luther, one immediately thinks of the strengths and weaknesses of Trump.

Donald Trump backs down from no one, and he is absolutely bull-headed in his convictions. If he feels he is right, he will take on the world, and I mean that quite literally. He will take on the American media; he will take on Congress; he will take on Russia and China. You oppose him, and he will fight you to the finish.

He is also an anti-establishment figure, and it is this quality that earned him many of his votes. His constituents were sick and tired of the status quo, sick and tired of politics as usual, and they wanted someone who would rock the boat. They wanted a wrecking ball and they got one.

But here too, Trump's strengths are his weaknesses. At times he has divided when he could have unified; he has alienated when he could have reconciled; he has used a sledgehammer when a scalpel was needed.

Do you see why I draw a parallel between these two men?

Luther was truly a world changer, one of the most influential men who ever lived, a man responsible for a massive amount of good, both spiritually and culturally. But at what cost?

Trump is in the process of writing his legacy, and he can still be a powerful and effective president. But at what cost?

To the extent he can harness his strengths while working on his weaknesses, the good will outweigh the bad. To the extent his weaknesses become dominant, the bad could outweigh the good.

Isn't this a good reason to pray for President Trump as we commemorate the 500th anniversary of Luther's reformation?

November 18, 2017

An Evangelical Appeal to President Trump Regarding His Al Franken Tweets

★ ★ ★ ★ ★

Dear Mr. President,

I write to you with the utmost respect and with great appreciation for all you have done for the pro-life cause and to help preserve religious liberties in our nation. And as an evangelical leader who voted for you last year, I write as a friend, not as a foe. Would you kindly consider if there might be some truth to my words?

I know that you were surprised and moved when you received so much support from evangelical Christians, since you were not exactly a poster boy for the conservative Christian faith. And to be totally candid, it was hard for many of us to support you, since sexual purity and marital faithfulness are very important to us.

Yet we believed you would be a strong leader willing to take on the Washington establishment, that you would stand with Israel, and that you would be a far better choice than Hillary for many obvious reasons. We also believed that you took our counsel seriously, although we hardly expected you to be a saint.

Even when that terribly embarrassing tape came out with your vulgar comments about women, we were still willing to vote for you. After all, the tape was over 10 years old, and you made clear that you weren't proud of it. And to be frank, you were hardly known for having a lofty sexual ethic back then.

In any event, your voters were willing to forgive and move forward, with the hope that scandals like this would remain in the past. And we weren't entirely convinced that the women raising further sexual charges against you were credible.

Either way, you got our vote, and I know you appreciated our support.

In that light, it strikes me (and many others) as quite inappropriate that you are gleefully tweeting against Senator Al Franken, asking, "Where do his hands go in pictures 2, 3, 4, 5 & 6 while [Leeann Tweeden] sleeps? ...And to think that just last week he was lecturing anyone who would listen about sexual harassment and respect for women. Lesley Stahl tape?"[1]

Certainly, Franken's actions are inexcusable, and he will face the heat for those actions in the Senate and beyond. But this happened more than 10 years ago, similar to your infamous conversation with Billy Bush about what you, as a star, could do to women. And so, if it was hypocritical of Franken to lecture people about sexual harassment and respect for women, is it proper for you to do so?

Jesus taught a parable about the importance of showing mercy to others after we ourselves have received mercy. If we don't, mercy will not be shown to us again. (When you can, please read Matthew 18:23-35.) Do you see how this could be relevant to you today?

I know Al Franken has been one of your political opponents, and I can understand why you jumped on the news of his misconduct in 2006. In fact, your staff has forcefully defended your "Al Frankenstien."[2] And without a doubt, it's appropriate that Senator Franken faces an uncertain political future.

I'm simply appealing to you as an evangelical leader to reconsider whether you should be leading the charge against him with your influential tweets.

I too have received much mercy from the Lord and in that spirit, I ask you to step back and spend a few quiet minutes before Him, reflecting on how much mercy He has had on you.

From that perspective, you might reconsider your approach to Senator Franken's current crisis.

November 28, 2017

Donald Trump and the Principle of Divine Upheaval

★ ★ ★ ★ ★

WHETHER you are a friend or foe of President Trump, there's no question that his political presence has produced unprecedented shaking and upheaval. How do we explain this phenomenon, and just how widespread is it? And is it possible that the Trump presidency is directly connected to women coming forward with claims of sexual abuse at the hands of the rich and powerful?

During last year's presidential campaign, Lance Wallnau, an evangelical strategist and speaker, wrote a bestselling book in which he described Donald Trump as "God's chaos candidate." (The full title of the book was *God's Chaos Candidate: Donald J. Trump and the American Unraveling*.) Wallnau also likened Trump to a divinely appointed "wrecking ball" against political correctness (and more). How much upheaval has President Trump brought in his wake?

Before getting into details, let me explain how it is that certain people have the effect of bringing hidden or suppressed things to the surface.

In biblical terms, and with wholly positive connotations, the Lord told His people that He would come as a "refiner's fire." Such a fire reveals the impurities of gold and silver when they are tossed into the mega-hot flames. (See Malachi 3:1-5.) The precious metals may look fine to the naked eye, but once they're subjected to the super-heated fire, all the dross rises up to the top, making for an ugly sight.

To use another biblical image, an old Jewish man named Simeon prophesied over the baby Jesus that, through Him, the "thoughts from many hearts may be revealed" (Luke 2:34-35). Jesus, by His words and deeds, would expose the secrets of people's hearts, as they came out radically for Him or against Him. When He came to town, you found out who people really were and where they really stood.

When it comes to Donald Trump, his strengths are as glaring as his weaknesses, and people line up to bless him or curse him based on whether they admire his strengths or despise his weaknesses.

So, in stark contrast to Jesus, whose perfections brought things to the surface, it is President Trump's imperfections that are bringing things to the surface today. But when someone like Trump comes on the scene, speaking his mind whether you like it or not, neutrality quickly vanishes. Sides are taken, and with great passion. Lines are drawn, and with great force. Inner thoughts are openly spoken, with little restraint or nuance.

This is part of the Trump effect, part of the wake that follows in his path.

Consider the effect on the media. The divisions between right and left, conservative and liberal, have never been clearer than they are today. It is almost impossible to be neutral to Trump. Those who are against him are really against him—overtly, consistently, doggedly, unashamedly. Those who are for him are really for him—always defending him, always taking his side, with no apologies or explanations needed.

In the larger world of politics, not only have Democrat and Republican divides deepened, but there are now cracks and fissures within the president's own party, separating the old guard from the new, the swamp dwellers from the swamp drainers. Trump is just as likely to feud with Paul Ryan or Mitch McConnell as he is with Nancy Pelosi or Chuck Schumer. Does anyone recall something like this under Presidents Obama, Bush II, Clinton, Bush I, or Reagan?

Looking at the society as a whole, the Trump phenomenon has heightened racial divisions, ethnic divisions, and even gender divisions.

Personally, I do not believe that the president is a white supremacist or a "male chauvinist pig," but his nationalistic appeals, his siding with the police rather than the victim (just as President Obama often did the opposite), and his history of sexist remarks make him into an easily caricatured figure.

Accordingly, because of Trump (and I'm neither blaming him nor praising him), both the alt-right and the radical left have emerged out of the shadows with much greater definition. And because of Trump, more and more women have decided to speak up and speak out, shouting to the world that he is not fit to be their president. This much is self-evident and hardly big news.

But is it possible that it is this very atmosphere that has led to so many women coming forward to accuse everyone from Harvey Weinstein to John Conyers of sexual misconduct? Is it possible that this is another aspect of the divinely appointed "wrecking ball" role of Trump?

Of course, the timing could be completely coincidental, perhaps related more to the Bill Cosby allegations than to anything else. At the same time, it's a bit uncanny that, with so much in our society shaking since candidate (and now President) Trump came on the scene, Hollywood and Congress are being shaken with sexual allegations.

If this is the case and the Trump presidency means that there will be a whole lot more shaking going on, then here's a word to the wise. Make sure your own house is in order, since your house might be the next to shake.

December 6, 2017

WILL GOD BLESS TRUMP FOR MOVING OUR EMBASSY TO JERUSALEM?

★ ★ ★ ★ ★

BEN Shapiro listed seven reasons why Trump's decision to move our embassy to Jerusalem is right, calling it "an act of not only political bravery but moral courage."[1] But is it an act that God Himself will bless? Is there spiritual significance to this decision as well?

Earlier this year, a pastor asked me if there was any way to get a message to the president. With great passion, he said to me, "During the campaign, Donald Trump promised to move the embassy his first day in office, but he didn't do it. And when did the protest marches against him begin? His second day in office! He will never see the full blessing of God until he makes good on his promise."

Others believe that Trump's decision will prove disastrous. As a headline on the *Daily Mail* proclaims, "'He's declaring war on 1.5 billion Muslims': Trump will recognise Jerusalem as Israel's capital TODAY despite international fury from the Pope, Britain, Russia, China and Palestinians."[2] In the words of the Palestinian Authority's Manuel Hassassian, "He is declaring war in the Middle East, he is declaring war against 1.5 billion Muslims [and] hundreds of millions of Christians that are not going to accept the holy shrines to be totally under the hegemony of Israel."

In reality, Trump is not declaring war in the Middle East, not declaring war against 1.5 billion Muslims, and in no way, shape, size, or form declaring war on hundreds of millions of Christians. In fact, the very notion that Christians will not accept "the holy shrines" being "totally under the hegemony of Israel" is absolute nonsense.

First, America's recognition of Jerusalem as Israel's capital changes nothing on the ground at all, especially when it comes to the Christian holy sites, which have been under Israeli hegemony for decades. Second, it is under Jewish hegemony that Middle Eastern Christians have access to these holy sites and freedom to practice their faith. The restrictions generally come under Islamic, not Israeli rule.

Still, the question must be asked: Why the uproar over Jerusalem? Why does the whole world care? Why does the Pope weigh in? Why are Muslim nations in such upheaval? Why are Russia and China concerned? What makes Jerusalem so important?

Jerusalem was never the capital of a Palestinian or Arab state. (For that matter, there was not even a concept of a Palestinian state until the middle of the 20th century and no such thing as a Palestinian people until after the Six Day War in 1967.)

Every other nation on the planet chooses its capital city and the other nations recognize that city and put their embassies there. Why won't the rest of the world recognize Jerusalem as Israel's capital? Why are the embassies located in Tel Aviv rather than Jerusalem?

Jerusalem is the historic capital of the Jewish people, going back to roughly 1,000 B.C. Jews face Jerusalem when they pray and synagogues in the West face East, while every year at Passover, the hopeful prayer is recited, "Next year in Jerusalem!" And in terms of functional reality, Jerusalem is the capital of the nation. There's nothing to discuss or debate. That's reality, plain and simple.[3]

When it comes to the peace process, more than two decades of negotiations have yielded precious little progress, so the idea that recognizing Jerusalem would hurt this process is ludicrous. Instead, if the Palestinians want peace with Israel, they can have wonderful, lasting, prosperous peace—without dividing Jerusalem.

But all these are political questions and issues. My question is spiritual in nature: Will God bless President Trump and the United States for making this bold and courageous move?

I believe He will, since: 1) in doing so the president is blessing Israel, and God still blesses[4] those who bless His covenant nation, despite that nation's sins; 2) out of all the cities on the earth, the Bible only calls us to pray for the welfare of Jerusalem (see Ps. 122; Isa. 62:1-8); 3) the tremendous resistance to the president's decision gives evidence to the intensity of the spiritual battle over this city; and 4) there are prophetic scriptures that speak of a Jewish Jerusalem welcoming back the Messiah, and so the decision to fortify the unity of the city is in explicit harmony with those scriptures (see especially Zech. 12 and 14).

And what about God's love for the Muslim world? What about justice for the Palestinians?

The answer is simple: If they want to be blessed, they too must recognize the Jewish claim to Jerusalem, a city that they do not need to possess or divide. They don't need to call for violence and war. Instead, they need to accept that East Jerusalem will not be the capital of a Palestinian state, that working with the Jewish people rather than against them will be in their best interests too, and that the Jewish people have a massively greater claim to Jerusalem than the Muslims do.

As for President Trump, he is convinced that this formal recognition of Jerusalem will aid and abet the peace process. But even if that is not the case, I truly believe that God will bless him and bless America for making this courageous and righteous decision.

Let's watch and see in the coming days.

January 5, 2018

HAS PRESIDENT TRUMP LOST HIS MIND OR HAS CNN LOST ITS BEARINGS?

★ ★ ★ ★ ★

HOUR after hour, with unrelenting intensity, CNN reporters bring the grim news. It appears that President Trump has lost his mind. This is a serious report about a serious story, without any bias or malice. It's looking really grim.

Yes, we are told, about a dozen senators and representatives met last month with Yale psychiatrist Bandy X. Lee, deeply concerned about the president's mental health. (Of course, they were not biased either.)

"Lawmakers were saying they have been very concerned about this, the President's dangerousness, the dangers that his mental instability poses on the nation," Lee told CNN by phone last Thursday. "They know the concern is universal among Democrats, but it really depends on Republicans, they said. Some knew of Republicans that were concerned, maybe equally concerned, but whether they would act on those concerns was their worry."[1]

Of course, Dr. Lee is not biased either. She is telling us the shocking facts.

And what did she tell the congressmen who met with her? One came on CNN to explain, sounding like a doctor who must inform the patient's family that there's nothing that can be done. Yes, the president's condition is untreatable and incurable. He's showing increasing signs of paranoia, delusion, and isolation. It's all downhill from here.

Politico reported[2] on the meeting on January 3 before CNN jumped on it, while leaks from the new, Trump-bashing tell-all book provided the perfect backdrop, not to mention the president's verbal attack on Steve Bannon adding further fuel to the fire.

And on and on the story goes on CNN, with the utmost seriousness and without the slightest self-consciousness that their "reporting" might appear to be in the least bit biased. Not at all. They're just doing their job. (Hey, at least they weren't advocating smoking pot[3] on the air, right?)

Unfortunately, not only does their anti-Trump prejudice jump off the screen, but their reporting hardly considers that this is the same old story being repackaged again.

Consider this headline from *Mother Jones* dated September 24, 2017: "A Group of Experts Wrote a Book About Donald Trump's Mental Health—and the Controversy Has Just Begun."[4]

In the words of Bill Moyers, who interviewed psychohistorian Robert Jay Lifton in the article, "Some of the descriptions used to describe Trump—narcissistic personality disorder, antisocial personality disorder, paranoid personality disorder, delusional disorder, malignant narcissist—even some have suggested early forms of dementia—are difficult for lay people to grasp. Some experts say that it's not one thing that's wrong with him—there are a lot of things wrong with him and together they add up to what one of your colleagues calls 'a scary witches brew, a toxic stew.'"

Note also that Dr. Lee was cited in this article as well.

Two months earlier, on July 25, 2017, Chelsea Schilling posted an op-ed piece on World Net Daily, stating:

It's a "gag rule" that mental-health professionals have followed for 44 years: It's unethical for psychiatrists to "diagnose" politicians or public figures based solely on that person's public actions or statements, without conducting an actual in-person examination.

But now that Donald Trump is president, a national psychology organization has given psychoanalysts the green light to publicly comment on Trump's mental health. And the move could usher in a flood of mental-health "experts" on TV news programs claiming the president is unstable or even unfit to serve in the White House.

Without ever having examined Trump, psychological professionals already have called the president "psychotic," "narcissistic," "paranoid," "hypomanic," "emotionally unstable," "delusional" and "psychologically isolated" and claimed he has a "dangerous mental illness." One physician suggested Trump could be suffering from an untreated sexually transmitted disease known as neurosyphilis.[5]

Three months before that, on May 16, 2017, the (totally unbiased) Huffington Post ran this headline: "Fears Over Trump's Mental State Gaining Traction In The Media." Then, "'We can't maintain the pretense that Trump is a sane and balanced adult, however much we'd like to,' says Andrew Sullivan."

Three months before that, on February 16, 2017, *Psychology Today* ran this two-part story: "Is Donald Truly Delusional? The president and mental incapacitation."

And four months before that, on October 16, 2016, an article on Slate noted:

Several people, spanning media and medicine, have tried to answer these questions, psychologizing Trump or at least discussing the propriety of psychologizing Trump. Can we blame the candidate's apparent insanity on an actual psychological condition? Are we watching the manifestation of a severe case of narcissistic personality disorder?

There have been cautiously speculative stories in the *New York Times*, here on *Slate,* in *Vanity Fair* and the *Washington Post* and the *Atlantic*, all of them seeming to grow from the same unspoken wish: to explain away the crazy by labeling it as a real disorder. We like to put a name to our monsters. Diagnosing Trump, whether doing so without examining him is proper or not, helps.

So, it looks like CNN's big story is the same old recycled story from the 2016 elections, with this one twist: This deluded, narcissistic candidate who was crazy enough to believe that he could become the President of the United States actually *did* become the president.

That, to CNN, is the scariest possible news of all.

Postscript: While doing research for this article, another headline popped on my screen: "Donald Trump SHOCKED After Daughter Publicly Admits to Taking Controversial 'Skinny Pill'—Behind Her Amazing Transformation!"

Upon further investigation, I discovered that this was just an ad, not news at all. These days, it's hard to tell what's real news and what's not.

January 13, 2018

As Evangelicals Our Ultimate Allegiance Is to the Lord, Not the President

★ ★ ★ ★ ★

I don't know why this is so difficult. When the president does the right thing, we commend him and encourage him. When he does the wrong thing, with full respect for his office, we express our differences. Is this really so hard?

That's what I did with President Obama, for whom I didn't vote and with whom I had much more occasion to be critical than to be positive. And that's what I've sought to do with President Trump, for whom I did vote and with whom I've had a lot to be positive about and a fair deal to be negative about.

As followers of Jesus, our ultimate allegiance should be to the Lord, to the truth, to righteousness, to justice, not to a party or a man.

We should be model citizens in terms of our conduct, and we should show honor to whom honor is due, as Paul exhorted in Romans 13. (Remember: Paul wrote Romans when the notorious Nero was the emperor of Rome. Yet as the leader of the empire, he was to be treated with respect.)

But when push comes to shove, we are not Republicans or Democrats or Independents. We are followers of Jesus. And so, when it comes to speaking the truth to power, we are "equal opportunity offenders" (although we need not be offensive in our speech; I'm just using the expression).

As for our relationship with President Trump, it's true that some evangelical leaders have had access to him behind closed doors, and it's appropriate for them to address their concerns to him in private. That means that, when he says or does something that is highly objectionable, they say to the public, "I understand why there is an uproar over this and I recognize why you are concerned. Be assured that I have spoken to the president about these very matters, and the president gave me a listening ear."

For the rest of us evangelical leaders who do not have access to the White House, if we are going to voice our approval when Mr. Trump does well, we should likewise voice our disapproval when he does poorly. Otherwise, we appear to be flunkies for the president, more committed to opposing the liberal media than for standing for what is right, more interested in political favor than in the smile of God.

Since when do we lose our voice once we vote for a candidate? Since when do we become yes men once that candidate begins to implement some of our key agenda items? Isn't our witness to the nation more important than the favor of a political leader? So what if liberal Christian leaders often act like flunkies for their candidates. Why should we do the same?

There is no one on the planet more loyal to me than my wife Nancy, but I would be shocked and disappointed if she didn't tell a colleague when asked, "Yes, I really disagreed with Mike on that one. We had totally opposite perspectives."

That only empowers her to tell my critics, "But you have no idea who he is. You could not be more wrong in your perceptions about my husband."

Her candor when it comes to my mistakes or shortcomings only makes her testimony of my character and strengths all the more believable.

Why can't do we the same with President Trump? Even those leaders who believed that God was raising him up to be our president likened him to Cyrus in the Bible, a man of whom the Lord said, "I give a name to you, though you do not know Me" (Isa. 45:4 HCSB). In today's terms, we would say, "The Lord is using him, even though he's not one of us."

Why must we always act as if he is 100 percent one of us already, as if he were a mature, exemplary Christian, a seasoned man of God?

One evangelical leader who strongly supports Trump called him "God's chaos candidate" and likened him to a divine wrecking ball. Must we defend everything that wrecking ball says and does? Will not there be some collateral damage that we regret? Why must we whitewash the White House to show loyalty or support?

Nancy voted for Trump with great reluctance, concerned that he would have a divisive, vulgarizing effect on the nation and wondering if that would be too great a price to pay for the good that he might do. (Under no circumstances, of course, was she going to vote for Hillary.)

You could say that her fears have been realized (most recently, with the "s—hole" comments, with that objectionable word now plastered everywhere and repeated non-stop). At the same time, she is totally aware of the extraordinary media bias against the president and she does appreciate the good he has done. She also knows it takes a forehead of steel to do the job.

But when it comes to the president's recent comments, why can't we say, "If this is an accurate quote, we reject it wholeheartedly, and we urge the president to clarify what he was saying and to reach out to the offended nations."

We don't need to parse his words, let alone defend them. We need to show integrity. Once we've done that, we can say, "What's amazing is that the media looked the other way when so-and-so said such-and-such," exposing their hypocrisy and agenda. And then we can say, "Where I think the president has a valid point (assuming there is one) is here."

But our first calling is not to defend the president, a man whom I love, pray for, and honor, and a man whose positive actions I deeply appreciate.

Our first calling is to stand as consistent witnesses for our Lord, to be ambassadors of righteousness and truth, and to be jealous for the reputation of Jesus.

Nothing is more important than our witness to a watching world.

January 21, 2018

AN HONEST CHALLENGE FOR
THE NEVER TRUMPERS

★ ★ ★ ★ ★

DURING the Republican primaries, I was very nearly a Never Trumper, so I'm quite sympathetic to that mindset. But I have a challenge for all of you who still identify as Never Trumpers: Are you willing to be as honest about the accomplishments of President Trump as you are about his failings?

For many of you who could not vote for Trump, it was a matter of conscience. How could you be a "values voter" and yet vote for a man with such abysmal moral values, a thrice-married playboy billionaire?

Put another way, your integrity compelled you to be a Never Trumper. But does your integrity now compel you to admit where he has done well? Where he has kept his promises? Where he has championed causes that really matter to "value voters"? Where he has stood strong for some of the great moral issues of the day?

Lest you think I'm being one-sided in my challenge to Never Trumpers, in June I wrote an article titled "Don't Sell Your Soul Defending the Words of President Trump." And earlier this month I penned, "As Evangelicals Our Ultimate Allegiance is to the Lord, Not the President," just to give two examples.

In short, I concur with prominent Never Trumper David French, who just last month counseled his colleagues to follow these guidelines: "Praise him when he's right, critique him when he's wrong, apply the same standards to your own side that you apply to ideological opponents, and keep your eyes fixed on the larger, more important cultural trends."[1]

But have Never Trumpers done this? On a regular basis, those of us who voted for Trump are called on to repudiate his latest ill-advised comment or tweet, or to condemn a past indiscretion. And with words similar to French's, I recently wrote, "When the president does the right thing, we commend him and encourage him. When he does the wrong thing, with full respect for his office, we express our differences. Is this really so hard?"

But I ask again, have you done this as Never Trumpers? Doesn't your integrity compel you to be even-handed, or, perhaps, to acknowledge where, at times, you may have been wrong?

Since the media bombards us 24/7 with the latest failings or alleged failings of the President, there's no need for me to rehearse them here. Only the most extreme pro-Trumpers view him as a flawless saint.

But will you, my Never Trumper friends, be as truthful in your praise as you have been in your criticism?

Consider the President's pro-life words and actions.

He appointed Neil Gorsuch to the Supreme Court, along with a score of fine justices for other federal positions. This alone is highly significant.

Last week, "The Department of Justice (DOJ) filed an amicus (or 'friend-of-the-court') brief at the Supreme Court Wednesday, urging the justices to overturn a California law requiring pro-life crisis pregnancy centers to post information about state-funded abortions."[2] Could anything be more anti-Obama than this?

Also last week, Trump made history as the first sitting president to address the March for Life in DC, which begs the question: Why didn't our previous pro-life presidents do this? And in his speech, he criticized Roe v. Wade by name.[3]

In terms of actions taken so far, was Vice President Pence exaggerating when he called Trump the "most pro-life" president in our history? Pence "boasted of a litany of anti-abortion measures by the Trump administration over its first year: Banning federal funds for global health groups that promote abortion under the 'Mexico City policy,' defunding the United Nations Population Fund, and over-turning an Obama administration rule that required states to provide funding for Planned Parenthood."[4]

How about Trump's actions opposing LGBT activism and standing for religious freedoms?

For the first time in eight years, last June was not gay pride month. In contrast, January 16 was just proclaimed "Religious Freedom Day."

Evaluating Trump's first year in office, a headline on The Hill announces, "Trump administration amasses striking anti-LGBT record in first year." Similarly, a headline on The Conversation describes 2017 as "the year of transgender moral panic."

To give one case in point, The Hill reported last October that, "Attorney General Jeff Sessions is reversing course on the Justice Department's policy that a 1964 civil rights law protects transgender individuals from discrimination."[5]

And in stark contrast with the Obama administration's aggressive pushing of transgender activism in our children's schools, the DOJ under Trump has reversed course here as well. This too is quite major. (It does not bring me joy that transgenders and their allies feel threatened or insecure; it does bring me joy that sanity is prevailing in our schools.)

Trump is also the first president to take a major step in repealing the onerous Johnson Amendment, although more still needs to be done to make this far-reaching and permanent.

And what of Trump's decision to move our embassy to Jerusalem, along with his calling out of the Palestinian authority's deception?

For many conservative voters, these are some of the most important issues—the sanctity of life and marriage, preserving religious freedoms, standing with Israel.

And what of the strength of the economy? The decimation of ISIS?

Do you have the integrity to commend the President for the good he has done?

Steve Deace says it well:

I was once NeverTrump. I have called our current president both a narcissist and a child. Compared him to both Peter Pan and former pro wrestling manager extraordinaire Bobby "The Brain" Heenan.

But...

The news that the Trump administration is setting up a new division within the Department of Health and Human Services to protect the conscience rights of doctors, nurses, and other health-care providers is unambiguously good. It allows HHS to come to the defense of conscientious objectors working in the health-care field by defending the God-given rights of those who opt out of "certain procedures"—like the killing field that is abortion or gender-bending sex-change operations.

This "is an outcome that simply wouldn't and couldn't have happened if Hillary Clinton was president," nor, Deace reasons, likely would have happened under an establishment candidate like Mitt Romney.

So, once more, my appeal to the Never Trumpers: Will you demonstrate your integrity by recognizing the good President Trump has done without overbalancing your statement with a litany of the negatives, at least just this one time? And might you even acknowledge that, in some important ways, he has done better than you expected?

I look forward to hearing your responses.

January 25, 2018

DOES TRUMP GET A MORAL MULLIGAN?

★ ★ ★ ★ ★

THERE is a firestorm of controversy over the comments of evangelical leader Tony Perkins that President Trump gets a "mulligan" for his past sexual indiscretions, as headline after headline reports on this apparently outrageous statement. To quote Perkins directly from his interview with Erin Burnett on CNN, "Yes, evangelicals, conservatives, they gave him a mulligan. They let him have a do-over. They said we'll start afresh with you and we'll give you a second chance."[1]

On the one hand, I can understand the outrage. We evangelicals didn't give Bill Clinton a mulligan, and we're certainly not giving Harvey Weinstein a mulligan. And since we claim to be champions of marital fidelity and sexual purity, we could not have picked a worst poster boy for our cause—at least that is what we're told.

As Michael Gerson wrote in the *Washington Post*, "The Trump evangelicals have lost their gag reflex."[2] Yes, we evangelicals have made our "political bargain with open eyes."

Trump, Gerson argues, "has made profanity an unavoidable part of our political culture. He is in the midst of a gathering corruption scandal that has left close aides under indictment. He tells repeated and obvious lies. He incites ethnic and racial resentment as a political strategy and was caught on tape bragging about sexual assault. Add to this something that could never be said of Nixon: the credible accusation that Trump paid hush money to a porn star to cover up an affair."

And how does Franklin Graham respond to this? "We certainly don't hold him up as the pastor of this nation and he is not. But I appreciate the fact that the president does have a concern for Christian values, he does have a concern to protect Christians whether it's here at home or around the world, and I appreciate the fact that he protects religious liberty and freedom."[3]

For Gerson and others, this is the height of hypocrisy, and there is no excuse for the fact that, in his words, Trump evangelicals have become "sycophants, cheerleaders and enablers."

From my perspective, to the extent we have minimized Trump's past transgressions or turned him into a modern-day saint, there is some truth to these allegations. We have lost our moral compass.

But that is only one side of the story, and this is what many people find impossible to grasp: We voted for Donald Trump with our eyes wide open and without compromising our faith.

If he did, in fact, have a fling with this porn star (which he denies) and pay to keep her quiet, we would not be surprised. And when he does use profanity (as many other presidents did before him), we are not surprised. And when he's caught in a lie, we are not surprised. Grieved, yes; surprised, no.

We don't overlook his past transgressions, we don't hail him as the exemplar of marital fidelity, and we don't say to our constituents, "Follow Trump, as he follows Christ" (to echo Paul's words in 1 Corinthians 11:1).

Rather, we say this: Babies are being slaughtered by Planned Parenthood, and this flawed man is willing to help us stop the slaughter. Christians are being massacred by ISIS, and this flawed man is willing to help stop the bloodshed. Our religious liberties are being threatened, and this flawed man is willing to take a stand on our behalf.

So, we appreciate him, we support him in carrying out his campaign promises, and as best as we can, behind closed doors and in other settings, we encourage him to step higher and to take the claims of Jesus seriously.

How is that hypocritical? How is that immoral? How is that compromised?

We weren't impressed when he held up his family Bible during the campaign, and we weren't surprised when he couldn't quote a single verse from memory. We know the man we voted for.

And he knows who he is too, saying in his acceptance speech at the Republican National Convention, "At this moment, I would like to thank the evangelical community because, I will tell you what, the support they have given me—and I'm not sure I totally deserve it—has been so amazing. And has been such a big reason I'm here tonight. They have much to contribute to our policies."[4]

A political insider even told me that, during the campaign, when he asked Trump to take a strong stand on a marriage-related issue, he said, "I can't do that, given my history."

I can't confirm this firsthand (although my source says he heard it for himself), but I can confirm that I've never heard Trump put himself forward as a paragon of marital virtue, which would make sense.

As for giving him a mulligan, that's what you call the gospel. God forgives us, and we forgive others, especially if they recognize their guilt and seek to make positive changes.

To this very moment, I feel confident that if Bill Clinton came forward and confessed to his past adulteries, taking full responsibility, seeking to make restitution, and asking for forgiveness, we would line up to be the first to forgive publicly. And should he then say, "I've had a change of heart regarding abortion," we would welcome him as a colleague on the front lines of the pro-life movement.

In certain ways, Trump has presented more of a mixed bag in that he continues to engage in unchristian behavior while, at the same time, making a clear break with his past. Yet he has consistently welcomed evangelical Christians into his life, he has listened attentively when they have spoken to him, and, to my knowledge, he has never rebuffed their calls for him to change.

So, while he remains a work in progress, he continues to champion many important causes, and with all his blemishes, he is our president.

Do we not, then, grant him a mulligan when it comes to his past? And if we were to learn that he committed adultery 50 times in his former life, would this change our view of him today?

To repeat: We voted for him with our eyes wide open (at least, most of us did), and we can support him, with the necessary caveats, without denying or compromising our faith.

What's so scandalous about that?

January 27, 2018

DONALD TRUMP
DID NOT DIE FOR MY SINS
★ ★ ★ ★ ★

I was scheduled to be on CNN this week to debate another commentator about evangelicals and President Trump, but due to breaking news, the debate was cancelled. Had I been on the air, I planned to make this point: With all respect to our president, and with my appreciation for the good things he has done, he did not die for my sins, and I have not staked my soul's salvation on his reputation. That distinction belongs to Jesus the Messiah, and to Jesus alone.

Why the need to state something that is so totally self-evident?

It's because evangelicals are being judged on the character and accomplishments of our president rather than on the character and accomplishments of our Lord, hence the need to remind a watching world that there is only one Savior, and His name is not Trump.

Unfortunately, in large part due to the media's anti-Trump frenzy, if you dared to vote for Trump, let alone speak a positive word of support on his behalf, you are considered complicit in his every failing, be it an adulterous affair in his past or an inappropriate tweet in the present. Wherever Trump is guilty (or perceived to be guilty), you are guilty. And if you dared endorse him, you have committed the unpardonable sin.

One of my ministry school grads was having a conversation with a stranger while they waited in line at an event. The conversation turned spiritual, and my former student began to share his faith. The stranger asked him, "Did you vote for Trump?" When he said yes, the man refused to talk anymore. Jesus was not the issue; Trump was.

A Christian woman told me that a close family member is no longer open to hear about Jesus because she voted for Trump. The conduct and character of this Christian woman no longer matter. The message of redemption through the cross does not matter. All that matters is that this family member perceives Trump to be a dangerous buffoon, and anyone who voted for him cannot be taken seriously.

May I suggest that, at least in part, this is a demonic attempt to turn people away from the Lord? May I suggest that our message has never been tethered to a politician? May I suggest that we fight against this aggressively, not by defending Trump but rather by asking more basic questions, such as: "If you were starving and I offered you free, healthy food, would you ask if I voted for Trump before you accepted it? If you were drowning and I reached out my hand to save you, would you choose to drown if you knew that I had voted for Trump?"

The point is that the gospel message states that people are perishing without Jesus, but through Him we can freely offer salvation. This is good news regardless of who we voted for. It saves the lost whether we who bring the message are Republicans or Democrats. We must proclaim this without fear and shame.

You might say, "But your analogies are not precise. Because you voted for Trump, we question your moral judgment, because of which we question your message."

I'm quite aware of that objection, and that's why I used the examples I did.

The issue here is one of eternal life and death, of salvation or damnation, which means it's even more pressing than the issue of starving or drowning. If you are guilty in God's sight and worthy of His judgment, and we have a message of eternal forgiveness and pardon, does it really matter who we voted for?

I agree that some evangelicals have so visibly hitched themselves to Trump and/or the Republican Party that we have compromised our integrity, as if political power was of greater importance to us than serving a lost and hurting world. We alone are to blame for this, and we alone can fix this. I do not minimize this for a moment.

At the same time, the very liberals who thrash us daily for our political affiliation as followers of Jesus had no problem with Christian support of Barack Obama and Hillary Clinton, despite their support of the slaughter of the unborn and despite their largely ignoring the Christian genocide in the Middle East. Why no shrill cries of hypocrisy? Why no protest marches in the streets? Why no one saying, "If you voted for Obama (or Hillary), I won't listen to your gospel message?"

For me, the solution is simple. When asked how I voted, I'm happy to say, "I voted for Donald Trump, but I did so with hope mixed with reservation. That's why on some days I'm tremendously proud of him while on other days, I cringe. But given the choice of Hillary or Trump, I'm glad I voted for him. At the same time, I find no need to defend him when he falls short, nor am I presenting him as a model Christian. That's also why I pray for him."

If I'm dealing with an honest, thinking human being, I don't see how this can be viewed as a hindrance to the gospel. That's why I'm not going to accept my vote for Trump as a conversation ender. I'll do my best to turn it into a conversation starter, one that quickly turns from our president to our Savior. He's the only one I want to proclaim.

March 13, 2018

I AGREE WITH CHUCK TODD

★ ★ ★ ★ ★

I F the presidential elections were held today and Donald Trump was running against Hillary Clinton, I would vote for Donald Trump without hesitation. But that doesn't mean that he doesn't embarrass me at times. And when it comes to his recent attack on NBC's Chuck Todd, I side with Todd.

That's not because I agree with Todd's ideology or that I feel his reporting is fair and balanced.

To be perfectly candid, I don't see much of Todd's reporting and so I can't really comment either way.

But what I do know is that the President of the United States debases himself by getting into juvenile, even profane name-calling. And while he may rally certain elements of his base with this kind of rhetoric, he alienates another part of his base. He also further inflames his adversaries and gives fresh fuel to his detractors. And to what purpose? To what gain?

Speaking in Pennsylvania on Saturday, President Trump referred to Todd as a "sleeping son of a b—h," a remark that lit up the Internet within minutes.

On Sunday Todd responded: "I bring my kids up to respect the office of the presidency and the president. I don't allow them to say anything negative, ever, about the president. It creates a challenge to all parents when he uses vulgarities like that."[1]

He is absolutely right. The "b" word is now everywhere, spelled out in full, and repeated on the airwaves, just as "s—thole" word became ubiquitous after the president's alleged comments in January.

Suddenly, that which used to be censored is now acceptable. The profane is no longer profane. Civility (or, whatever is left of it) is further crushed underfoot.

This contributes to a general coarsening of the culture, while the ugly insults multiply exponentially as all sides fire back.

Without a doubt, having Donald Trump as our president has its big pluses and big minuses.

Of course, ardent Trump supporters will lambaste me, accusing me of prudery, of focusing on inconsequential details, of being a secret leftist at heart.

"Just look at what he's done for the economy, for Israel, for the courts, for our religious rights. And he's about to meet with the President of North Korea in what could be one of the greatest diplomatic breakthroughs of our era. Plus, he's virtually destroyed ISIS."

Again, that's why I would vote for him today against the likes of Hillary Clinton.

But the fact is that President Trump could have accomplished these same goals without degrading himself, without debasing the office of the president, without attacking others with crudeness and vulgarity, and without further dividing an already divided nation. Can anyone tell me how his cruelty helps his cause?

My appeal is that our president step higher, that he be aggressive and bold without acting like a child, that he be fearless without being frivolous. Only the blindly loyal will defend him at every turn, just as those blindly loyal to President Obama could see no wrong in him.

Appearing on "Face the Nation" on Sunday, *Washington Post* columnist Michael Gerson was asked, "What do you think the evangelicals who support President Trump make of the Stormy Daniels scandal?"

He replied, "Well, I think that it is the height of hypocrisy.... If any other Democratic president had been guilty of what is alleged in these cases, evangelicals would be, you know, off the reservation."[2]

But Gerson is only partly right since: 1) no Democratic president fought for the things Trump is fighting for, meaning that the overall picture is quite mixed; and 2) there are evangelicals who support President Trump while not endorsing his crude behavior or passing over his marital transgressions.

That being said, I agree with Gerson that evangelicals who downplay Trump's moral failings are guilty of hypocrisy and do compromise their witness. This is something I've addressed many times before.

Gerson further stated that, "Evangelicalism really has had a good tradition. And now they are really undermining that reputation of their faith."

This prompted Margaret Brennan to ask, "But, in that judgment, you are saying the transactional part of this relationship isn't worth the trade-off?"

Gerson replied:

Well, they are acting like, you know, slimy political operatives, not moral leaders.

They are essentially saying, in order to get benefits for themselves, in a certain way—they talk about religious liberty and other issues—but to get benefits for themselves, they are willing to wink at Stormy Daniels and wink at misogyny and wink at nativism.

And that, I think, is deeply discrediting, not just in a political sense, but actually in a moral and religious sense.[3]

Are some evangelicals acting like "slimy political operatives, not moral leaders"? Perhaps some are, just as some liberal Christian leaders have gotten into political bed with their Democratic counterparts.

But once again, Gerson is only partly right.

As evangelicals, we're not trying "to get benefits" for ourselves as much we're trying to advocate for what is best for our nation and the world. And when it comes to fighting against abortion, fighting against the genocide of Christians in the Middle East, fighting against the radical left's takeover of America—just to name some of our biggest issues—we absolutely support President Trump. We believe he's the man for the job.

Yet we don't pretend he is a virtuous Christian, while we are grieved over many things he says and does. As for the Stormy Daniels' allegations, if they are true, many of us would not be surprised. But we would urge our president to confess his past sins publicly and ask for forgiveness.

That's what true support looks like, and frankly, I fail to see what is hypocritical in taking a stand like this. As an evangelical leader I'm often embarrassed by our president, but I voted for him with my eyes wide open, weighing the good with the bad.

So, I will praise him for the great things he accomplishes and share my disappointment when he falls short.

That means that one day I'm celebrating President Trump for his bold and courageous leadership while the next day I'm regretting his cruel and crude attacks.

Today is one of those days when it's important for me to say, "Chuck Todd, I'm sorry for what our president said about you, and I agree with the sentiments you expressed."

Hopefully, tomorrow will be a different day.

March 13, 2018

JOY BEHAR, MIKE PENCE, DONALD TRUMP, AND THE QUESTION OF PUBLIC APOLOGIES

★ ★ ★ ★ ★

ACCORDING to Vice President Pence, Joy Behar needs to make a public apology for the anti-Christian comments she made on the View. According to Pastor Robert Jeffress, if President Trump did indeed commit adultery in the past with porn star Stormy Daniels, no public apology is needed. It's a matter between his family and God. How do we sort this out?

To Joy Behar's credit, she did call Mike Pence to apologize for her ugly comments, since her words were directed at him. As he told Sean Hannity, "I give Joy Behar a lot of credit. She picked up the phone. She called me. She was very sincere, and she apologized and one of the things my faith teaches me is grace; forgive as you've been forgiven."[1]

However, since she made the comments on national TV, Pence said, "I'm still encouraging her, to use the forum of that program or some other public forum, to apologize to tens of millions of Americans who were equally offended."

He's absolutely right, and it will be for Behar's own good to follow his advice. Sins committed publicly require public apologies. And in this case, because she sinned against people who are taught to forgive, I believe she will receive an outpouring of forgiveness if she is humble and sincere. Some will still scorn and mock her, but those with a true faith will forgive.

What about President Trump and his alleged affair with Stormy Daniels?

According to Pastor Jeffress, "Evangelicals knew they weren't voting for an altar boy when they voted for Donald Trump. We supported him because of his policies and his strong leadership."[2]

As to whether the president owes America an apology (if guilty), Jeffress explained that "evangelicals understand the concept of sin and forgiveness" since "we're all sinners" and "we all need forgiveness." That forgiveness, Jeffress continued, is available to everyone through Christ, and whether or not Trump needs that forgiveness (meaning, whether he's guilty of the porn star's charges) "is between him, his family, and his God."

Is Jeffress correct?

On the one hand, if a man committed adultery ten years ago, confessed that sin to his wife and family, and made things right with anyone else involved, there's no need for that to be disclosed publicly. As the Scriptures teach, "love covers a multitude of sins" (1 Pet. 4:8). Why put someone to shame for a privately committed sin, if it has been confessed and rectified? (We're not talking something like committing murder in private. That must be dealt with in public under the law, for many obvious reasons.)

There would be, however, one exception regarding private sins and private apologies: If the private sins related to someone's public responsibilities, then a public apology would be appropriate.

When it comes to allegations against the President of the United States, there are several factors involved.

First, if the allegations are true, then he is presently lying about them. That requires public confession and apology.

Second, the charges involve the payment of hush money to prevent election embarrassment, which is also a public issue.

Third, because the allegations have become public, they raise further questions about his character in the past, perhaps even beyond what some of us understood.

Speaking for myself, if the allegations are true, that wouldn't surprise me at all. This is pretty much who I understood him to be in the past. For others, this would be a disappointment.

Either way, while I appreciate Pastor Jeffress's gracious pastoral sentiments, if I were counseling the president, I would say this: "Sir, if the charges are true, even if

God, Melania and your family have already forgiven you, why not be honest with the nation? Americans are forgiving people, and, since it's true that we knew we weren't electing an altar boy to be president, it will be easy for us to show mercy. In fact, we'll remember your humility and contrition more than your past misdeeds. That's the way forgiveness works."

Of course, if the charges are false, then the president should remain steadfast in his denials. But if true, let him say to the nation, "As you know, there are many things in my past of which I'm not proud, and this is one of them. Years ago my family forgave me, but today I'm asking you to forgive me. I've also made significant changes since then, and those old days are long since behind me."

By humbling himself, he will be lifted up.

The same would hold true for Joy Behar. The more she recognizes the wrongness of what she said and the more she humbles herself before her Christian viewers, the more they will forgive her and offer her a fresh start.

As the Scriptures state, "For whoever exalts himself will be humbled, and he who humbles himself will be exalted" (Luke 14:11 NKJV). And, "God resists the proud, but gives grace to the humble" (1 Pet. 5:5 NKJV).

If you've never humbled yourself, taken full responsibility for your actions without blaming others, and asked for forgiveness, you should try it. It's painful and beautiful at one and the same time. And more than that, it's wonderfully liberating.

March 15, 2018

THE HYPOCRISY OF
THOSE ACCUSING WHITE
EVANGELICALS OF HYPOCRISY

★ ★ ★ ★ ★

SINCE President Trump was elected in 2016 with the help of white evangelicals, we have been told that in voting for him, we compromised our ethics and can no longer be taken seriously. The latest alleged evidence for this is found in reports that black evangelicals are leaving white evangelical churches because of the latter's support of Trump.[1] What are we to make of this?

The charge of white evangelical hypocrisy has been leveled most recently by Michael Gerson, writing in the *Atlantic*'s April edition. The title and subtitle of his major, nearly 7,000-word article read: "The Last Temptation: How evangelicals, once culturally confident, became an anxious minority seeking political protection from the least traditionally religious president in living memory."[2]

According to Gerson, who speaks positively of his own experience growing up as an evangelical Christian and who claims to be jealous of our tradition, "One of the most extraordinary things about our current politics—really, one of the most extraordinary developments of recent political history—is the loyal adherence of religious conservatives to Donald Trump. The president won four-fifths of the votes[3] of white evangelical Christians. This was a higher level of support than either Ronald Reagan or George W. Bush, an outspoken evangelical himself, ever received."

He notes that, "Trump's background and beliefs could hardly be more incompatible with traditional Christian models of life and leadership.... Trump's strength-worship and contempt for 'losers' smack more of Nietzsche than of

Christ. *Blessed are the proud. Blessed are the ruthless. Blessed are the shameless. Blessed are those who hunger and thirst after fame.*"

In spite of this, "According to Jerry Falwell Jr., evangelicals have 'found their dream president,' which says something about the current quality of evangelical dreams."

To be sure, I share some of Gerson's concerns, and I have raised them frequently myself.

But what Gerson seems to have missed—quite glaringly so—is that many of us who voted for Donald Trump did so because a vote for him was a vote against Hillary Clinton. In other words, we were not so much voting *for* Trump as *against* Hillary. Yet, in a 7,000-word article, the name Hillary Clinton does not occur once. How can this be?

I'm currently conducting polls on my Facebook and Twitter pages, asking if those who voted for Trump did so primarily because they were voting *for* him or *against* Hillary. Of the votes which have come in so far (about 2,000 on Facebook and 500 on Twitter), the Facebook vote is 56 percent for Trump and 44 percent against Hillary, while the Twitter vote is 40 percent for Trump and 60 percent against Hillary.

Now, go back to the last two elections and ask Democrats who voted for Barack Obama: Were you primarily voting *for* him or *against* his candidate. I'm confident the numbers would be overwhelmingly in the *for* Obama column, in stark contrast with the Trump numbers. This makes Gerson's omission of Hillary Clinton all the more surprising.

It also underscores a major blind spot in his article, namely, his failure to recognize how deeply many white evangelicals feel that our nation has lurched in a very dangerous direction, which calls for some extraordinary measures. That means that when we see a candidate (now, a president) who has the potential of changing the makeup of the Supreme Court (and perhaps helping to overturn Roe v. Wade), who is genuinely concerned about our religious liberties, who is in the process of relocating our embassy to Jerusalem, we say: That man will have our support, despite his many flaws and failings. What is so hypocritical about that?

As Roman Catholic columnist Monica Showalter noted, "Evangelicals (and most Catholics—something [Gerson] forgets to notice) voted for Trump because not only does he *not hate* them, but he is willing to defend their values."[4]

In the confused and troubled days in which we live, that goes a long way.

As David French, himself a Never Trumper, pointed out, "While Gerson ably explains that Evangelicals feel as if they're under siege, he doesn't give an adequate explanation as to *why*. He communicates the reality that Evangelicals feel embattled without providing sufficient explanation for that belief, belittling their concerns as hysterical and self-pitying. The effect is to make Evangelicals appear irrational when, in fact, Evangelicals made their political choice in response to actual, ominous cultural and legal developments that jeopardized their religious liberty and threatened some of their most precious religious and cultural institutions."[5]

I ask again, against this backdrop, what makes our vote for Trump an act of hypocrisy? And isn't it the height of hypocrisy to accuse us of betraying our values when Gerson, according to Showalter, voted for Hillary? Is this not a classic example of the pot calling the kettle black?

This brings us back to the question of black Christians allegedly leaving white evangelical churches because of the latter's support of Trump. According to African American pastor Van Moody, "The exodus of blacks from white evangelical churches is real and understandable. People tend to gravitate towards communities that they can identify with and that they believe identifies with them. Unfortunately, the political positions many white evangelical pastors and churches have taken have eroded that sense of identification for many black people."[6]

Now, I'm not aware of any major studies that back up the anecdotal evidence supplied by the *New York Times*,[7] and to my knowledge, most white evangelical pastors do not get into politics that much from the pulpit.

But even if these reports are true, doesn't the sword cut both ways? Haven't black evangelicals consistently voted for pro-abortion, pro-LGBT candidates like Barack Obama and Hillary Clinton? Haven't some African-American megachurches even prayed by name for the election of candidates like Obama and Al Gore? Why then weren't *they* called on the carpet for hypocrisy? Why aren't *they* guilty of tarnishing the evangelical tradition?

Personally, I believe we all have blind spots and there's more than enough hypocrisy to go around. And I think leaders like Van Moody and Franklin Graham would profit greatly by spending time with each other, if they haven't already. Let us hear one another out, let us share our respective perspectives, and let us commit to being holistic in our ethics and concerns, with the help of God.

But I'm a little suspicious whenever left-leaning Christians (and/or the leftist secular media) raise charges against white evangelicals, people who just happen to be strong social conservatives.

Perhaps the bigger issue is not our alleged hypocrisy but rather our counter-cultural convictions? Could this be where the conflict really lies?

April 1, 2018

ADULTERY, CHARACTER, AND LEADERSHIP: A RESPONSE TO DENNIS PRAGER

★ ★ ★ ★ ★

IN light of the media's obsession with Stormy Daniels and her alleged tryst with Donald Trump, Dennis Prager has returned to the question of whether one can be both a good president and an adulterer.[1] (He had previously addressed this in 2011 in his article, "What Does Adultery Tell Us About Character?")

Without a doubt, Prager is correct in stating that, while adultery is always sinful, we should recognize that:

- The calling of a president is different than that of a religious leader.

- The same left that wants to crucify Trump for his alleged (past) affairs gave Ted Kennedy a free pass, defended Bill Clinton against his accusers, and has no problem celebrating Martin Luther King, Jr., despite his many alleged infidelities. In Prager's words, "It should be clear that this whole preoccupation with Trump's past sex life has nothing to do with morality and everything to do with humiliating Trump—and, thereby, hopefully weakening the Trump presidency—the raison d'etre of the media since he was elected."

- The Never Trump conservatives shouldn't be so focused on the president's alleged past failings; they should look, instead, at his positive accomplishments in the White House.

Accordingly, if America was under attack by ISIS militants, I would rather have a philandering, battle-tested general leading our troops than a faithfully married pacifist who was afraid of his own shadow. And, with Prager (in his 2011 article), I agree that a twice-married Ronald Reagan was a far more effective president than a once-married, Sunday-school-teaching Jimmy Carter.

I also concur with Prager when he writes, "That '60 Minutes' correspondent Anderson Cooper and many in our country found it acceptable to ask a woman, 'Did he use a condom?' on national TV is a far graver reflection of America's moral malaise than a man having a one-night affair 12 years ago." (Here are my own reflections on this.[2])

At the same time, I don't believe we are left with an either-or question. Could it be that Trump and Clinton and Kennedy and King could have done their jobs better without the adultery? Is it possible that we are being too compartmentalized? And what of the larger, moral effect that a president has on the nation?

According to a 2010 article on CBSNews.com, "Researchers point to former President Clinton's infamous statement, 'I did not have sexual relations with that woman,' as the pivotal turning point in society's changing views about oral sex. The attitude shift has been dubbed the 'Clinton-Lewinsky' effect."[3] And with that, "virginity" took on a new meaning as well. What will be the ripple effect of the constant talk of Trump and a porn star?

To be clear, though, my purpose here is not to throw stones from some imaginary moral high ground. How many of us have committed adultery in our hearts, numerous times? According to Jesus, that is quite serious too (see Matt. 5:27-30). On the flip side, every sin can be forgiven in God's sight, and even adultery can be overcome within a marriage.

But are there serious consequences to adultery, even for the President of the United States? And does adultery tell us something about character?

The person who commits adultery violates the deepest trust two human beings can have. He or she engages in deception, makes choices based on carnal desires rather than integrity and faithfulness, and is certainly guilty of impaired judgment. Doesn't this speak seriously to the issue of character?

And what of the question of marital strife? Is it improbable that a president enjoying a solid marriage with his wife could lead more effectively than a president who was emasculated by his wife because of her reaction to his womanizing? Or, could he govern better if he were not constantly squabbling with his wife?

And what of the distractions caused by adultery? Was Bill Clinton's presidency unaffected by the Monica Lewinsky affair? Has Donald Trump not been at least a little bit hamstrung by the constant accusations from his past? Was Dr. King at all impaired by the (alleged) threats from J. Edgar Hoover to expose King's (alleged) indiscretions? Was nothing hanging over his head when he was alone (or with his wife and family)?

I can only imagine the pressure that a president (or a leader like King) lives with. Is it farfetched to think that, without the unneeded pressure of affairs and their messy aftermath, those leaders could think more clearly?

We all think of King David as a man loved by God and used by God. But he was also a man who committed adultery, had numerous wives, and even commissioned a murder. Yet to this day, he is a hero of the faith and a man whose songs (psalms) we sing and recite. At the same time, biblical history demonstrates that his actions had a negative impact on his leadership, ultimately impacting the nation.

When it comes to President Trump, if all the allegations about his past prove true, that would not surprise me. As I've said repeatedly, we knew who we were voting for. And if the leftist media decided not to focus on his (allegedly) sordid past, focusing instead on his presidential actions, the distractions would be minimized.

Still, we do well to recognize that adultery and sexual indiscretions are not without consequences, even for presidents and world leaders. And while they do not automatically disqualify one from office (or "invalidate" in Prager's words), they can certainly hinder effectiveness.

Prager correctly wrote, "If a president is also a moral model, that is a wonderful bonus. But that is not part of a president's job description."[4] Yet an immoral president can negatively affect the morals of a nation, not to mention negatively impact his own presidency.

So, while I concur with many of the points made by my rightly esteemed colleague, I do so with caveats.

May 9, 2018

IT'S TIME TO GIVE
PRESIDENT TRUMP HIS DUE

★ ★ ★ ★ ★

TO all the Never Trumpers and Trump-haters, it's time to give the man his due. Not only did he do the right thing in backing out of our deal with Iran, but he stood in full presidential stature in denouncing this terrorist-funding regime and sending a message of hope and liberation to the people of Iran. Well done, Mr. President!

On a personal level, I have every right to ask my anti-Trump friends to commend him, since I have spoken out when the president's words or actions grieved me. And I have made clear that, as evangelical followers of Jesus, we must not sell our souls in his defense.

My policy has been simple: When the president does well, we should commend him. When he doesn't do well, we should constructively criticize him. That's what loyal citizens do.

Today is a day to commend him. He hit the ball out of the park with his decision and speech[1] regarding Iran. And in doing so, he presented himself as the ultimate anti-Obama.

Let's examine the contrasts carefully.

First, Trump properly identified Iran for the dangerous nation it has become. In his words:

The Iranian regime is the leading state sponsor of terror. It exports dangerous missiles, fuels conflicts across the Middle East, and supports terrorist proxies and militias such as Hezbollah, Hamas, the Taliban, and al-Qaeda.

Over the years, Iran and its proxies have bombed American embassies and military installations, murdered hundreds of American servicemembers, and kidnapped, imprisoned, and tortured American citizens. The Iranian regime has funded its long reign of chaos and terror by plundering the wealth of its own people. No action taken by the regime has been more dangerous than its pursuit of nuclear weapons and the means of delivering them.

This is all patently true, and only the most strident supporters of Iran would dispute it.

Did President Obama ever make a statement about Iran on this level? Did he ever call a spade a spade in such forthright, categorical terms?

Second, President Trump said no to a really bad deal with Iran, a deal that put tens of billions of dollars back into the hands of radical Muslim leaders committed to war and upheaval in the Middle East and beyond.

Yet it was Obama who helped get us into this mess. In fact, according to a lengthy report on Politico, "In its determination to secure a nuclear deal with Iran, the Obama administration derailed an ambitious law enforcement campaign targeting drug trafficking by the Iranian-backed terrorist group Hezbollah, even as it was funneling cocaine into the United States, according to a POLITICO investigation."[2]

The headline and sub-heading to the story were even more damning: "The Secret Backstory of How Obama Let Hezbollah Off the Hook. An ambitious U.S. task force targeting Hezbollah's billion-dollar criminal enterprise ran headlong into the White House's desire for a nuclear deal with Iran."

If this report is true, not only did we make a foolhardy deal with Iran. We also helped to enable to Hezbollah, one of Iran's terrorist allies. And we did it to our direct detriment.

It's also worth noting that our treaty with Iran was multinational, thereby bringing an aggressive, radical regime into a coalition with other nations (including the United Kingdom, Russia, China, and countries in the European Union).

The president, in his speech, further isolated Iran when he stated that "at this very moment, Secretary Pompeo is on his way to North Korea in preparation for my upcoming meeting with Kim Jong-Un. Plans are being made, relationships are building, hopefully a deal will happen, and with the help of China, South Korea, and Japan, a future of great prosperity and security can be achieved for everyone."

He was saying to Iran, "Get with the program, and you'll have a bright future. Dig in your heels, and you'll regret it."

Third, Trump told the oppressed people of Iran they had a friend here in the United States. He said, "Finally, I want to deliver a message to the long-suffering people of Iran: The people of America stand with you. It has now been almost 40 years since this dictatorship seized power and took a proud nation hostage. Most of Iran's 80 million citizens have sadly never known an Iran that prospered in peace with its neighbors and commanded the admiration of the world. But the future of Iran belongs to its people. They are the rightful heirs to a rich culture and an ancient land and they deserve a nation that does justice to their dreams, honor to their history, and glory to their god."

What a message this sends to the people of Iran, who also understand from Trump's remarks that a new government means a prosperous Iran. This stands in stark contrast to the relatively weak[3] support offered by President Obama during the protests of 2009. (Note also that, according to one Iranian dissident and defense expert, the country could fall within a year.[4])

So, to those who questioned whether Trump would keep his word about Iran and to those who are quick to criticize him when he does wrong, here's your chance to prove your impartiality. Give the man his due today, without caveat. He deserves it.

May 19, 2018

Am I Tuning In at the Wrong Times, or Does CNN Really Have Trump Derangement Syndrome?

★ ★ ★ ★ ★

MAYBE it's a matter of timing. Maybe I'm not giving this a fair shake. But whenever I happen to tune in to CNN, there's a panel of talking heads discussing President Trump and the porn star. Or President Trump and the Mueller investigation. Or President Trump and whether he'll be impeached.

As for President Trump and Jerusalem. Or President Trump and Saudi Arabia. Or President Trump and Iran. Or President Trump and North Korea. Or President Trump and the American economy. Or President Trump and pro-life legislation. Or President Trump and national security—or whatever the major topic is—I almost never hear CNN talking about it.

As for CNN talking about a subject that didn't mention Trump at all, I can't remember the last time I witnessed that personally.

Now, I want to be totally honest. I watch very little TV news, so my sampling is quite small.

I get almost all my news reading online, and in that regard, my sampling is quite large.

Perhaps, if I sampled Fox News on TV the same way, I would get similarly skewed results, just in a different direction.

Again, I'm asking a question here rather than claiming scientific accuracy.

Still, I have to wonder: Is CNN giving even the slightest pretense to being fair and balanced? Is there even a modicum of desire to say, "We are not just here to slam the president"?

The fact is, although my sampling is small, it's somewhat representative. That's because the TVs in our home are programmed to start with CNN. (I'm not sure who set it up like that, but we've never changed it.)

So, when I want to watch some sports (perhaps while eating dinner at night when Nancy is not with me, or while winding down a little between writing projects), the first thing I see and hear is CNN.

The times of day can vary. The days of the week can vary. But one thing never varies.

I mean day after day. Week after week. Broadcast after broadcast. CNN anchor or talking head panel.

They're breathlessly discussing President Trump and the latest alleged scandal. They're examining the newest dirt in fine detail. They're talking about chaos and upheaval and crisis. They're talking about Trump melting down. Things are really bad, and they're getting worse by the moment!

Watching CNN, you're surprised when you hear the president under a single sane word. I thought he was out of his mind!

Watching CNN, you're shocked to see that his administration survived another day. And you can hardly believe that Trump and Melania are still together.

Through the lens of CNN, the White House sky seems to be falling multiple times a day, as crisis after crisis comes crashing down. At least that's how CNN's reporting sounds in my ears.

So, again I ask, is it just me? Are my impressions simply the result of my poorly timed, too-short, random sampling?

I don't watch much TV in general, so maybe that's the problem. Maybe I'm not giving CNN a fair shake.

On the other hand, what are the chances of my random sampling being that skewed?

As for CNN reporting on Trump's major accomplishments, those can only be reported in the negative. He acted hastily. It was all for political gain. This is about Trump, not helping others. He's making a total mess of things.

There is nothing good about the man or his administration. Nothing praise-worthy. Nothing positive. Not one thing.

And on a daily basis, aside from a major news headline—like another tragic school shooting—the big news is not the world news. The big news is the latest scandalous accusation against the president. At least, that's the big news according to CNN.

So, is it just me? Am I tuning in at the wrong times or not watching for long enough periods? Or does CNN suffer from Trump Derangement Syndrome?

May 26, 2018

WHY SO MANY ISRAELIS LOVE TRUMP

★ ★ ★ ★ ★

I knew that President Trump was popular in Israel. I just didn't know how popular. Talk about enthusiastic support!

I asked one man if we could talk with him on camera about religious subjects. He was quite happy to do so. But since we were Americans, he first wanted to talk about Trump. "Make America great!" he shouted with a big smile. "Make Israel great!"

To be sure, Trump has his detractors in Israel. Opinions here are anything but monolithic, and divisions are fierce and intense.

One of my friends is the Israeli equivalent of an Evangelical Christian Never Trumper. When it comes to politics, he is very liberal and normally sides with the Palestinians. Obviously, he is not a fan of Donald Trump.

Some cab drivers we spoke with, including Israeli Muslims, expressed indifference toward Trump. One was downright hostile (he happened to be a secular Israeli Jew).

He said Trump was good for nothing and that he had the support of only two people, a Texas farmer and Putin.

We asked him, "How then, did he get elected?"

He replied, "Christians didn't vote for him. Jews didn't vote for him. Blacks didn't vote for him. Mexicans didn't vote for him."

We asked again, "Then who voted for him? How did he get elected?"

He replied, "A farmer in Texas and *Putin*," with the strong emphasis on Putin. The Russian conspiracy lives on.

This driver even told us, "No one wants Trump. Not even his wife Melania. I saw it on Fox News. He tried to hold her hand and she pulled it away."

But he was in the clear minority among those we spoke with, and over and over we heard the same two things.

It was not just that his slogan, "Make America great again," had reached Israel. A slogan alone is just that—words. Why be so excited about words?

But that's what separated Trump from other politicians in the minds of many Israelis. He was not just a man of words. Instead, as they said repeatedly—and with enthusiasm—Trump gets things done.

Their support for Trump, then, can be boiled down to these two things. First, when he says something, he does it. He keeps his word. Second, in doing so, he is not like other politicians. That's why they loved Trump.

It was clear that their opinion of him was based on sound bites and caricatures. He was almost an exaggeration of himself, if such a thing were possible.

But that's what travels around the world. Not subtle differences in policies. Not partisan squabbling. Not journalistic opinions.

Instead, it is the bold strokes of what a political leader says and does that carry. Who is Putin to you? What about Kim Jong-Il? What about Netanyahu? What about Macron?

We know them from a distance, and we know them in simplified (or exaggerated) form.

Here in Israel (from whence I write), political scandals are a dime a dozen. Vicious political divisions are the norm.

Like Trump, Prime Minister Netanyahu has been married three times. He even confessed to adultery in the past. And, like Trump, he presents the figure of a strong, no-nonsense leader.

In a nation like Israel, surrounded by sworn, mortal enemies, strength and decisiveness are highly valued. And that's how Trump is perceived.

A Russian-born Israeli said to us with enthusiasm, "He says it and he does it! He's not a politician. He keeps his word."

Seeing that this man stood guard in front of the American Embassy in Jerusalem, it was easy to understand his enthusiasm. Trump did what Clinton, Bush, and Obama did not do. He literally made international history by keeping the same political promise many others had made.

This Russian-Israeli said to us, "Even before he was a politician, I liked him. But my friends said he was dumb."

"Yes," I replied, "dumb enough to get elected President of the United States."

And now dumb enough to have his name engraved on the wall of our historic embassy. Even dumb enough to have his face on a newly-minted "Temple Coin," along with the face of the ancient Persian king, Cyrus.

"Make America great again! Trump, Trump!"

Talk about marketing skills. The Trump brand is thriving here in Israel.

July 3, 2018

I'M NOT PLAYING THE NEW GAME OF "DENY TRUMP TO PROVE YOUR LOVE FOR JESUS"

★ ★ ★ ★ ★

W^E hear this on a daily, if not hourly basis. Evangelicals have hurt their witness by voting for Trump. Evangelicals have lost their credibility by supporting Trump. Evangelicals can no longer be taken seriously because they're in bed with Trump. And on and on it goes.

It doesn't matter who he appoints to the Supreme Court. It doesn't matter if he improves the economy. Or strengthens the military. Or helps stabilize the Middle East.

Not at all. Trump is a heartless, misogynistic, immoral, narcissistic, xenophobic monster, and whoever voted for him (or continues to support him) is not worthy of the name "Christian."

This has almost become the new orthodoxy: Prove your allegiance to Jesus by denouncing Trump. Failure to denounce him is proof positive that you have compromised your witness.

Sorry, but I'm not playing this game. In fact, I refuse the premise of this game.

First, the very ones driving this narrative are the ones who didn't take our faith seriously before. They branded us bigots and homophobes. They criticized us as Bible-bashers and rightwing extremists. And they're the ones now saying, "We would take you more seriously if you denounced Trump."

I don't think so. They didn't take us seriously before. Why should they suddenly say, "Now that you've put a distance between yourselves and that crazy man in the White House, we'd love to hear your views on abortion and homosexuality. Yes, please tell us why abortion is murder and why same-sex marriage is illegitimate in God's sight. You have so much to offer us."

Not quite!

This reminds me of some criticism I got for our video "Can You Be Gay and Christian?" A lot of hateful viewers vilified me as an "old man" (and much worse, of course). This prompted me to ask, "So, if I was a cool-looking young guy, would you like what I had to say?" I think not.

It's the position we take that primarily brings us rejection, not our age or appearance.

Second, there are plenty of evangelicals and conservatives who didn't vote for Trump (some were Never Trumpers), yet they still get hated and ridiculed by the left for their conservative views. Did journalists like Ben Shapiro and David French earn the respect of the liberal world by not voting for Trump? Have they become less hated? Are liberal campuses opening their doors saying, "Please speak to us, now that you've proved your credibility by not voting for Trump"?

Third, many of us who did vote for Trump said from the start that we had grave concerns about his character. That we thought he could be very divisive. That some of his rhetoric could be dangerous. And plenty of us have expressed our disagreement with the president since he was elected.

How, then, does our vote for him impinge on our faith?

I've said repeatedly that Donald Trump didn't die for my sins and that he's not my savior. And I will not sell my soul in support of him.

But you better believe I'd vote for him against Hillary Clinton any day of the week. I'd far rather have him picking Supreme Court nominees than Hillary. Or standing against LGBT extremism. Or protecting our religious freedoms. Or standing with Israel. Or facing down Iran.

Please tell me, then, how a vote (with hesitation) for a man who would stand for the life of the unborn and resist LGBT activism in our schools and push back against the assault on our liberties and challenge radical Islam and support Israel is somehow a compromise of my faith.

Yes, when I was a Cruz supporter and a Trump opposer, I was personally sick of the line, "We're not voting for a pastor. We're voting for a Commander in Chief."

Yet it's true. That's who we voted for, with the hopes of him getting certain things done. Some of us loved him from the start and others held their noses as they voted. But to make this a test of our faith is nonsense.

Fourth, the media is framing the narrative and deciding when outrage is called for. "If you don't speak out against the separation of children at the borders you're a hypocrite!"

Frankly, I don't know anyone who likes this, whether the policy goes back to George W. Bush or Barack Obama, or whether Trump is the main cause of it. Of course we want better solutions. But why are we required to join some leftwing, Trump-hating rally to prove we're not evil people?

The fact is, an incredible amount of social good is done every day by evangelicals around the country, from feeding the poor to housing the homeless to fighting human trafficking to adopting rejected children to helping addicts get free to sponsoring refugees. (This is just the tip of a giant iceberg of evangelical good works.)

We don't have to prove our morality by giving our "Amen" to the left's latest cause. (And to repeat: I don't know anyone who was pleased with kids being separated from their parents, and many of my colleagues raised their voices too. But we don't have to dance to the media's tune.)

Of course, there are evangelicals who seem to idolize Trump, who will never differ with him, let alone criticize him, who seem to have double standards when it comes to this president. I concur with those who believe that those types of actions can hurt our witness and make us seem hypocritical. Absolutely.

But to make the denouncing of Trump a litmus test of Christian orthodoxy is utterly ridiculous. I urge my colleagues and friends not to be lured into this game.

July 13, 2018

MUSINGS ON THE PRESIDENT, THE RELIGIOUS RIGHT, DEMOCRATS, AND THE SUPREME COURT

★ ★ ★ ★ ★

S INCE there are many legal pundits far more qualified than I to debate the merits and demerits of Justice Brett Kavanagh, I'll focus here on some larger, related issues.

1. This is the main reason many of us voted for Donald Trump.

We do well to remember that many of us who identify as evangelicals had grave reservations about candidate Trump. Many of us said that, out of the 17 Republican candidates, he was our last choice.

Some of us (including me) frequently spoke and wrote against him during the primaries. (See, for example, the video I posted on November 27, 2015 titled, "Why Evangelical Christians Should Have a Problem with Donald Trump."[1] Because it was my position at the time, for the sake of integrity and honesty, we have kept it online even though I ultimately voted for Trump.)

Yet the major reason we voted for Trump in large numbers was because we hoped he would keep his word about Supreme Court nominees. And we voted for him because we were voting against Hillary, which leads us to reflect on this stark reality: Had Hillary been elected, President Obama would probably have been able to get his pick for the Court, namely, Merrick Garland, while Hillary would be making her first pick now.

So, you would have Garland instead of Neil Gorsuch, plus a presumably far-left pick rather than Frank Kavanagh. And maybe Justice Ginsberg would be more ready to step down, allowing for a young liberal to take her place and giving Democrats a third pick already.

The implications for America's future—at least for the next 30-40 years—are massive.

To date, Donald Trump has not disappointed us in his picks, both for Supreme Court as well as for the many other federal appointees. This is a major reason, if not *the* major reason, many of us voted for him.

2. President Trump is not the puppet of the religious right.

In the days leading up to the president's Supreme Court nominee, this was a common charge. Yet it is one that can easily be dismissed.

Simply stated, if anything is clear about Trump it is that he is his own man. No one can bridle him or rein him in, to the consternation of many. And he has sometimes embarrassed conservative Christian leaders with his rhetoric and temperament. That is not the behavior of a puppet.

I'm close to faith leaders who got close to Donald Trump during his candidacy, and some of them are part of his Faith Advisory Council. While he listens to them with respect, to a person they would tell you that he makes his decisions independently.

As one of the leaders told me face to face when I asked about him tempering his tweets, "It's unlikely that a 70-year-old man is going to change."

What is remarkable, though, is that he seems to have embraced the convictions of Christian conservatives when it comes to crucial issues such as abortion, religious liberties, and the meaning of marriage. It is a providential, quite unexpected, and apparently sovereign union, one that goes beyond Trump's formula for victory. (In other words, it's more than just good campaign strategy.) Somehow, these issues became important to him, because of which he became close to many evangelical believers, who then earned his respect and loyalty. Again, this is a far cry from being a puppet.

3. President Obama nominated two far-left justices to the Supreme Court. What's so terrible about President Trump nominating two solid conservatives to the Court?

Comedian Dennis Miller tweeted two days ago, "Just to keep things in perspective, or not, Trump could nominate either Amy Coney Barrett or Vladimir Putin tomorrow and the headlines would be exactly the same. #DennisMillerOption."[2] Exactly so.

The one thing that was certain was this: Whoever Trump nominated, there would be an outcry from the left. The sky is falling! This is the end of the world! We must go to the streets and protest!

Fox News even played video clips Monday night of college students weighing in on the Trump nominee. They were interviewed hours (if not days) *before* Trump's announcement was made, but already they were denouncing the pick as racist. One student suggested the nominee wear white robes rather than black robes!

Yet President Obama was able to make his picks, and when it comes to their ideological base, you could easily argue that they are much farther to the left than Gorsuch and Kavanagh are to the right.

For example, in September, 2014, Justice Elena Kagan "officiated for the first time at a same-sex wedding, a Maryland ceremony for her former law clerk and his husband."[3] Yet the Court did not rule to redefine marriage until one year later.

Already in 2010, CBS News ran this headline: "EXCLUSIVE: Documents Show Kagan's Liberal Opinion on Social Issues." Her decisions to date have been consistently to the left, sometimes in extreme form.

As for Justice Sonia Sotomayor (to give just one example), when it came to the Hobby Lobby decision, she claimed that it compromised "hundreds of Wheaton [University's] employees and students of their *legal entitlement* to contraceptive coverage" (my emphasis).[4]

Yet I don't recall the same level of outcry against Obama's nominees when compared to Trump's. Was there very strong concern about Obama's nominees from those on the right? Absolutely. Was there the same kind of hysteria? Not to my memory.

The real issue is that everyone knows that one of the greatest sacred cows of the left (and of the Democratic Party) is now at risk, namely, Roe v. Wade. Even the possibility of this landmark, horrific ruling being threatened sends shock waves into the liberal world, and the reaction will no doubt be intense. The reaction will go far beyond words. It will turn to acts of violence.

My hope is that the extreme, shrill, and over-the-top reaction of the left will turn moderates away.

For the moment, though, expect things to get ugly. Really ugly. May cooler heads prevail.

July 13, 2018

WHAT CHRISTIAN LEADERS CAN
LEARN FROM DONALD TRUMP

★ ★ ★ ★ ★

THERE are plenty of things followers of Jesus *cannot* learn from Donald Trump. That is self-evident. But there *are* things he can teach us, especially those of us in leadership.

First, though, let me list some things that the president *cannot* teach us, including: 1) how to cultivate humility; 2) developing effective tools for personal Bible study; 3) treating your opponents with civility and respect; 4) how to avoid divorce; 5) keys to sexual purity; 6) how to deny yourself; 7) developing a distinctive hairstyle for TV preachers. (Wait. That one might work!)

Yet there are many things the president can teach us—again, speaking of leaders in particular—even if we don't like the specific way he has modeled some of these things.

Here's a short list.

1. Don't avoid confrontation.

We often try so hard to be "nice." At all costs, we do not want to offend. But sometimes confrontation is necessary and important, and there are scores of biblical examples for this.

Nathan the prophet confronted King David (2 Sam. 12). Paul confronted Peter (Gal. 2). Proverbs even says, "Better is open rebuke than hidden love" (Prov. 27:5). And the New Testament calls us to "speak the truth in love" (Eph. 4:15 NLT).

Again, I'm not implying that all of Trump's confrontational tactics are called for or that the way he confronts is always right. But it's clear that he will speak up and speak out when he feels the need, no matter how uncomfortable things become. Mixed with grace and wisdom, this is something we must learn to do as well. Don't be so afraid of uncomfortable confrontations.

2. Don't be a slave of public opinion.

It's becoming increasingly clear that Trump controls the media much more than the media controls Trump. This is not to say that he doesn't care about polling and negative reports. Nor is this to say that we should turn a deaf ear to the voices of others. Shepherds need to be attentive to their sheep.

But all too often, as Christian leaders, we are more concerned with human opinion than divine opinion, more wanting to please other people than to please the Lord. And all too often, we tell people what they want to hear rather than what they need to hear.

And how many pastors and leaders are slaves to congregational numbers, to budgetary constraints, to the sensitivities of the community?

"I dare not speak out on this, lest I lose long-term members. I dare not take this stand, lest our donor base evaporates. I dare not get involved in this controversy, lest the community view me negatively."

This is slavery, not freedom. Trump can teach us a lesson here too. Do what's right because it's right, not because it's convenient.

In the oft-quoted words of Dr. King, "The ultimate measure of a man is not where he stands in moments of comfort and convenience, but where he stands at times of challenge and controversy."

3. Don't be afraid to ride out the storm.

Some would call this stubbornness, others conviction, others foolishness. But it's clear that Trump is not afraid to take a stand, take some hits (as in day and night media bombardment), and hold to his guns, believing that, over time, he will be proven right.

Again, he has done this at times when I wish he would not. He has appeared to be tone deaf. He has alienated people he might have won over. He has seemed to be more pigheaded than pragmatic—hence my caveats.

But he has also proven that if you stand for a particular principle, then refuse to move from that principle regardless of how much flack you receive, you can ride out almost any storm.

How many times do we waffle when the pressure builds? How often do we cave in right before the breakthrough? How frequently are we marked by cowardice rather than courage?

Proverbs states, "If you falter in a time of trouble, how small is your strength!" (Prov. 24:10 NIV).

President Trump sets an example of strength, whether you love him or loathe him, and that's why so many have rallied around him.

We can learn a thing or two from him in the midst of his flaws and imperfections. And if we can merge courage and forthrightness and tenacity with Christlikeness, we will be unstoppable. (The truth be told, true Christlikeness requires courage and forthrightness and tenacity, does it not?)

And perhaps, as we stand strong and tall and unashamed, we'll be able to teach our president a thing or two as well.

July 17, 2018

DID TRUMP MAKE THE RIGHT PLAY OR DID TRUMP GET PLAYED?

★ ★ ★ ★ ★

FROM accusations of "treason"[1] to blunt assessments that, "The President of the United States made a fool of himself in his meeting in Helsinki on Monday with Russian dictator Vladimir Putin,"[2] the majority consensus is that Putin won and Trump lost. Even the pro-Trump Drudge Report headlined with, "PUTIN DOMINATES IN HEL."[3] (The accompanying picture[4] of a confident, smiling Putin and a slump-shouldered Trump said it all.) But is it totally clear that Trump got played?

Naturally, the liberal media and the Democrats bashed Trump. But that was a foregone conclusion. No matter what the outcome of the summit, Trump would be lambasted by his opponents.

It's the fact that a number of Republican congressmen also lined up to denounce Trump that is so concerning. (In particular, they were shocked at his trashing of American intelligence and his near-defense of Russia.)[5]

Where was the expected bravado? Where was the alpha-male leader who got in the face of Germany's Angela Merkel and Britain's Teresa May and challenged the EU and NATO? Did he finally meet his match? Or was it simply a matter of Trump's ego obscuring his vision? (In other words, he was more upset with Robert Mueller and the Democrats than he was concerned with speaking the truth to Putin.)

It's possible that all the above (and more) are true.

It's possible that Trump was thinking more about himself and his reputation than he was thinking about the good of America. It's possible that he was outmaneuvered by the more politically savvy Putin. It's possible he was even *outmanned* by Putin.

I don't mean to defend his words, and I don't claim to know his intentions.

And it's clear that he has totally had it with the Mueller investigation. An investigation that has dragged on for endless months. An investigation that was triggered by leaks from the just-fired James Comey. An investigation that still offers no proof that Trump colluded with Russia.

What if, in the end, Trump will be found *not guilty* of collusion by Mueller? Just think of the hundreds of thousands of hours lost, of the millions of words spilled, of the dark suspicions aroused. And all because of what? A political (or, worse still, personal) vendetta? It is for good reason that Trump is upset.

But does that excuse what he said today, comparing American intelligence (and/or guilt) to Russian intelligence (and/or guilt)?

Ironically, the same liberals who cheered President Obama when he spoke freely of America's failing when abroad are the very ones ready to crucify Trump. Conversely, the same conservatives who excoriated Obama as anti-patriotic are now scrambling to find ways to defend Trump. So much for unbiased media.

Putin, for his part, made some interesting remarks to Chris Wallace in a testy, post-press conference interview.

He explained there was no reason to meet if they were just going to insult each other, asking, "Why should this come as a surprise? Was it worth going all the way to Helsinki, going through the Atlantic, to just insult one another and—well, it's not exactly the diplomatic standard in the world. There is no need to go and meet a person if you just want to insult another person. We met to try to find a way for improving our relationship and not aggravating it or destroying it completely."[6]

Could this be what Trump had in mind as well?

As for Wallace's probing question as to whether Russia had any dirt on Trump, Putin said, "I don't want to insult President Trump when I say this—and I may come as rude—but before he announced that he will run for presidency, he was of no interest for us. He was a rich person, but, well, there's plenty of rich persons in the United States. He was in the construction business. He organized the beauty pageants. But no, it would never occur to anyone that he would think of running for president. He never mentioned his political ambitions. It sounds like it's utter nonsense."

He has a point. Why in the world would Russia have taken Trump as a serious candidate for president before 2015? He was merely a rich guy in the construction business who organized beauty pageants.

And this leads me back to the initial question: Did Trump make the right play, or did he get played?

On the one hand, it's easy to see how he appeared weak, not to mention unpatriotic. He certainly didn't sound like Mr. "America first" when he threw some of our agencies under the bus.

But others, like Al Perotta on the Stream, have noted that, "Trump didn't learn his politics in the posh lounges of academia. He learned them on the hard streets of New York. Let Obama quote U Thant. Trump will quote Don Corleone: 'Keep your friends close and your enemies closer.'

"There is also another saying that used to have some meaning in our culture. 'Actions speak louder than words.'"[7]

Perotta continued, "Last March, a bunch of Russian mercenaries in Syria started advancing on a U.S. position. The U.S. warned the Russians several times to back off. They didn't. And they were destroyed. Our military killed 200 to 300 Russians."

And he asked, "If you are Vladimir Putin, what message have you already received? What informs your decisions more? A few nice words at a press conference or the bodies of your comrades?

"It's okay to speak softly when you've already hit someone with a big stick."

Was this a large, unspoken part of the dynamic?

Interestingly, Senator Rand Paul has defended the president's actions, saying, "It's gotten so ridiculous that someone has to stand up and say we should try to engage even our adversaries and open up our lines of communication. We're going to talk to the president about some small steps in order to try to thaw the relations between our countries."

That, for me, is the ultimate question.

Yes, it's true that our president allowed partisan politics to play into the Helsinki news conference. But those very politics—specifically, the Mueller investigation—were about the only thing the media spoke of for days. And these were the issues raised by the media in the immediate aftermath of the summit. Why is it so shocking that Trump addressed it from his perspective, with lots of distrust toward our intelligence?

The big thing for me is this: Did Trump positively engage an adversary? Did he open a door wider that previously had been almost shut? In five or ten years, will our countries be on better terms?

It could well be that some of Trump's public comments were ill-advised, if not indefensible. But maybe, just maybe, he also did something very positive. Maybe he worked toward befriending an enemy. Time will tell.

August 11, 2018

Some Candid Questions for Evangelical Supporters of President Trump

★ ★ ★ ★ ★

D O you remember when candidate Trump said that he could stand on Fifth Avenue in New York City and shoot someone and he wouldn't lose any voters? It was quite a statement, but there was some truth to it. Trump's loyal supporters are doggedly loyal. The question is: Are his evangelical supporters just as loyal? The deeper question is: Should they be?

For the record, while I strongly opposed candidate Trump during the Republican primaries, I did vote for him over Hillary Clinton. And I'm glad I did. If the elections were held tomorrow and it was Trump vs. Hillary, he would have my vote without question.

But he does not have my undivided loyalty. Why should he? As I wrote previously, President Trump didn't die for my sins and he is not my Savior and Redeemer.

Of course, every evangelical Christian could echo those words. (We do not worship Lord Trump.) Yet sometimes I wonder: What would it take for some of us to differ publicly with the president? What would it take for us to say, "He's my president and I deeply appreciate the many good things he has done. But I wish he didn't say (or do) this."

So, to repeat my question: What would it take for some of us to differ publicly with the president?

Cal Thomas recently offered some unsolicited counsel to President Trump, suggesting that rather than attacking LeBron James via Twitter, he should have invited him to the White House.[1]

It's true that James has been openly critical of the president. And it's true he made negative comments about him on CNN, speaking with Don Lemon, no less.

But what he said this time was hardly outlandish. (His exact words were: "He's dividing us. And what I've noticed over the past few months [is] he's kind of used sport to kind of divide us, and that's something that I can't relate to, because I know that sport was the first time I ever was around someone white, and I got an opportunity to see them and learn about them, and they got an opportunity to learn about me, and we became very good friends.")

And part of the CNN interview focused on James's education initiative to help at-risk kids.

What a great opportunity for Trump to say, "Let's unite to help these kids. Let's put aside our differences for the sake of young Americans."

Instead, our president ignited a fresh firestorm, mocking both James and Lemon. (His exact words were: "Lebron James was just interviewed by the dumbest man on television, Don Lemon. He made Lebron look smart, which isn't easy to do. I like Mike!")

I really wish he hadn't done that. Yet I'm sure some of you reading this (I'm referring specifically to evangelical Christian readers) were glad he did: "I'm glad he put that basketball player in his place! Who does James think he is, speaking against the President of the United States?"

To my surprise, I've heard evangelical leaders defend Trump's harsh tweets, saying things like, "Well, he's the president, not a Christian leader." Or, "It's about time someone put politics aside and spoke his mind."

But when I hear this, I wince. Yes, it's true that Trump is not a Christian leader, but we are still Christians. And some of us are Christian leaders. (As for Trump, if he is a Christian at all, God knows; but he is clearly not a Christian leader.)

Does the nasty rhetoric not bother us at all? Do the insults never offend us? Do we never think to ourselves, "He could get even more done if he didn't constantly alienate people?"

And this leads to another question: Have we ourselves become caustic? In our reaction against the savage, unrelenting, often unfair attacks from the left, have we decided to defend the president no matter what, even if it means compromising our values? Has the "this is war" mentality hardened us rather than honed us?

A colleague of mine forwarded to me an article by Pete Enns titled, "Is it OK for Christians to protest against their political leaders?"

His answer: "It is the Christian's *duty* in civic affairs to hold powers to account when they see injustice done."[2]

He adds, "In my opinion, nowhere do Christians have a more visible and obvious responsibility to be salt and light, to embody the will of God, than when other humans are disenfranchised, treated unjustly, or unfairly—which is to say, treated less than fully human."

He even writes that, "Christians should never say to someone like that, 'If you don't like it, move to Denmark,' or 'He's your president and you owe him your allegiance.'"

Perhaps his article will step on some toes. Perhaps some will feel he made a good point but took it too far.

At the least, though, as evangelical followers of Jesus who support Trump, we should ask ourselves some honest questions. First and foremost would be this: Has my allegiance to Donald Trump in any way compromised my allegiance to Jesus?

That's the biggest question of all.

A Final Word

EVANGELICALS AND THE ELECTIONS: WHERE DO WE GO FROM HERE?

★ ★ ★ ★ ★

THE relationship between Donald Trump and evangelicals has been unique. On the one hand, he has been the least "Christian" candidate to gain widespread evangelical support, and in that sense our support for him has been a paradox. How can we stand with a man like this? On the other hand, he has kept his promises and turned his words into action more than his "Christian" predecessors. Who cares about his vile behavior when he is enacting critically important policies?

Either way, these years with Trump have been a learning experience, and if we will seize this teachable moment, we'll be able build on our positive actions and learn from our mistakes. Here are seven final points for consideration.

1. We must rise above the political fray.

According to the Word of God, as followers of Jesus we are citizens of another kingdom, seated in heavenly places, with ultimate allegiance to another Lord (see Phil. 3:20; Eph. 2:6; Col. 3:1-4). And while we live in this world, we are not like this world (see John 17:15-16). That means we cannot get caught up in a partisan political spirit. We must step higher.

Every four years (and less so, every two years), our nation gets worked up into an emotional frenzy as we choose our next president (and other elected officials). Billions of dollars are spent on campaigns, trillions of words are spilled, and emotions beyond counting are poured out. How emotional and worked up and divided we become! For the last ten years, have any two names elicited more spirited responses than the names of Obama and Trump?

We cannot get caught up in this volatile, political fray. It cannot dominate our lives. It must be made subject to the everyday priorities that matter more, namely, how we relate to God; how we live our lives; how we raise our families; how we love our neighbors. Those things transcend the world of politics, and rather than getting caught up in that frenzied arena, we must bring balance and perspective to it.

Let's be the ones who keep our cool. Let's stay in the Spirit. Let's set a good example for others to follow rather than be caught up in their bad example.

2. Regardless of party affiliation, we must remain independent.

Some of my friends are registered Republicans; others (far less in number) are registered Democrats; still others Libertarian or simply Independent. What matters, though, is that we identify more with God's cause than with a political party, since: 1) every party is mixed, and 2) no party, in itself, can bring about national transformation. In that sense, we stand as God's holy, alternative party, offering our votes and support to those who stand for what is right.

I wrote on January 30, 2017, "Let's put our faith before our politics, lest we make the mistake the religious right made in generations before and become an appendage of the Republican Party." To the extent we become an appendage to a party, to that extent we sell ourselves short, and to that extent we lose our ability to bring about change. Let the political parties come to us rather than us going to them. No one should be able to bribe us or gain our votes by offering us a seat at the table.

3. We must stay involved.

It's easy to get discouraged when we look at some of our options. What if no candidate meets our ideals? What if no party consistently stands for our values? But it is disastrous to drop out. Part of our calling is to continue to shine the light in dark places, and if our light goes out, darkness prevails. That must not happen on our watch.

I'm glad that evangelical leaders stayed with Donald Trump, and I'm glad they continue to be involved in his life and presidency. These men and women have made a difference in his life, and it has been a difference for the good. And while it's true that he is far from being "Saint Donald," it's also true that he appears to be taking many steps in the right direction, at least in terms of pro-Christian policies, for the good of the nation. (Again, I'm not saying this about all his policies and, obviously, about all his actions.)

Looking back to my warnings about Trump during the primaries (coupled with my expressed hope that I'd be proven wrong and would have to eat my words), I truly believe that prayer on his behalf, along with godly leaders speaking into his life, has made a positive impact. By all means, we should keep praying and speaking.

As for voting, what if evangelical voters stayed home and let Hillary Clinton win? I believe the results would have been terrible on many fronts, in particular those of deep Christian concern.

So, stay involved. Just do so with the right perspective, remembering that involvement does not mean absolute trust. Nor does it mean total allegiance.

4. God uses unlikely vessels, but character still matters.

During the presidential campaigns, I grew very tired of hearing people saying, "We're electing a president, not a pastor," but there is some truth to this statement. More importantly, the Lord sees things differently than we do, and His purposes far transcend ours.

When it comes to President Trump, during the primaries, I had a hard time seeing what some others saw because of his many, evident flaws. This was only highlighted by what seemed to be better Republican alternatives. I was also aware that a bull in a china shop can do a lot of damage. Yet it's clear to me (and millions of others) that there was a specific divine purpose in raising up a rough and tumble leader like Trump, and it often takes a bullish personality to get things done in Washington.

At the same time, character does count, and character flaws can make things much messier than they need to be. In the case of Trump, while he stands to get a lot of good done, it may come at a high cost. So, as stated throughout this book, if the presidential elections were today, I would vote for him once more against Hillary Clinton (or another like-minded opponent). But I will not downplay the importance of personal integrity for a leader, and I will continue to look for future candidates whose character matches their convictions.

5. We must stand for the issues near and dear to the Lord's heart.

My friend Professor Darrell Bock wrote a book titled, *How Would Jesus Vote?: Do Your Political Views Really Align With The Bible?* In this book, Darrell covers a wide range of subjects, including healthcare, immigration, the size of the government, gun control, education, and more. How, indeed, would Jesus vote? Or, more to the point for each of us, how would He have us vote?

All too often, we vote out of political habit, often carrying on family or ethnic or racial traditions for generations. But are we carrying God's heart? Are we standing for the most vulnerable in our society? Are we being responsible with our vote when it comes to what really matters in our society?

Sadly, many of us vote in selfish ways, primarily asking, "What will be best for my personal income?" or, "How will this tax plan affect me?" Instead, we should look at the things that Scripture prioritizes—the sanctity of life, justice for all, the stability of the family, right sexual order—and vote accordingly. In a country like ours, there's no reason to sit on the sidelines.

6. Sometimes, we must function as the president's loyal opposition.

In my aforementioned January 30, 2017 article, I referenced a Jewish scholar named Yochanan Muffs who wrote a profound article in 1980 titled, "His Majesty's Loyal Opposition: A Study in Prophetic Intercession." Professor Muffs argued that, "Prophecy is a dialectical tension between passive transmission of divine anger and active intercession in the name of prophetic love."[1] He added, "The life of Moses is a vivid illustration of the prophet as intercessor. The stories of the Exodus are marked by periodic eruptions of divine anger which are soothed by the wise intercession of Moses."[2]

Muffs' point is that God relied on the prophets to intercede, to plead the case of their people, to appeal for mercy, to ask for a respite, to oppose the divine decree of judgment. And, Muffs notes, "When the dialogue between mercy and anger is silent, there arises an imbalance of divine emotion."[3]

You ask, "But what does that have to do with evangelicals and President Trump (or, for that matter, believing Christians and any president)?"

Simply this: At times, our calling is to oppose the president, with respect and honor and love. At times, being loyal means disagreeing. At times, being a true friend involves conflict, since no one needs a bunch of yes men—in particular, the President of the United States.

7. Our calling goes beyond patriotism.

America is an amazing country, one that many other nations seek to emulate. We really have been richly blessed with freedoms and resources and opportunities. And in many ways, we are blessed to be Americans.

But America is far from perfect, and even though we have done so much good worldwide, we have also done evil. We export pornography around the globe. We model carnality and narcissism. We have birthed false religions. Not all of our military ventures are for the good. And as much as America has some amazing Christian roots, we cannot equate America with the kingdom of God.

That's why, rather than pray, "God bless America," I prefer to pray, "Your kingdom come to America." The former can sometimes be taken to mean, "God, make us bigger and stronger and richer!" The latter really means, "Father, bring us to repentance for our sins and turn our hearts to righteousness that we may be truly blessed!"

If we remember this, we will keep political involvement in the right perspective, namely, something important, but something subservient to a higher cause. And we will never look to the government or to a political leader to do what only Jesus and the gospel can do.

When it comes to President Trump, I do believe he has been raised up as a significant, 21st-century leader, but as a divine wrecking ball, accomplishing much good (with the potential of even more good in the coming years) but with many unneeded casualties. We do well as evangelical followers of Jesus (and others of like mind) to respect his office, to encourage him to do right, to support him however we can, but not to identify ourselves primarily as followers of (or defenders of) Trump. As I wrote on June 30, 2017, "I will not sacrifice my ethics and demean my faith to defend his wrongful words. To do that is to lose all credibility before a watching world."

As the title of this book says, Donald Trump is not our Savior. But he is our president, and as such, one of the most powerful men in the world. Let's not scorn him; let's not glorify him; and by all means, let's not give up on him.

Notes

Introduction: Evangelicals and Donald Trump: A Match Made in Heaven or a Marriage with Hell?

1. See Jim Hoft, "FLASHBACK: On June 19, 2015 Ann Coulter Predicted Trump Would Win—And the Liberal Audience Laughed," May 5, 2016, Gateway Pundit, https://www.thegatewaypundit.com/2016/05/flashback-june-19-2015-predicted-trump-win-liberal-audience-laughed/.

2. See Sarah Pullam Bailey, "White evangelicals voted overwhelmingly for Donald Trump, exit polls show," November 9, 2016, *Washington Post*, https://www.washingtonpost.com/news/acts-of-faith/wp/2016/11/09/exit-polls-show-white-evangelicals-voted-overwhelmingly-for-donald-trump/?noredirect=on&utm_term=.867adff73567. For caveats to these figures, see Joe Carter, "No, the Majority of American Evangelicals Did Not Vote for Trump," November 15, 2016, The Gospel Coalition, https://www.thegospelcoalition.org/article/no-the-majority-of-american-evangelicals-did-not-vote-for-trump/.

3. Kate Shellnutt and Sarah Eekhoff Zylstra, "Who's Who of Trump's 'Tremendous' Faith Advisers," June 22, 2016, *Christianity Today*, https://www.christianitytoday.com/ct/2016/june-web-only/whos-who-of-trumps-tremendous-faith-advisors.html. For the purpose of this council—which is to advise, not endorse, see "Should Trump's Evangelical Advisors Abandon Him?"

4. Rev. Robison shared this with me on my radio show as well; he also shared it at the FRC's Watchmen on the Wall event on May 25, 2017. I was in attendance when he spoke.

5. See "Who's Who of Trump's 'Tremendous' Faith Advisers."

6. Jeremiah Johnson, "Trump Shall Become the Trumpet," https://avemariaradio.net/prophecy-donald-trump-shall-become-the-trumpet/. (This was originally posted on a *Charisma Magazine* blog, April, 2015.) See further Joe Kovas, "Firestorm Erupts Over Trump's 'Bible Connection,'" August 8, 2015, WND, https://www.wnd.com/2015/08/firestorm-erupts-over-trumps-bible-connection/. See also Lance Wallnau, *God's Chaos Candidate: Donald J. Trump and the American Unraveling* (Keller, TX: Killer Sheep Media, 2016).

7. It was Jeb Bush who first dubbed Trump the "chaos candidate" and said he would be the "chaos president." His exact words in a December, 2015 primary debate were, "Donald, you know, is great at the one-liners. But he's a chaos candidate. And he'd be a chaos president. He would not be the commander-in-chief we need to keep our country safe." See Candace Smith, "Jeb Bush on Donald Trump: He's a 'Chaos Candidate' and He'd Be a 'Chaos President,'" December 15, 2015, ABC News, https://abcnews.go.com/Politics/jeb-bush-donald-trump-chaos-candidate-hed-chaos/story?id=35788736.

8. Ben Shapiro, "Another Prominent Anti-Trump Republican Just Went Down in Minnesota. Here's Why This Keeps Happening," *Daily Wire*, August 15, 2018, https://www.dailywire.com/

news/34530/another-prominent-anti-trump-republican-just-went-ben-shapiro.

9. See Bob Eschliman, "Charismatic Pastor: Donald Trump Is the New World Order's Worst Nightmare," Charisma News, March 17, 2016, https://www.charismanews.com/politics/primaries/55914-charismatic-pastor-donald-trump-is-the-new-world-order-s-worst-nightmare. The charismatic pastor is Rodney Howard-Browne.

10. See "I'm Not Playing the New Game of 'Deny Trump to Prove Your Love for Jesus,'" below, [000].

11. Michael L. Brown, *Saving a Sick America: A Prescription for Moral and Cultural Transformation* (Nashville, TN: Thomas Nelson, 2016), 39.

September 25, 2015: Donald Trump and the Difference Between Chutzpah and Rudeness

1. Bernard Weinraub, "Wiesel Confronts Reagan on Trip; President to Visit Bergen-Belsen; Survivor of Holocaust Urges Him Not to Stop at German Cemetery," April 20, 1985, https://www.nytimes.com/1985/04/20/us/wiesel-confronts-reagan-trip-president-visit-bergen-belsen-survivor-holocaust.html.

November 30, 2015: Why Evangelical Christians Should Not Support Donald Trump

1. Mark Mooney, "Donald Trump denies mocking reporter's disability," November 26, 2015, https://money.cnn.com/2015/11/25/media/donald-trump-serge-kovaleski/.

2. Erin Durkin, "Donald Trump denies he mocked disabled reporter: 'I have no idea who this reporter, Serge Kovlaski, is,'" Novebmer 27, 2015, http://www.nydailynews.com/new-york/trump-denies-mocking-disabled-reporter-article-1.2447814.

3. Ibid.

4. Ray Nothstine, "Trump: 'Why Do I Have to Repent or Ask for Forgiveness If I Am Not Making Mistakes?'" July 23, 2015, https://www.christianpost.com/news/trump-why-do-i-have-to-repent-or-ask-for-forgiveness-if-i-am-not-

making-mistakes-video-141856/.

5. Michael L. Brown, "Why Evangelical Christians Should Have a Problem with Donald Trump," ASKDrBrown, November 27, 2015, https://www.youtube.com/watch?v=CZJ7X5p0CBA.

January 18, 2016: Is Donald Trump a Double-Minded Man?

1. See "Donald Trump on Abortion," sections: "I have evolved on abortion issue, like Reagan evolved"; "I changed my views to pro-life based on personal stories," http://www.ontheissues.org/Celeb/Donald_Trump_Abortion.htm.

2. Daniel Reynolds, "No, Donald Trump Has Never Supported Same-Sex Marriage," January 17, 2016, http://www.advocate.com/election/2016/1/17/no-donald-trump-has-never-supported-same-sex-marriage.

3. Zeke J. Miller, "When Donald Trump Praised Hillary Clinton," July 17, 2015, http://time.com/3962799/donald-trump-hillary-clinton/.

4. Daniel White, "Donald Trump Calls Clinton's Bathroom Break 'Disgusting,'" December 22, 2015, http://time.com/4158303/donald-trump-hillary-clinton-disgusting-schlonged/.

5. Jennifer Jacobs, "Trump rents Iowa theater to show Benghazi movie," January 14, 2016, http://www.desmoinesregister.com/story/news/elections/presidential/caucus/2016/01/14/donald-trump-rents-urbandale-iowa-theater-free-showing-benghazi-movie-13-hours/78823046/.

6. Miller, "When Donald Trump Praised Hillary Clinton."

7. Ted Cruz, "Trump on Hillary," January 17, 2016, https://www.youtube.com/watch?v=xM8jfZTC6Mo.

8. Ibid.

9. Peter Weber, "Donald Trump Walks Back Calling Ted Cruz a 'Maniac' with 'Wrong Temperament' to Be President," December 15, 2015, http://theweek.com/speedreads/594555/donald-trump-walks-back-calling-ted-cruz-maniac-wrong-temperament-president.

10. John Santucci, "Donald Trump Ramps up Attacks on Ted Cruz, Says 'He's a Nasty Guy,'"

January 17, 2016, http://abcnews.go.com/Politics/donald-trump-ramps-attacks-ted-cruz-hes-nasty/story?id=36335768.

January 27, 2016: An Open Letter to Jerry Falwell Jr.

1. Robert Costa and Jenna Johnson, "Evangelical leader Jerry Falwell Jr. endorses Trump," January 26, 2016, https://www.washingtonpost.com/news/post-politics/wp/2016/01/26/evangelical-leader-jerry-falwell-jr-endorses-trump/?noredirect=on&utm_term=.88c7faa12d3e.

April 21, 2016: Donald Trump Is Not Your Protector: A Warning to Evangelical Christians

1. Ben Johnson, "Donald Trump would liberalize the Republican Party platform on abortion," April 21, 2016, https://www.lifesitenews.com/news/donald-trump-would-change-the-republican-party-platform-on-abortion-video.

2. Ben Johnson, "Trump has 'zero chance' of changing GOP platform on abortion: pro-life leaders," April 21, 2016, https://www.lifesitenews.com/news/trump-has-zero-chance-of-changing-gop-platform-on-abortion-conservative-and.

3. Candace Smith, "Donald Trump OK With Caitlyn Jenner Using Any Bathroom in His Tower," April 21, 2016, https://abcnews.go.com/Politics/donald-trump-caitlyn-jenner-bathroom-tower/story?id=38566263.

4. "Ted Cruz: Transgender 'Bathroom Bills' Are 'Perfectly Reasonable,'" April 14, 2016, http://talkingpointsmemo.com/livewire/ted-cruz-supports-hb2-north-carolina.

5. Michael L. Brown, "It's Time to Stand Up to Transgender Activism," April 21, 2016, http://www.charismanews.com/opinion/in-the-line-of-fire/56645-it-s-time-to-stand-up-to-transgender-activism.

6. The Right Scoop, "Ted Cruz SLAMS Trump on Transgenders: HAVE WE GONE STARK RAVING NUTS?" April 21, 2016, http://therightscoop.com/ted-cruz-slams-trump-on-transgender-bathroom-position-have-we-gone-stark-raving-nuts/.

April 28, 2016: When Bible-Quoting Trump Supporters Drop the F-Bomb

1. Michael L. Brown, "Why We Should Boycott Target," ASKDrBrown, April 27, 2016, https://www.youtube.com/watch?v=v-VSCUJebvE.

2. Michael L. Brown, "Is Israel an Evil Occupier?" ASKDrBrown, May 23, 2013, https://www.youtube.com/watch?v=zueuZ8GSjJc.

3. Michael L. Brown, "A Warning to Conservative Christians Supporting Trump," ASKDrBrown, April 21, 2016, https://www.youtube.com/watch?v=c1nOt4k5nHo.

May 3, 2016: Donald Trump: The *National Enquirer* Candidate

1. Family Policy Institute of Washington, "Gender Identity: Can a 5'9, White Guy Be a 6'5, Chinese Woman?" April 13, 2016, https://www.youtube.com/watch?v=xfO1veFs6Ho.

May 30, 2016: If Obama Was Not the Political Savior, Neither Is Trump

1. Jenna Johnson, "Even in victory, Donald Trump can't stop airing his grievances," May 29, 2016, https://www.washingtonpost.com/politics/even-in-victory-donald-trump-cant-stop-airing-his-grievances/2016/05/29/a5f7a566-2526-11e6-8690-f14ca9de2972_story.html?utm_term=.7524437a22aa.

2. Brandon Morse, "This Feels Less Like An Election and More Like the Establishment Of Religion," May 30, 2016, http://www.redstate.com/brandon_morse/2016/05/30/298390.

3. M.G. Oprea, "What The Arab Spring Can Teach Us About America's Populist Revolution," May 28, 2016, http://thefederalist.com/2016/05/28/what-the-arab-spring-can-teach-us-about-americas-populist-revolution.

June 30, 2016: Why I'm Actually Rooting for Donald Trump

1. Wayne Allyn Root, "A Message For Christians About Donald Trump," June 24, 2016, https://townhall.com/columnists/wayneallynroot/2016/06/24/a-message-for-christians-about-donald-trump-n2182796.

2. Leon H. Wolf, "Evangelical Leaders Continue to Prove that there's a Sucker Born Every Minute," June 26, 2016, http://www.redstate.com/leon_h_wolf/2016/06/26/evangelical-leaders-continue-prove-theres-sucker-born-every-minute.

3. Leon H. Wolf, "Tom DeLay Hammers Servile 'Evangelical' 'Leaders' for their Softball Treatment of Trump," June 23, 2016, http://www.redstate.com/leon_h_wolf/2016/06/23/tom-delay-hammers-servile-evangelical-leaders-softball-treatment-trump.

4. Samuel Smith, "James Dobson Says Paula White Led Donald Trump to Jesus Christ," June 29, 2016, http://www.christianpost.com/news/james-dobson-says-paula-white-led-donald-trump-to-jesus-christ-165844.

5. Michael L. Brown, "A Compromised Gospel Produces Compromised Fruit," March 12, 2013, http://ministrytodaymag.com/news/main/19922-the-fruit-of-a-compromised-gospel.

6. Michael L. Brown, "David French on Trump, Radical Islam, and Brexit," ASKDrBrown, June 28, 2016, https://www.youtube.com/watch?v=Tj-CWJftTas.

7. Right Wing Watch, "RWW News: Lance Wallnau Says Donald Trump Is Being Raised Up And Protected By God," RWW Blog, December 3, 2015, https://www.youtube.com/watch?v=gDvs-KsZHdw.

8. Kyle Mantyla, "Leading Dominionist Says Donald Trump Is A Modern-Day Lincoln Anointed By God," December 3, 2015, http://www.rightwingwatch.org/content/leading-dominionist-says-donald-trump-modern-day-lincoln-anointed-god.

9. "White House Watch: Clinton Edges Ahead," November 7, 2016, http://www.rasmussenreports.com/public_content/politics/elections/election_2016/white_house_watch.

July 9, 2016: The Irony of Democrats Calling Donald Trump Anti-Semitic

1. Jared Kushner, "The Donald Trump I Know," July 6, 2016, http://observer.com/2016/07/jared-kushner-the-donald-trump-i-know.

2. Rabbi Shmuley Boteach, "Donald Trump needs help with his values, but he's no anti-Semite," July, 8, 2018, http://www.nydailynews.com/opinion/shmuley-boteach-trump-values-no-anti-semite-article-1.2704377.

3. "Jerusalem And God Vote Gets Booed At Dem Convention," September 5, 2012, http://www.realclearpolitics.com/video/2012/09/05/jerusalem_and_god_get_booed_at_dem_convention.html.

4. Ron Kampeas, "Bernie Sanders picks three Israel critics to help draft Democratic platform," May 23, 2016, http://www.jta.org/2016/05/23/news-opinion/politics/dems-panel-drafting-platform-includes-critics-of-israel-friends-of-israel-and-a-bds-backer.

5. Judea Pearl, "An open letter to Cornel West," April 21, 2015, http://www.danielpearl.org/home/media/op-ed-archive/an-open-letter-to-cornel-west.

6. Andrea Peyser, "If you're Jewish, don't vote for Bernie Sanders," April 10, 2016, http://nypost.com/2016/04/10/if-youre-jewish-dont-vote-for-bernie-sanders.

August 4, 2016: Hillary Clinton, Donald Trump, the Presidential Elections, and the Sovereignty of God

1. Michael L. Brown, "Does God Have a Political Affiliation?" July 19, 2016, https://stream.org/does-god-have-a-political-affiliation.

August 19, 2016: Has Donald Trump Turned a New Leaf?

1. Jeremy Diamond and David Mark, "Campaign reboot: Trump expresses regret for saying 'the wrong thing,' doesn't specify," August 19, 2016, http://www.cnn.com/2016/08/18/politics/trump-i-regret-sometimes-saying-wrong-thing.

2. Joe Crowe, "Kellyanne Conway: Trump's Regret Is for 'Anyone' Who Felt Offended," August 19, 2016, http://www.newsmax.com/Headline/kellyanne-conway-trump-regret-offended/2016/08/19/id/744370.

September 5, 2016: Do Conservative Christians Have the Love of Christ for Obama and Hillary?

1. Christopher Hitchens, "Faith-Based Fraud,"

May 16, 2007, http://www.slate.com/articles/news_and_politics/fighting_words/2007/05/faithbased_fraud.html.

October 10, 2016: Why All the Fuss Over the Trump Sex-Comments Tape?

1. Wayne Grudem, "Trump's Moral Character and the Election," October 9, 2016, http://townhall.com/columnists/waynegrudem/2016/10/09/trumps-moral-character-and-the-election-n2229846.

2. Michael L. Brown, "On the Danger of Christian Leaders Endorsing Candidates," October 8, 2016, https://askdrbrown.org/library/danger-christian-leaders-endorsing-candidates.

October 13, 2016: Is Donald Trump "God's Chaos Candidate"?

1. Eric Hananoki, "Trump's White Nationalist Supporters Find Culprit For Sexual Assault Tape Release: 'The Jews Did It,'" October 11, 2016, http://mediamatters.org/blog/2016/10/11/trump-s-white-nationalist-supporters-find-culprit-sexual-assault-tape-release-jews-did-it/213762.

2. Paul Farhi, "In debate, Trump takes on moderators almost as much as Clinton," October 9, 2016, https://www.washingtonpost.com/lifestyle/style/in-debate-trump-takes-on-moderators-almost-as-much-as-clinton/2016/10/09/b668c192-8e7f-11e6-a6a3-d50061aa9fae_story.html.

October 23, 2016: Why I Will Vote for Donald Trump

1. Michael L. Brown, "Since God Hates the Shedding of Innocent Blood, Can a Christian Vote for Hillary?" July 26, 2016, https://stream.org/since-god-hates-shedding-innocent-blood-can-christian-vote-hillary.

2. Michael L. Brown, "Christian Conservatives, Be Assured That President Hillary Clinton Will Declare War on You," October 15, 2016, https://stream.org/be-assured-president-hillary.

3. Michael L. Brown, "An Interview with Lance Wallnau on 'God's Chaos Candidate,'" ASKDrBrown, October 20, 2016, https://www.youtube.com/watch?v=NFhHknCytuQ.

November 1, 2016: Donald Trump Waves the Gay Flag

1. Michael Lambert, "Donald Trump Waves LGBT Rainbow Flag at Colorado Rally," October 31, 2016, http://www.advocate.com/2016/10/31/donald-trump-waves-lgbt-rainbow-flag-colorado-rally.

2. HRC Staff, "Donald Trump's Courting of Hate Movement Dangerous to LGBTQ People," August 25, 2016, http://www.hrc.org/blog/donald-trumps-courting-of-hate-movement-dangerous-to-lgbtq-people.

November 9, 2016: Donald Trump, President of the United States by the Sovereign Intervention of God

1. Jeremiah Johnson, "2018: Cancer, Baby Boomers, Trump, and the Nations," January 21, 2018, http://jeremiahjohnson.tv/blog/2018-cancer-baby-boomers-trump-nations.

2. Michael L. Brown, "An Interview with Lance Wallnau on God's Chaos Candidate," October 20, 2016, https://askdrbrown.org/library/interview-lance-wallnau-gods-chaos-candidate.

November 15, 2016: Donald Trump, Same-Sex "Marriage," and the Church

1. Dustin Siggins, "Trump: 'Very Important' Supreme Court Nominee Will Overturn Roe v. Wade, Let States Control Abortion," November 14, 2016, https://stream.org/trump-very-important-supreme-court-nominee.

2. Ariane de Vogue, "Trump: Same-sex marriage is 'settled,' but Roe v Wade can be changed," November 15, 2016, http://www.cnn.com/2016/11/14/politics/trump-gay-marriage-abortion-supreme-court.

3. Michael L. Brown, "Equivocating or Evolving, President Obama is Wrong Either Way," May 12, 2012, http://townhall.com/columnists/michaelbrown/2012/05/12/equivocating_or_evolving_president_obama_is_wrong_either_way.

4. Michael L. Brown, *Revolution: Jesus' Call to Change the World* (Bellingham, WA: Kirkdale Press, 2012).

November 16, 2016: Have Evangelicals Lost Their Credibility by Voting for Trump?

1. Kate Shellnutt, "Global Evangelical Leaders: Trump's Win Will Harm the Church's Witness," November 15, 2016, http://www.christianitytoday.com/gleanings/2016/november/global-evangelical-leaders-trump-win-will-harm-churchs-witn.html.

2. William J. Bennett, *The Death of Outrage: Bill Clinton and the Assault on American Ideals* (New York, NY: Touchstone, 1998), 9.

3. Jonathon Van Maren, "The painfully obvious reason Christians voted for Trump (that liberals just don't understand)," November 12, 2016, https://www.lifesitenews.com/blogs/the-painfully-simple-reason-christians-voted-for-donald-trump-that-liberals.

December 12, 2016: Why Many Americans Trust Donald Trump More Than the CIA

1. "Confidence in Institutions," Gallup.com, http://www.gallup.com/poll/1597/confidence-institutions.aspx.

2. Cortney O'Brien, "Clinton Campaign to Support the Electoral College's Request for Intel Brief on Russian Hack," December 12, 2016, http://townhall.com/tipsheet/cortneyobrien/2016/12/12/clinton-campaign-supports-the-electoral-colleges-request-for-intel-brief-on-russian-hack-n2258882?utm_source=thdailypm&utm_medium=email&utm_campaign=nl_pm&newsletterad=.

December 19, 2016: Why Donald Trump Is Catching Hell for Planning to Move Our Embassy to Jerusalem

1. Rabbi Shraga Simmons, "What is the capital of Israel: Jerusalem or Tel Aviv?" May 7, 2013, https://unitedwithisrael.org/jerusalem-or-tel-aviv.

2. Ibid.

3. Bethan McKernan, "Donald Trump's Israel ambassador pick is told that moving US embassy to Jerusalem would be 'declaration of war,'" http://www.independent.co.uk/news/world/middle-east/donald-trump-david-friedman-israel-ambassador-pick-anger-arabs-palestinians-jerusalem-a7480041.html.

4. Ibid.

5. Elder of Ziyon, "Four articles in the NYT against David Friedman in one day," December 17, 2016, http://elderofziyon.blogspot.com/2016/12/four-articles-in-nyt-against-david.html.

6. Noah Pollack, "The NYT Is Having a Meltdown Over Trump's Israel Nominee," December 17, 2016, http://freebeacon.com/blog/nyt-meltdown-trumps-israel-nominee.

7. Brad Wilmouth, "Friedman Sees 'Madness' in Trump Amb Pick Talk of Moving Embassy to Jerusalem," December 17, 2016, https://www.newsbusters.org/blogs/nb/brad-wilmouth/2016/12/17/friedman-sees-madness-trump-amb-pick-talk-moving-embassy-jerusalem.

8. Brent Griffiths, "Conway: Moving U.S. Embassy to Jerusalem 'big priority' for Trump," December 12, 2016, http://www.politico.com/blogs/donald-trump-administration/2016/12/us-embassy-to-jerusalem-big-priority-for-trump-232505.

9. Michael L. Brown, "Oh Jerusalem, Jerusalem," September 7, 2012, http://townhall.com/columnists/michaelbrown/2012/09/07/oh_jerusalem_jerusalem.

10. Dana Milbank, "Anti-Semitism Is No Longer an Undertone of Trump's Campaign It's the Melody," November 7, 2016, https://www.washingtonpost.com/opinions/anti-semitism-is-no-longer-an-undertone-of-trumps-campaign-its-the-melody/2016/11/07/b1ad6e22-a50a-11e6-8042-f4d111c862d1_story.html?utm_term=.cb5e1f03809a.

December 20, 2016: "Islamist Terrorists Continually Slaughter Christians": Trump Says What Obama Refused to Say

1. See http://www.thereligionofpeace.com.

2. Michael L. Brown, "When a Mass-Murdering Soldier of Allah Is Not a Terrorist," August 2, 2013, https://askdrbrown.org/library/when-mass-murdering-soldier-allah-not-terrorist.

3. Michael L. Brown, "Workplace Violence or Islamic Terrorism?" November 5, 2015, https://askdrbrown.org/library/workplace-violence-or-islamic-terrorism.

4. Matt Hunter, "Trump says terrorists 'must be eradicated from the face of the earth' after 12 die and 48 are hurt when lorry ploughs into Berlin market," December 19, 2016, http://www.dailymail.co.uk/news/article-4049952/World-leaders-unite-condemn-Berlin-terror-attack-lorry-packed-steel-crashes-Christmas-market-shoppers-killing-nine-injuring-45.html#ixzz4TO0h3SdI.

5. Chris Hughes, "Berlin 'terror attack': Europe was warned that ISIS planned Christmas market assaults 25 days ago," December 19, 2016, http://www.mirror.co.uk/news/world-news/berlin-terror-attack-europe-warned-9487129.

6. Chris Perez, "ISIS claims responsibility for Berlin Christmas market attack," December 19, 2016, http://nypost.com/2016/12/19/isis-claims-responsibility-for-berlin-christmas-market-attack.

January 11, 2017: Donald Trump, the Johnson Amendment, and the Question of Christian Cowardice

1. Heather Clark, "Study Reveals Most American Pastors Silent on Current Issues Despite Biblical Beliefs," August 12, 2014, http://christiannews.net/2014/08/12/study-reveals-most-american-pastors-silent-on-current-issues-despite-biblical-beliefs.

2. Ibid.

January 23, 2017: An Attempted Impartial Reading of President Trump's Inaugural Speech

1. Joe Concha, "MSNBC's Chris Matthews: Trump inauguration speech 'Hitlerian,'" January 20, 2017, http://thehill.com/homenews/media/315324-msnbcs-chris-matthews-trump-inauguration-speech-hitlerian.

2. Ben Shapiro, Twitter, January 22. 2017, https://twitter.com/benshapiro/status/823203046867931136.

3. Peter Hasson, "Trump Inaugural Address Focuses On 'We,' Leaves Himself Out Of Speech Almost Entirely," January 20, 2017, http://dailycaller.com/2017/01/20/trump-inaugural-address-focuses-on-we-leaves-himself-out-of-speech-almost-entirely.

4. J'na Jefferson, "Ray Lewis And Jim Brown Speak About Their Meetings With Donald Trump," December 14, 2016, http://www.vibe.com/2016/12/ray-lewis-jim-brown-donald-trump.

January 30, 2017: Five Things Bothering Me About the Response to Trump's Executive Order on Refugees

1. Cris, Twitter, January 29, 2017, https://twitter.com/ThePatriot143/status/825857379489214464.

2. The Editorial Board, "Donald Trump's Muslim Ban Is Cowardly and Dangerous," January 28, 2017, https://www.nytimes.com/2017/01/28/opinion/donald-trumps-muslim-ban-is-cowardly-and-dangerous.html.

3. Lee Stranahan, "Terror-Tied Group CAIR Causing Chaos, Promoting Protests & Lawsuits as Trump Protects Nation," January 28, 2017, http://www.breitbart.com/big-government/2017/01/28/terror-tied-group-cair-causing-chaos-promoting-protests-lawsuits-as-trump-protects-nation.

4. Nahal Toosi, "Trump ratchets up defense of immigrant ban as outrage mounts," January 29, 2017, http://www.politico.com/story/2017/01/trump-refugees-234320.

5. Paris Shutz, Twitter, January 28, 2017, https://twitter.com/paschutz/status/825474435402469376.

6. Elana Shor, "Christian groups oppose Trump's preference for Christian refugees," January 29, 2017, http://www.politico.com/story/2017/01/trump-immigration-christians-234341.

7. Patrick Goodenough, "13,210 Syrian Refugees So Far in 2016; Up 675% from 2015; 99.1% Are Muslims," November 1, 2016, http://www.cnsnews.com/news/article/patrick-goodenough/13210-syrian-refugees-admitted-year-through-october-675-99-are.

8. ABC News, Twitter, January 29, 2017, https://twitter.com/ABC/status/825818969911214082.

9. David French, "Trump's Executive Order on Refugees—Separating Fact from Hysteria," January 28, 2017, http://www.nationalreview.com/article/444370/donald-trump-refugee-executive-order-no-muslim-ban-separating-fact-hysteria.

10. Dan McLaughlin, "Refugee Madness: Trump Is Wrong, But His Liberal Critics Are Crazy," January 28, 2017, http://www.nationalreview.com/article/444373/donald-trump-refugees-critics-wrong.

February 3, 2017: Four Major Takeaways from President Trump's Nomination of Justice Gorsuch

1. Ian Schwartz, "Trump Nominates Gorsuch To Supreme Court: I Promised To Select A Representative Of Our Constitution," January 31, 2017, http://www.realclearpolitics.com/video/2017/01/31/trump_nominates_gorsuch_to_supreme_court_i_promised_to_select_a_representative_of_our_constitution.html.

2. WND, "Michael Savage cautions Trump about inner circle," February 2, 2017, http://www.wnd.com/2017/02/michael-savage-cautions-trump-about-inner-circle.

3. Jason Sattler, "Time for outrageous obstruction against Gorsuch: Jason Sattler," January 31, 2017, http://www.usatoday.com/story/opinion/2017/01/31/democrats-must-fight-gorsuch-supreme-court-column/97297614.

4. Eric Bradner, "Pelosi on Gorsuch: 'A very hostile appointment,'" February 1, 2017, http://www.cnn.com/2017/01/31/politics/nancy-pelosi-town-hall-highlights.

5. Christian Schneider, "Pay no attention to the Gorsuch hysteria: Christian Schneider," February 1, 2017, http://www.usatoday.com/story/opinion/2017/02/01/gorsuch-supreme-court-trump-conservative-hysteria-christian-schneider-column/97355702.

6. Aaron Klein, "Ex-Obama Official Suggests 'Military Coup' Against Trump," February 2, 2017, http://www.breitbart.com/big-government/2017/02/02/ex-obama-official-suggests-military-coup-trump.

7. Fox News, "Sarah Silverman calls for military to overthrow President Trump," February 02, 2017, http://www.foxnews.com/entertainment/2017/02/02/sarah-silverman-calls-for-military-to-overthrow-president-trump.html.

8. Cody Derespina, "Democrats fuming over Gorsuch backed him in 2006," February 02, 2017, http://www.foxnews.com/politics/2017/02/02/democrats-fuming-over-gorsuch-backed-him-in-2006.html.

9. Chris Field, "12 Must-Read Quotes from Scalia's Blistering Same-Sex Marriage Dissent," June 26, 2015, http://www.theblaze.com/stories/2015/06/26/12-must-read-quotes-from-scalias-blistering-same-sex-marriage-dissent.

February 5, 2017: The Election of Donald Trump Tells Us That Anything Is Possible

1. Anna M. Tinsley, "James Robison, Trump's prayer warrior, wishes president would 'start tweeting Proverbs,'" February 03, 2017, http://www.star-telegram.com/news/politics-government/article130596509.html#storylink=cpy.

2. Ibid.

3. *The Line of Fire with Dr. Michael L. Brown*, December 15, 2015, http://thelineoffire.org/2015/12/15/two-new-books-on-homosexuality-and-the-church.

February 15, 2017: My Response to Huffington Post Contributor Wanting to Talk with a White, Christian Supporter of Trump

1. Susan M. Shaw, "Dear White, Christian Trump Supporters: We Need To Talk," February 11, 2017, http://www.huffingtonpost.com/entry/an-open-letter-to-white-christian-trump-supporters_us_589f5ce4e4b0e172783a9cef.

2. Zeke J. Miller, "Axelrod: Obama Misled Nation When He Opposed Gay Marriage In 2008," February 10, 2015, http://time.com/3702584/gay-marriage-axelrod-obama.

3. Boteach, "Donald Trump needs help with his values, but he's no anti-Semite."

4. Tom Blumer, "O'Reilly Rips Press Coverage of ICE Raids: 'A Low Point in American Journalism,'" February 14, 2017, http://www.newsbusters.org/blogs/nb/tom-blumer/2017/02/14/oreilly-rips-press-coverage-ice-raids-low-point-american-journalism.

5. Sarah Pulliam Bailey, "Conservative Evangelicals Join Letter Denouncing Trump's Order On Refugees," February 8, 2017, https://www.

washingtonpost.com/news/acts-of-faith/
wp/2017/02/08/conservative-evangelicals-
join-letter-denouncing-trumps-order-on-
refugees/?utm_term=.4808d4fd0c98.

**March 1, 2017: Please Don't Tell Me Trump's Speech
to Congress Was Racist**

1. Erin Kelly, "GOP lawmakers cheer Trump's
   speech as Democrats sit stone-faced," February
   28, 2017, http://www.usatoday.com/story/
   news/politics/2017/02/28/congress-reaction-
   trump-speech-republicans-democrats/98547048.

2. Jeff Stein, "Just one Senate Democrat
   applauded Trump's call to 'make America
   great,'" March 1, 2017, http://www.vox.
   com/2017/3/1/14761076/senate-democrats-
   trump.

3. John Podhoretz, "Trump's speech to Congress
   marks the real start of his presidency," March 1,
   2017, https://nypost.com/2017/03/01/trumps-
   speech-to-congress-marks-the-real-start-of-his-
   presidency/amp.

**March 2, 2017: When Trump Is Presidential, His
Critics Are Left Out in the Rain**

1. GOP War Room, "Fox News' Chris Wallace:
   One Of The Best Joint Session Speeches I've
   Ever Heard A President Give," February 28,
   2017, https://www.youtube.com/watch?v=yd-
   bLYO3kDQ&feature=youtu.be.

2. News2Share, "Rosie O'Donnell Speaks
   Back Against Trump Address," February
   28, 2017, https://www.youtube.com/
   watch?v=cYRCCO2rzfM.

3. Karma Allen, "Rosie O'Donnell leads anti-Trump
   protest in DC before congressional address,"
   March 1, 2017, http://abcnews.go.com/Politics/
   rosie-odonnell-leads-anti-trump-protest-dc-
   ahead/story?id=45823164.

4. Jason Kurtz, "Van Jones on Trump: 'He became
   President of the United States in that moment,
   period,'" March 1, 2017, http://edition.cnn.
   com/2017/03/01/politics/van-jones-trump-
   congress-speech-became-the-president-in-that-
   moment-cnntv.

5. Ibid.

6. Ronna, McDaniel, "'Trump At His Absolute
   Best,' See What They Are Saying About Trump's
   Speech," February 28, 2017, https://www.gop.
   com/trump-at-his-absolute-best-see-what-they-
   are-saying-about-trumps-speech.

7. Ibid.

8. Kathryn Blackhurst, "Maddow Pans 'Small
   and Stunty' Democratic Response," February
   28, 2017, http://www.lifezette.com/polizette/
   maddow-calls-dem-response-trump-speech-
   small-stunty.

9. Lisa Hagen, "DNC chair: Trump's speech was
   'Bannon on steroids with a smile,'" February
   28, 2017, http://thehill.com/homenews/
   campaign/321728-dnc-chair-trumps-speech-
   was-bannon-on-steroids-with-a-smile.

10. Daniel Nussbaum, "Celebrities React as Trump
    Speaks to Congress: 'Suck a Bag of Soiled
    D*cks,'" March 1, 2017, https://www.breitbart.
    com/big-hollywood/2017/03/01/hollywood-
    reacts-trumps-joint-address-congress-sck-bag-
    spoiled-dcks/?utm_source=facebook&utm_
    medium=social.

11. Rebecca Savransky, "Van Jones: Trump 'became
    president' in moment honoring Navy SEAL
    widow," February 28, 2017, http://thehill.com/
    homenews/administration/321722-van-jones-
    on-trumps-honoring-of-widow-of-navy-seal-
    trump-became.

**April 19, 2017: "America First" Does Not Mean
"America Only"**

1. Ann Coulter, "Lassie, Come Home," April
   12, 2017, http://www.anncoulter.com/
   columns/2017-04-12.html#read_more.

2. Jeff Stein, "Some of Trump's biggest
   supporters are furious about his strikes
   in Syria," April 6, 2017, http://www.vox.
   com/2017/4/6/15215376/alt-right-trump-syria.

3. "The Inaugural Address," January 20, 2017,
   https://www.whitehouse.gov/briefings-
   statements/the-inaugural-address.

4. Jeremy Diamond, "Trump pushes 'Buy American,
   Hire American' policy in Wisconsin," April 18,
   2017, http://www.cnn.com/2017/04/17/politics/
   trump-wisconsin-buy-american/index.html.

April 27, 2017: Donald Trump Disappoints the Anti-Semites

1. Sam Kestenbaum, "Trump Gives a Holocaust Speech—And The 'Alt Right' Screams 'Betrayal,'" April 26, 2017, http://forward.com/news/370132/trump-gives-a-holocaust-speech-and-the-alt-right-screams-betrayal.

2. "Remarks by President Trump at United States Holocaust Memorial Museum National Days of Remembrance," April 25, 2017, https://www.whitehouse.gov/briefings-statements/remarks-president-trump-united-states-holocaust-memorial-museum-national-days-remembrance.

3. Kestenbaum, "Trump Gives a Holocaust Speech."

4. Tovah Lazaroff, "Netanyahu: Trump is a great friend of the Jewish people," February 16, 2017, http://www.jpost.com/Israel-News/Netanyahu-Trump-is-a-great-friend-of-the-Jewish-people-481681.

5. Kestenbaum, "Trump Gives a Holocaust Speech."

6. "Statement by President Donald J. Trump on Armenian Remembrance Day 2017," April 24, 2017, https://www.whitehouse.gov/the-press-office/2017/04/24/statement-president-donald-j-trump-armenian-remembrance-day-2017.

7. Rabbi Shmuley Boteach, "President Trump an anti-Semite? Talk about #FakeNews," February 22, 2017, http://thehill.com/blogs/pundits-blog/foreign-policy/320605-president-trump-an-anti-semite-talk-about-fakenews.

May 10, 2017: Five Things Ann Coulter Got Wrong About Donald Trump

1. Alex Pfeiffer, "Ann Coulter Is Worried The 'Trump-Haters Were Right,'" May 14, 2017, http://dailycaller.com/2017/05/14/ann-coulter-is-worried-the-trump-haters-were-right.

May 19, 2017: The Importance of Trump's Saudi Arabia Speech Denouncing Islamic Terrorism

1. Raheem Kassam, "Kassam: From Cairo to Riyadh, Trump Urged Action on Terror Where Obama Offered Islamic Apologism," May 21, 2017, http://www.breitbart.com/big-government/2017/05/21/kassam-from-cairo-to-riyadh-trump-urged-action-on-terror-where-obama-offered-islamic-apologism.

2. Harriet Sinclair, "Full Transcript: Donald Trump Calls on Saudi Arabia and Arab Leaders to Combat 'Crisis of Islamist Extremism,'" May 21, 2017, http://www.newsweek.com/full-transcript-donald-trump-saudi-arabia-speech-islamist-extremism-radical-613040.

3. Angela Dewan, "Trump's new tune on Islam unconvincing, experts in Mideast say," May 21, 2017, http://www.cnn.com/2017/05/21/politics/trump-islam-saudi-arabia-reaction/index.html.

4. Ibid.

June 1, 2017: Kathy Griffin Is Not the Only One Guilty of Anti-Trump Hysteria

1. Jerome Hudson, "Madonna Drops F-Bombs at Anti-Trump Rally: 'I've Thought a Lot About Blowing Up the White House,'" January 21, 2017, http://www.breitbart.com/live/womens-march-washington-live-updates/madonna-drops-f-bombs-anti-trump-rally-ive-thought-lot-blowing-white-house.

2. Lisa Respers France, "Madonna: 'Blowing up White House' taken out of context," January 23, 2017, http://www.cnn.com/2017/01/23/entertainment/madonna-white-house.

3. Sarah Stites, "Media Blast Charlie Sheen For Tweeting Trump Death Wish," December 30, 2016, http://www.newsbusters.org/blogs/culture/sarah-stites/2016/12/30/media-blast-charlie-sheen-tweeting-trump-death-wish.

4. "Some of the Trump damage is 'SELF-INFLICTED' says Ted Cruz," May 19, 2017, http://therightscoop.com/some-of-the-trump-damage-is-self-inflicted-says-ted-cruz.

5. Pam Key, "Maxine Waters: American Public 'Getting Weary' That Trump Not Impeached Yet," May 28, 2017, http://www.breitbart.com/video/2017/05/28/maxine-waters-american-public-getting-weary-that-trump-not-impeached-yet.

6. Katie Pavlitch, "Clapper: We Still Have No Evidence of Collusion Between The Trump Campaign And The Russians," May 30, 2017 https://townhall.com/tipsheet/

katiepavlich/2017/05/30/clapper-we-still-have-zero-evidence-wrongdoing-on-russia-n2333267.

7. John Nolte, "CNN Got a Rodeo Clown Fired For Obama Mask. CNN Still Employs Kathy Griffin," May 31, 2017, http://www.dailywire.com/news/17021/cnn-got-rodeo-clown-fired-cnn-still-employs-kathy-john-nolte.

June 2, 2017: Trump Not Moving Our Embassy to Jerusalem—Yet

1. Eric Cortellessa, "Trump signs waiver, won't move US embassy to Jerusalem," June 1, 2017, http://www.timesofisrael.com/trump-signs-waiver-to-keep-us-embassy-in-tel-aviv.

2. TOI Staff, "Trump yelled at Abbas: 'You tricked me in DC,' Israeli TV reports," May 28, 2017, http://www.timesofisrael.com/trump-said-to-yell-at-abbas-over-incitement-you-lied-to-me.

3. "Prime Minister's Office Statement," June 1, 2017, http://gpoeng.gov.il/media-center/pm-news/prime-ministers-office-statement-1-june.

4. Cortellessa, "Trump signs waiver."

June 26, 2017: President Trump, This Advice Could Really Help You

1. Ken Hanner, "Top 10 Democratic attacks on Mitt Romney," September 8, 2012, http://humanevents.com/2012/09/08/top-10-democratic-attacks-on-mitt-romney.

June 30, 2017: Don't Sell Your Soul in Defense of President Trump

1. James Barrett, "Coulter: Hannity Would Endorse Communism For Trump. Hannity Responds," June 29, 2017, http://www.dailywire.com/news/18084/coulter-hannity-would-endorse-communism-trump-james-barrett.

July 18, 2017: Is It "Theological Malpractice" for Ministers to Pray for Trump?

1. Jeff Poor, "NAACP's Rev Dr William Barber: 'Form of Theological Malpractice That Borders on Heresy' to Pray for Trump," July 15, 2017, http://www.breitbart.com/video/2017/07/15/naacps-rev-dr-william-barber-form-theological-malpractice-borders-heresy-pray-trump.

2. James Robison, "Faith & Prayer in the Oval Office: James Robison Speaks With Jack Graham," July 14, 2017, https://stream.org/faith-prayer-oval-office-james-robison-speaks-jack-graham.

3. Leslie Salzillo, "Watch Rev. Barber 'shock' the DNC, shame religious hypocrisy & lead with love," July 28, 2016, https://www.dailykos.com/stories/2016/7/28/1553896/-Moral-Monday-s-Rev-William-Barber-IGNITES-the-DNC-Lead-With-Love.

July 26, 2017: Was I Wrong About Donald Trump?

1. Annie Karni, "Ivanka Trump and Jared Kushner worked to sink LGBT order," February 23, 2017, http://www.politico.com/story/2017/02/ivanka-trump-jared-kushner-lgbt-order-234617.

2. Pete Baklinski, "Trump officials, Mike Pence have weekly prayer, Bible study," Aril 28, 2017, https://www.lifesitenews.com/news/mike-pence-sponsors-bible-study-for-trump-cabinet.

July 29, 2017: What the Hiring of Anthony Scaramucci Tells Us About President Trump

1. Ryan Lizza, "Anthony Scaramucci Called Me to Unload About White House Leakers, Reince Priebus, and Steve Bannon," July 27, 2017 http://www.newyorker.com/news/ryan-lizza/anthony-scaramucci-called-me-to-unload-about-white-house-leakers-reince-priebus-and-steve-bannon.

2. Josh Delk, "Scaramucci deleting old tweets to avoid 'distraction,'" July 22, 2017, http://thehill.com/homenews/administration/343297-scaramucci-admits-to-deleting-old-tweets-bashing-trump.

August 2, 2017: The Old Lady, the Devil, and Donald Trump

1. German Lopez, "It's not only the military. Trump's administration just took another big anti-LGBTQ step," July 27, 2017, https://www.vox.com/identities/2017/7/27/16049306/trump-sessions-justice-department-lgbtq.

2. Michelangelo Signorile, "Jeff Sessions' Assault On Gay Workers Revealed Yet Another Lie He Told At Confirmation Hearings," July 30,

2017, http://www.huffingtonpost.com/entry/
jeff-sessions-assault-on-gay-workers-revealed-yet-
another-lie-he-told-at-confirmation-hearings_
us_597c8d94e4b02a8434b6b2f3.

August 20, 2017: Should Trump's Evangelical Advisors Abandon Him?

1. Tom, Gjelten, "Trump's Evangelical Advisers Stand By Their Man," August 18, 2017, http://www.npr.org/2017/08/18/544531424/trumps-evangelical-advisers-stand-by-their-man.

2. Ibid.

3. A.J. Willingham, "Trump made two statements on Charlottesville. Here's how white nationalists heard them," August 15, 2017, http://www.cnn.com/2017/08/14/politics/charlottesville-nazi-trump-statement-trnd/index.html.

4. Meghan Keneally, "Trump lashes out at 'alt-left' in Charlottesville, says 'fine people on both sides,'" August 15, 2017, http://abcnews.go.com/Politics/trump-lashes-alt-left-charlottesville-fine-people-sides/story?id=49235032.

September 19, 2017: President Trump Calls Out North Korea's "Rocket Man" Before the UN

1. Michael D'Antonio, "'Rocket man' is awkward Dad Trump's attempt to be cool," September 19, 2017, http://www.cnn.com/2017/09/19/opinions/rocket-man-trump-north-korea-opinion-dantonio/index.html.

2. George Congdon, "Netanyahu Says He's Never Heard A More Courageous Speech Than Trump's At UN," September 19, 2017, http://dailycaller.com/2017/09/19/netanyahu-says-hes-never-heard-a-more-courageous-speech-than-trumps-at-un.

3. Chemi Shalev, "Trump Delights Netanyahu With Belligerent and Nationalist Right-wing UN Speech," September 19, 2017, http://www.haaretz.com/us-news/.premium-1.813291.

4. Becca Stanek, "John Bolton declares Trump's U.N. debut his 'best' speech ever," September 19, 2017, http://theweek.com/speedreads/725516/john-bolton-declares-trumps-un-debut-best-speech-ever.

5. Kaileen Gaul, "Hillary Clinton slams Trump's

UN speech as she tells Stephen Colbert the President should not have called Kim Jong-un 'Rocket Man,'" September 19, 2017, http://www.dailymail.co.uk/news/article-4901088/Hillary-Huma-arrive-outside-Late-Show.html.

6. Shalev, "Trump Delights Netanyahu."

7. Gaul, "Hillary Clinton slams Trump's UN speech."

8. Edward, "Kim Jong-Un's favorite songs," February 19, 2016, http://alt77.com/kim-jong-uns-favorite-songs.

September 25, 2017: What Do We Make of the Battle Between President Trump and the NFL?

1. Michael McClymont, "Robert Kraft 'deeply disappointed by the tone' of Trump's comments," https://www.thescore.com/nfl/news/1381478.

2. Brant James, "NASCAR owners side with Trump, take firm stance against anthem protests," September 24, 2017, https://www.usatoday.com/story/sports/nascar/2017/09/24/nascar-owners-trump-protests-response-petty-ganassi-childress/698122001.

3. Brian Stelter, "With 'son of a bitch' comments, Trump tried to divide NFL and its players," September 23, 2017, http://money.cnn.com/2017/09/23/media/donald-trump-nfl-protest-backlash/index.html.

4. Daniel Politi, "James' 'U Bum' Tweet Is Way More Popular Than Any of the President's Messages," September 24, 2017, http://www.slate.com/blogs/the_slatest/2017/09/24/lebron_james_tweet_calling_trump_u_bum_is_way_more_popular_than_anything.html.

5. Chris Haynes, "Warriors' Kevin Durant: 'Sports is what brings us all together,'" September 25, 2017, http://www.espn.com/nba/story/_/id/20808125/golden-state-warriors-players-support-nfl-players-protests-light-president-donald-trump-remarks.

6. Joel B. Pollack, "5 Stupid Arguments in Favor of the NFL Protests of the National Anthem," September 24, 2017, http://www.breitbart.com/big-government/2017/09/24/5-dumb-arguments-nfl-protests-national-anthem.

7. Ryan Vooris, "10 Athletes Who Made Bold Political and Social Statements," August 30, 2010, http://bleacherreport.com/articles/446420-ten-athletes-who-made-major-political-and-social-statements.

8. Bonnie Kristian, "First MLB player joins NFL protest: 'I'm kneeling for the people that don't have a voice,'" September 24, 2017, http://theweek.com/speedreads/726685/first-mlb-player-joins-nfl-protest-im-kneeling-people-that-dont-have-voice.

October 2, 2017: Donald Trump Wins Again

1. John Nolte, "Nolte: Trump Wins Bigly as Every NFL Player Stands for Thursday Night Anthem," September 29, 2017, http://www.breitbart.com/sports/2017/09/29/nolte-trump-wins-bigly-as-every-nfl-player-stands-for-thursday-night-anthem.

2. Michael L. Brown, "A Practical Suggestion for NFL Players," September 29, 2017, https://stream.org/practical-suggestion-nfl-players.

October 16, 2017: Have Evangelical Leaders Become Disciples of Donald Trump?

1. Kimberly Ross, "Trump's Cheap 'Merry Christmas' Christianity Continues to Sway Evangelicals," October 15, 2017, https://www.redstate.com/kimberly_ross/2017/10/15/trumps-merry-christmas-christianity.

November 18, 2017: An Evangelical Appeal to President Trump Regarding His Al Franken Tweets

1. Herman Wong, "'Where Do His Hands Go?' Trump Takes Aim at Franken over Groping Claims," November 17, 2017, https://www.washingtonpost.com/news/politics/wp/2017/11/16/trump-takes-aim-at-al-franken-over-groping-claims/?utm_term=.20f548dbe58c.

2. Jonathan Easley, "White House adviser: No hypocrisy in Trump attacking Franken," November 17, 2017, http://thehill.com/homenews/administration/360914-wh-adviser-trump-is-not-a-hypocrite-for-attacking-franken.

December 6, 2017: Will God Bless Trump for Moving Our Embassy to Jerusalem?

1. Daily Wire, "Trump's Jerusalem Decision 'An Act Of Not Only Political Bravery But Moral Courage,'" December 6, 2017, http://www.dailywire.com/news/24376/watch-shapiro-fox-and-friends-trumps-jerusalem-daily-wire.

2. David Martosko, "My act of political courage," December 6, 2017, http://www.dailymail.co.uk/news/article-5150649/Amid-warnings-Trump-forges-ahead-Jerusalem-capital.html.

3. Shmuel Rosner, "Of Course Jerusalem Is Israel's Capital," December 5, 2017, https://www.nytimes.com/2017/12/05/opinion/jerusalem-capital-israel-trump.html?action=click&pgtype=Homepage&clickSource=story-heading&module=opinion-c-col-left-region&region=opinion-c-col-left-region&WT.nav=opinion-c-col-left-region&smid=tw-nytopinion&smtyp=cur.

4. Michael L. Brown, "Does God Bless Those Who Bless Israel?" October 28, 2017, https://askdrbrown.org/library/does-god-bless-those-who-bless-israel.

January 5, 2018: Has President Trump Lost His Mind or Has CNN Lost Its Bearings?

1. Sunlen Sarfaty and Ryan Nobles, "Yale psychiatrist briefed members of Congress on Trump's mental fitness," January 5, 2018, http://www.cnn.com/2018/01/04/politics/psychiatrist-congress-meeting-trump/index.html.

2. Annie Karni, "Washington's growing obsession: The 25th Amendment," January 3, 2018, https://www.politico.com/story/2018/01/03/trump-25th-amendment-mental-health-322625.

3. Brian Flood, "Outrage grows over CNN's pot-infused New Year's segment," January 2, 2018, http://www.foxnews.com/entertainment/2018/01/02/outrage-grows-over-cnns-pot-infused-new-years-segment.html.

4. Karni, "Washington's growing obsession."

5. WND Exclusive, "Psychs crack up over 'psychotic,' 'paranoid' Trump," July 25, 2017, http://www.wnd.com/2017/07/crazy-talk-psychs-crack-up-over-psychotic-paranoid-trump/#SzMBPAl1iOYpoZFV.99.

6. Susan Matthews, "We've Misdiagnosed the Problem With Donald Trump," October 26, 2016, http://www.slate.com/articles/health_and_science/medical_examiner/2016/10/we_ve_misdiagnosed_donald_trump.html.

January 21, 2018: An Honest Challenge for the Never Trumpers

1. David French, "It's Important to Distinguish Between Never Trump and Never Trump/Never Hillary Conservatives," December 29, 2017, http://www.nationalreview.com/corner/454999/its-important-distinguish-between-never-trump-and-never-trumpnever-hillary.

2. Kevin Daley, "DOJ Backs Effort to Repeal California Law Requiring Pro-Lifers to Promote Abortion," January 19, 2018, https://stream.org/doj-backs-effort-repeal-california-law-requiring-pro-lifers-promote-abortion.

3. The Hill Staff, "Addressing March for Life, Trump touts gains in anti-abortion policy," January 19, 2018, http://thehill.com/opinion/white-house/369761-full-speech-addressing-march-for-life-trump-touts-advances-in-anti.

4. Gregory Korte, "Trump is the 'most pro-life president in American history,' Pence says," January 18, 2018, https://www.usatoday.com/story/news/politics/2018/01/18/trump-most-pro-life-president-american-history-pence-says/1046812001.

5. Max Greenwood, "Sessions reverses DOJ policy on transgender employee protections," October 5, 2017, http://thehill.com/blogs/blog-briefing-room/news/354023-sessions-reverses-doj-policy-on-transgender-employee.

6. Steve Deace, "Here's why evangelicals don't have to feel guilty for supporting Trump," January 19, 2018, https://www.conservativereview.com/articles/heres-evangelicals-dont-feel-guilty-supporting-trump.

January 25, 2018: Does Trump Get a Moral Mulligan?

1. Jennifer Hansler, "Conservative evangelical leader: Trump gets a 'mulligan' on his behavior," January 23, 2018, https://www.cnn.com/2018/01/23/politics/tony-perkins-trump-affairs-mulligan/index.html.

2. Michael Gerson, "The Trump Evangelicals Have Lost Their Gag Reflex," January 22, 2018, https://www.washingtonpost.com/opinions/the-trump-evangelicals-have-lost-their-gag-reflex/2018/01/22/761d1174-ffa8-11e7-bb03-722769454f82_story.html?utm_term=.6aad74f4faf0.

3. Anugrah Kumar, "Franklin Graham Responds to Trump-Porn Star Allegations: 'He Is Not President Perfect,'" January 21, 2018, https://www.christianpost.com/news/franklin-graham-trump-porn-star-allegations-not-president-perfect-214549.

4. Brad Plumer, "Full transcript of Donald Trump's acceptance speech at the RNC," July 22, 2016, https://www.vox.com/2016/7/21/12253426/donald-trump-acceptance-speech-transcript-republican-nomination-transcript

March 12, 2018: I Agree with Chuck Todd

1. Fox News, "Chuck Todd responds to Trump's 'son of a b—h' jab: 'It creates a challenge to parents,'" March 11, 2018, http://www.foxnews.com/politics/2018/03/11/chuck-todd-responds-to-trumps-son-b-h-jab-it-creates-challenge-to-parents.html.

2. Pam Key, "WaPo's Michael Gerson: Evangelicals Who Support Trump Are 'Slimy Political Operatives, Not Moral Leaders,'" March 11, 2018, http://www.breitbart.com/video/2018/03/11/wapos-michael-gerson-evangelicals-support-trump-slimy-political-operatives-not-moral-leaders.

3. Ibid.

March 13, 2018: Joy Behar, Mike Pence, Donald Trump, and the Question of Public Apologies

1. Brian Flood, "Pence calls for ABC News star Joy Behar to apologize for 'slander' against Christians," March 12, 2018, http://www.foxnews.com/entertainment/2018/03/12/pence-calls-for-abc-news-star-joy-behar-to-apologize-for-slander-against-christians.html.

2. Fox News, "Pastor Jeffress talks evangelical

reaction to Stormy Daniels," March 8, 2018, https://www.youtube.com/watch?time_continue=101&v=icGlGHVeFAk.

March 15, 2018: The Hypocrisy of Those Accusing White Evangelicals of Hypocrisy

1. Campbell Robertson, "A Quiet Exodus: Why Black Worshipers Are Leaving White Evangelical Churches," March 9, 2018, https://www.nytimes.com/2018/03/09/us/blacks-evangelical-churches.html.

2. Michael Gerson, "The Last Temptation," April 2018, https://www.theatlantic.com/magazine/archive/2018/04/the-last-temptation/554066.

3. Gregory A. Smith and Jessica Martínez, "How the faithful voted: A preliminary 2016 analysis," November 9, 2016, http://www.pewresearch.org/fact-tank/2016/11/09/how-the-faithful-voted-a-preliminary-2016-analysis.

4. Monica Showalter, "Playing Pope, Michael Gerson upbraids Evangelicals for their love of Trump," March 12, 2018, https://www.americanthinker.com/blog/2018/03/pope_michael_gerson_upbraids_evangelicals_for_their_love_of_trump.html.

5. David French, "The True Sin of American Evangelicals in the Age of Trump," March 13, 2018, https://www.nationalreview.com/2018/03/evangelicals-support-donald-trump-political-realities-2016-election.

6. Van Moody, "Why Blacks Are Really Leaving White Evangelical Churches," March 12, 2018, https://www.christianpost.com/voice/why-blacks-are-really-leaving-white-evangelical-churches.html.

7. Robertson, "A Quiet Exodus."

April 1, 2018: Adultery, Character, and Leadership: A Response to Dennis Prager

1. Dennis Prager, "Trump, Adultery, Morality," March 31, 2018, https://www.dailywire.com/news/28864/prager-trump-adultery-morality-dennis-prager.

2. Michael L. Brown, "We Have Forgotten How to Blush," March 26, 2018, https://stream.org/we-have-forgotten-how-to-blush.

3. Kelli Stacy, "Most Young Adults: Oral Sex Is Not Sex," April 9, 2010, https://www.cbsnews.com/news/most-young-adults-oral-sex-is-not-sex.

4. Prager, "Trump, Adultery, Morality."

May 9, 2018: It's Time to Give President Trump His Due

1. Lena Felton, "Read Trump's Speech Withdrawing From the Iran Deal," May 8, 2018, https://www.theatlantic.com/politics/archive/2018/05/full-transcript-iran-deal-trump/559892.

2. Josh Meyer, "The secret backstory of how Obama let Hezbollah off the hook," 2017, https://www.politico.com/interactives/2017/obama-hezbollah-drug-trafficking-investigation.

3. Josh Levs, "Fact Check: Was Obama 'silent' on Iran 2009 protests?" October 9, 2012, https://www.cnn.com/2012/10/08/politics/fact-check-romney-iran/index.html.

4. Anthony Blair, "Iran 'Will Fall': Regime faces triple treat and could be brought down later this year," March 17, 2018, https://www.dailystar.co.uk/news/world-news/684265/Iran-regime-fall-protest-Ayatollah-Khamenei-President-Rouhani-Iraq-Saudi-Arabia-IRGC-hijab.

July 13, 2018: Musings on the President, the Religious Right, Democrats, and the Supreme Court

1. Michael L. Brown, "Why Evangelical Christians Should Have a Problem with Donald Trump," ASKDrBrown, November 27, 2015, https://www.youtube.com/watch?v=CZJ7X5p0CBA.

2. Dennis Miller, Twitter, July 8, 2018, https://twitter.com/DennisDMZ/status/1016004073055608832.

3. Paul Morigi, "Supreme Court justice performs her first same-sex wedding," September 22, 2014, https://www.cbsnews.com/news/supreme-court-justice-elena-kagan-performs-her-first-same-sex-wedding.

4. Adrianna McIntyre, "The Supreme Court sided against birth control again, and Sotomayor is not happy about it," July 7, 2014, https://www.vox.com/2014/7/7/5873611/the-supreme-courts-other-contraceptives-ruling-explained.

July 17, 2018: Did Trump Make the Right Play or Did Trump Get Played?

1. John O. Brennan, Twitter, https://twitter.com/JohnBrennan/status/1018885971104985093.

2. Ben Shapiro, "Trump SLAMS His Own Intelligence Agencies, Insists Putin Might Be Right That Russia Didn't Hack Hillary," July 16, 2018, https://www.dailywire.com/news/33123/trump-slams-his-own-intelligence-agencies-insists-ben-shapiro.

3. Brett Samuels, "Drudge Report: 'Putin dominates' Trump in Helsinki," July 16, 2018, http://thehill.com/homenews/media/397257-drudge-report-putin-dominates-trump-in-helsinki.

4. Rob Tornoe, "Trump's comments alongside Putin criticized by both parties as 'disgraceful,' 'treasonous' and 'shameful,'" July 16, 2018, http://www.philly.com/philly/news/politics/presidential/trump-putin-summit-russia-mueller-hacking-emails-hillary-clinton-20180716.html.

5. Ali Rogin, "'Bizarre' and 'shameful': Republicans lead responses to Trump news conference with Putin," July 16, 2018, https://abcnews.go.com/Politics/bizarre-shameful-republicans-lead-responses-trump-news-conference/story?id=56622621.

6. Ryan Saavedra, "Putin Answers Tough Questions From Fox News' Chris Wallace," July 16, 2018, https://www.dailywire.com/news/33145/watch-putin-answers-tough-questions-fox-news-ryan-saavedra.

7. Al Perrotta, "Trump-Putin Meltdown...by the Media," July 16, 2018, https://stream.org/trump-putin-meltdown-by-the-media.

August 11, 2018: Some Candid Questions for Evangelical Supporters of President Trump

1. Cal Thomas, "Mr. President: Take This Advice Please," August 7, 2018, https://calthomas.com/columns/mr-president-take-this-advice-please.

2. Pete Enns, "Is it OK for Christians to protest against their political leaders?" January 2017, https://peteenns.com/is-it-ok-for-christians-to-protest-against-their-political-leaders.

A Final Word: Evangelicals and the Elections: Where Do We Go from Here?

1. Yochanan Muffs, *Conservative Judaism*, Vol. 33, No. 3, 1980, 25-37.

2. Ibid., 27.

3. Ibid., 35. Muffs also notes, "When there is no prophet to intercede, the Lord Himself comes to the defense of His people" (ibid.).

DR. MICHAEL L. BROWN holds a Ph.D. in Near Eastern Languages and Literatures from New York University and has served as a visiting or adjunct professor at seven top seminaries. The author of more than thirty books, he hosts the *Line of Fire* radio program, a syndicated, daily talk show, where he serves as "your voice of moral, cultural, and spiritual revolution," and his syndicated columns appear on many Christian and conservative websites He also hosts TV programs airing on NRBTV, GOD TV, and METV, and he has appeared as a guest on secular and Christian media (including Piers Morgan, Tyra Banks, Phil Donahue, *700 Club*, and Daystar). He has conducted debates or outreach lectures on major campuses, including Oxford University, the Hebrew University (Jerusalem), Ohio State University, Yale, and USC. Michael and his wife, Nancy, have two children and four grandchildren. They live near Charlotte, NC.

Connect with Dr. Brown on

Facebook (AskDrBrown),
YouTube (AskDrBrown),
Twitter (@drmichaellbrown),
Instagram (@drmichaelbrown).